ROUTLEDGE LIBRARY EDITIONS: HISTORIOGRAPHY

Volume 5

HISTORY AND COMMUNITY

HISTORY AND COMMUNITY
Essays in Victorian Medievalism

Edited by
FLORENCE S. BOOS

LONDON AND NEW YORK

First published in 1992 by Garland Publishing, Inc.

This edition first published in 2016
by Routledge
4 Park Square, Milton Park, Abingdon, Oxon OX14 4RN
605 Third Avenue, New York, NY 10017

Routledge is an imprint of the Taylor & Francis Group, an informa business

© 1992 Florence S. Boos

All rights reserved. No part of this book may be reprinted or reproduced or utilised in any form or by any electronic, mechanical, or other means, now known or hereafter invented, including photocopying and recording, or in any information storage or retrieval system, without permission in writing from the publishers.

Trademark notice: Product or corporate names may be trademarks or registered trademarks, and are used only for identification and explanation without intent to infringe.

British Library Cataloguing in Publication Data
A catalogue record for this book is available from the British Library

ISBN: 978-1-138-99958-9 (Set)
ISBN: 978-1-315-63745-7 (Set) (ebk)
ISBN: 978-1-138-12478-3 (Volume 5) (hbk)
ISBN: 978-1-138-12479-0 (Volume 5) (pbk)
ISBN: 978-1-315-64794-4 (Volume 5) (ebk)

Publisher's Note
The publisher has gone to great lengths to ensure the quality of this reprint but points out that some imperfections in the original copies may be apparent.

Disclaimer
The publisher has made every effort to trace copyright holders and would welcome correspondence from those they have been unable to trace.

HISTORY AND COMMUNITY
Essays in Victorian Medievalism

edited by

Florence S. Boos

GARLAND PUBLISHING, INC. • NEW YORK & LONDON
1992

© 1992 Florence S. Boos
All rights reserved

Library of Congress Cataloging-in-Publication Data

History and community : essays in Victorian medievalism /
edited by Florence S. Boos.
    p.   cm. — (Garland reference library of the humanities ;
vol. 1563)
  ISBN 0-8153-0792-6
  1. Great Britain—Civilization—19th century. 2. Great Britain—
History—Victoria, 1837–1901. 3. Medievalism—Great Britain—
History—19th century. 4. English literature—19th century—
History and criticism. 5. Art, British—19th century. I. Series.
DA533.H57   1992
941.081—dc20   92-3196
                                                                                   CIP

Printed on acid-free, 250-year-life paper
Manufactured in the United States of America

Contents

List of Illustrations	vii
Acknowledgments	ix
Introduction *Florence S. Boos*	xi
• Alternative Victorian Futures: "Historicism," *Past and Present* and *A Dream of John Ball* *Florence S. Boos*	3
• Interpreting Victorian Medievalism *Charles Dellheim*	39
The Myth of Merrie England in Victorian Painting *Rebecca Jeffrey Easby*	59
• Tennyson's Hierarchy of Women in *Idylls of the King* *Rebecca Cochran*	81
William Morris's Late Romances: The Struggle Against Closure *Hartley S. Spatt*	109
• Marxism, Medievalism, and Popular Culture *Chris Waters*	137
Ralph Adams Cram: Last Knight of the Gothic Quest *Charlotte H. Oberg*	169

Reviews

The Return to Camelot: Chivalry and the English Gentleman by Mark Girouard *Debra Mancoff*	209
The Image of the Middle Ages in Romantic and Victorian Literature by Kevin L. Morris *Carolyn Collette*	221
Bibliography of Victorian Historicism and Medievalism	229

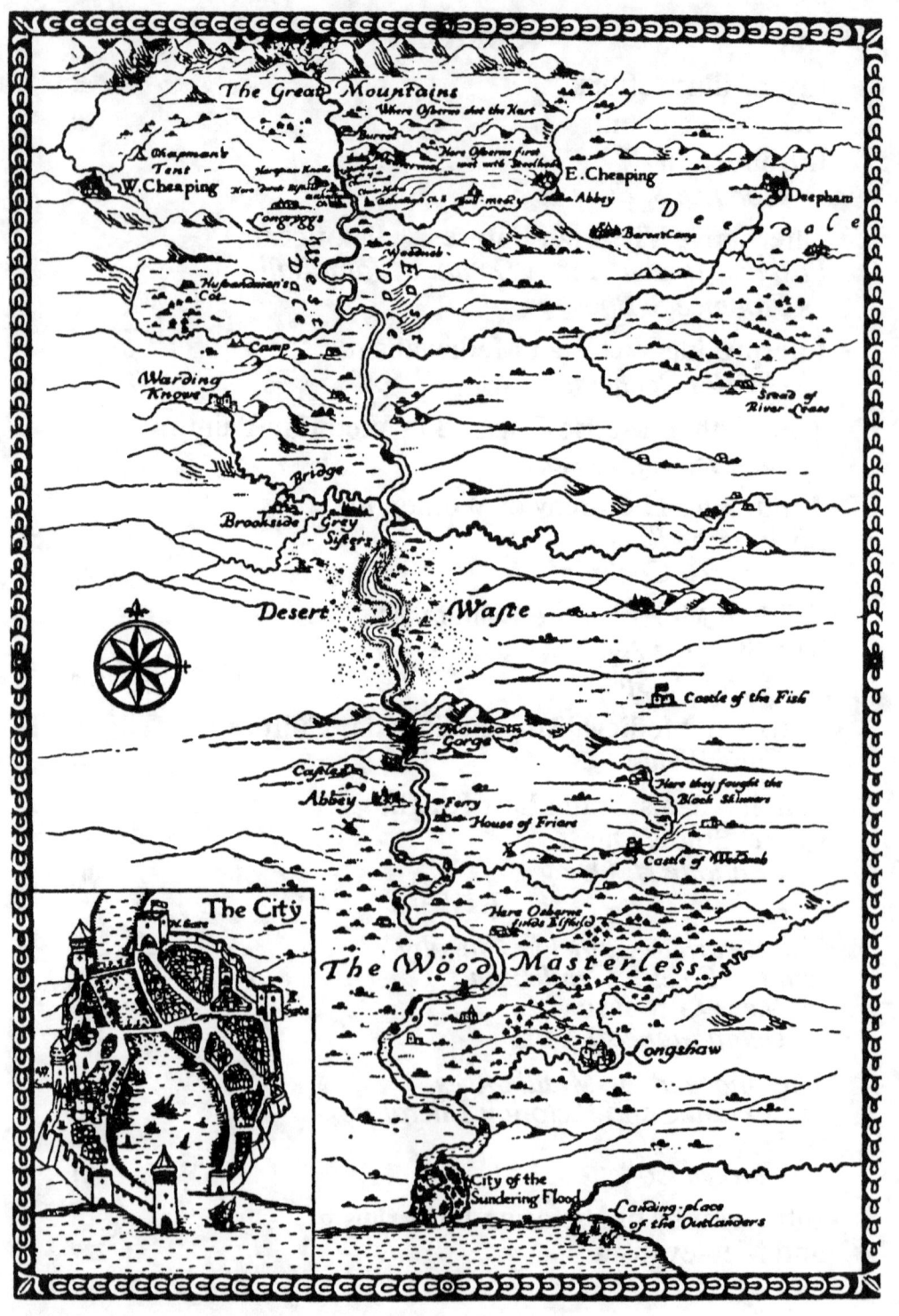

Frontispiece: Illustration for *The Sundering Flood*, Kelmscott edition (1897).

Illustrations

Frontispiece: Illustration for *The Sundering Flood*, Kelmscott edition (1897).	*frontispiece*
	facing page
Jacob Thompson, *The Rush Bearers* (1872); *Irish Harvest Home* (1849).	64
William Powell Frith, *Coming of Age in the Olden Time* (1849).	66
William Powell Frith, *An English Merry-Making A Hundred Years Ago* (1847); Frederick Goodall, *The Village Festival* (1847); *Spring in the Olden Time* (1843).	68
Charles Knight, *Maypole Before St. Andrew's Undershaft* (1844); C. Cousens, after Joseph Nash, *The Maypole*; Anthony, *May-Day in the Last Century* (1844).	69
Daniel Maclise, *Merry Christmas in the Baron's Hall* (1838); Joseph Nash, *Penshurst Castle, Kent* (1839-49); *Christmas Eve* (1848); *The Procession of the Wassail Bowl* (1849).	70
Edwin Landseer, *Bolton Abbey in the Olden Time* (1834).	73
John Rogers Herbert, *The Monastery in the 14th Century: Boarhunters Refreshed at St. Augustine's Monastery, Canterbury*; Augustus Welby Pugin, *Contrasted Residences for the Poor* (1841).	75
The Knight Errant, volume one, number one (1892), title page.	178
St. Thomas Church, New York City.	186

facing page

St. John the Divine, New York City, front arch, entrance; interior.   **187**

United States Military Academy at West Point, New York (1951); Rice University (1990).   **188**

University Chapel, Princeton University; Graduate College and Cleveland Tower, Princeton University.   **189**

University of Richmond, Sarah Brunett Hall.   **191**

Acknowledgments

For permission to reproduce photographs, I am grateful to the Cathedral of St. John the Divine, New York City; Christie's, New York; the Fogg Art Museum, Harvard University; The Forbes Magazine Collection, New York; The National Gallery of Ireland, Dublin; Princeton University; St. Thomas' Church, New York City; the Trafalgar Galleries, London; the United States Military Academy at West Point; and the University of Richmond.

I am also indebted to the acquisitions editor of Garland Publishing Company, Gary Kuris, and the manuscript editor, Phyllis Korper, for their helpfulness and good advice.

I am grateful to Peter Powers for assistance in annotating entries for the bibliography. In addition, I wish to thank Brian Schellberg for his accurate aid in preparing bibliographic citations, and Alice Adams for her characteristically adroit preparation of the manuscript for publication.

Introduction

All history is contemporary history.
    Benedetto Croce, *History, Its Theory and Practice*.

For he to whom the present is the only thing that is present, knows nothing of the age in which he lives.
    Oscar Wilde, *The Critic as Artist, Works*, X, 191.

Therefore, when we build, let us think that we build forever.... let it be such work as our descendants will thank us for.
    John Ruskin, "The Lamp of Memory," *Seven Lamps of Architecture*, 176-77.

In a "high" culture defined by transient technologies and self-conscious "discourses" of "postmodernism," one must pause to (re)conceive a society in which reflective people sometimes expressed their deepest hopes and demands for *change* in evocations of an idealized *"past."* A century and a half now separate us from the rise of Victorian medievalism, a period of paradigm shifts as radical as any which separated the Victorians from their pre-industrial ancestors, and perhaps from their medieval ones as well.

Students of the Victorian period quickly encounter the all-pervasiveness of historical models and recreations in all aspects of its cultural and intellectual life. Architects realized a "Gothic" Revival in hundreds of new and "restored" churches, civic buildings, private dwellings, and railroad stations. Musicians wrote and performed an extensive literature of sacred music which claimed indebtedness to medieval and Renaissance precedents. Theologians of the Tractarian Movement and Catholic Revival asserted their identification with an authentically unified medieval Christian church. Conventional artistic depictions of "Merrie England" and assorted Arthurian motifs appealed to fantasies of a harmoniously stratified feudal society, and the members of the Pre-Raphaelite movement tried to evoke medieval antecedents in more realistic and less conventional ways.

    Mid- and late-century historians also bequeathed a remarkable array of developmental narratives. A few, like Henry Prescott, in his histories of the conquests of Mexico and Peru, and Samuel Laing in his introduction to a translation of the *History of the Kings of Norway*, explored other civilizations. Others, such as John Neale (*The History of the Eastern Church*), and Henry Hallam (*The History of Medieval Europe*), reworked the familiar terrain of Gibbon's 1775 *The Decline and Fall of the Roman Empire*, a Victorian favorite. Still others, such as George Stubbs (*Constitutional History*) and Edward A. Freeman (*The History of the Norman Conquest in England*), provided new accounts of medieval and Renaissance British history. Contemporary social and political debates were often conducted by historical proxy, through a medium of competing historical interpretations. John Ruskin, for example, chastised the rapacity of mid-century capitalists in the unlikely context of *The Stones of Venice*, his three-volume account of medieval and Renaissance Venetian art. Friedrich Engels found a countermodel to bourgeois family structures in historically derivative speculations about classical, medieval Germanic, and Iroquois kinship systems in *The Origin of the Family, Private Property, and the State.* Even Walter Pater, in *The Renaissance*, used art criticism as a vehicle to express muted resistance to various forms of sexual as well as religious orthodoxy.

Dominant paradigms have always overridden subdominant reactions, of course, as successive generations quietly erased (part of) what they did not themselves create, and relegated to the status of trivial and commonplace (some of) what their predecessors struggled to understand and put into effect. Even if one rejects Freud's grim hypothesis in *Totem and Taboo* that sons consume their fathers (though not daughters their mothers; perhaps this offers unintended hope?), it is sometimes difficult to be fair to one's intellectual and emotional parents and grandparents. Precisely *because* of their compelling nature, radically persuasive ways of (re)organizing experience come to seem so self-evident that we struggle to conceive them unconceived. Perhaps romantic metaphors of organic life and Victorian conceptions of evolution, for example, scored the music of consciousness so powerfully that massive over- and counter-reactions were needed before other harmonies could become audible. It seems likely that there will always be a spontaneous response to the metaphysical pathos of "organic" metaphors such as Carlyle's great mythic tree Igdrasil, moreover, and processive metaphors seem to satisfy a deep desire for an answer to the restless question(s) which arise when *any* story is interrupted, "So what (will happen) happened next?"

The essays in this volume examine some of the pervasive implications of Victorian medievalism, and assess its creative manifestations and dual capacities for expression of reformist anger and escapist retreat. In "Alternative Victorian Futures: *Past and Present* and *A Dream of John Ball*," I reconsider some of the emotional and intellectual reasons for the strong Victorian attraction to "medieval" history and literature, and contrast two emblematic responses to this attraction: Thomas Carlyle's (literally) reactionary *Past and Present*, and William Morris's communal and open-ended *A Dream of John Ball*. In "Interpreting Victorian Medievalism" Charles Dellheim argues that Victorians coopted medieval motifs both to impose fixed political interpretations on the period, and to suggest more fluid schemes of social justice, and serve socialist (or at least radical-democratic) ends. In "The Myth of Merrie England in Victorian Painting," Rebecca Easby comments on the widespread predilection for sentimental artistic medievalism which roughly paralleled the rise of Young England sentiment in the 1840's.

Two articles discuss Victorian uses of medievalism in imaginative literature. In "Tennyson's Hierarchy of Women in the *Idylls,*" Rebecca Cochran examines Tennyson's creation of an elaborate 'moral' calculus and gender hierarchy in his Arthurian poem, and in "William Morris's Late Romances: The Struggle Against Closure," Hartley Spatt finds in Morris's late medieval and post-medieval romances an evolving dialectic of realism and fiction in which Morris struggled to transcend mere recreation of medieval legend. In "Marxism, Medievalism, and Popular Culture," Chris Waters evaluates nineteenth-century socialists' attempts to appropriate a "medieval" language and assumptions for the cause of "the Social Revolution," and offers several reasons for these efforts' ultimate failure. Charlotte Oberg's study of "Ralph Adams Cram: Last Knight of the Gothic Quest" considers the American architect's idiosyncratic mixture of conservative political ideology and neo-medieval design of turn-of-the-century Gothic buildings such as the Graduate College at Princeton University and the Cathedral of St. John the Divine. Finally, Debra Mancoff and Carolyn Collette review two earlier discussions of Victorian medievalism, Mark Girouard's *The Return to Camelot*, and Kevin Morris's *The Image of the Middle Ages in Romantic and Victorian Literature*, and mark some directions they consider essential for future studies of the subject.

The essays in this volume thus reexamine several more (and less) attractive aspects of a now-historical attitude toward a still more remote historical past. Inevitably, our own attempts at historical reconstruction will recapitulate some of that movement's limitations and mistakes. May we also recreate some of its imaginative insight into the recurrent continuities of human experience.

Florence S. Boos
Iowa City, Iowa
December, 1991

History and Community

Alternative Victorian Futures:
"Historicism," *Past and Present* and *A Dream of John Ball*

Florence S. Boos

European and American intellectuals have often debated the uses and abuses of "historicism," a term which has itself had a complicated history since Friedrich Schlegel first used it in 1789. At its broadest it simply records the truistic recognition that all human phenomena undergo historical change. Critics of "historicism" have long since exposed some of the more reactionary normative uses of nineteenth- and early twentieth-century European developmental histories-- crude causal or teleological models which made specious national or political unities "inevitable," and suppressed structural inequity and social conflict. More recently, Michel Foucault and his "new historicist" descendants have argued for an "archeology of the human sciences"--a metaphor that would have appealed to many Victorians--that would forego "uniform, simple notion[s] of. . . causality" for more holist consideration of "dependencies" in "discursive formation[s]."[1] One such "discursive formation" might be found in the Victorians' tendency to find themselves prefigured in past cultures, or overshadowed by them.

Such instances of historical reconstruction and identification have sometimes been called "existential"; I will call them "projective." "Projective" historicism of this sort was one of the more pervasive aspects of Victorian literature: it can be found not only in historical novels and dramas, but also in a wide range of prose romances, essays, and poetry of the period. My attempts to understand this phenomenon will begin with a brief allusion to the ideas of one of its foremost continental proponents, the late nineteenth-century philosopher of "human studies" (*Geisteswissenschaften*), Wilhelm Dilthey. Against the background of these Diltheyan arguments, I will then ask why Victorian women were less ardent medievalizers, and examine some views of historical reconstruction in Elizabeth Barrett Browning's *Aurora Leigh* and George Eliot's *Daniel Deronda*. After this, I will examine two Victorian reconstructions in some detail: Thomas Carlyle's *Past and Present*, and one of the finest set pieces of nineteenth-century historicism, William Morris's treatment of the Peasant Uprising of 1381 in *A Dream of John Ball*. Finally, I will attempt a concluding evaluation of the range, limitations, and strengths of Victorian historicism as a whole, and consider some ways in which it might enlarge in turn our own sense of human identity and its future.

Victorian intellectuals notoriously encountered a decline of religious certainty and rise of scientific methods and disciplines (geology, physics) which seemed to ignore or deny the centrality of human concerns. One nineteenth-century response to these cultural modifications was to search for forms of historical and literary art which might preserve--in memory at least--certain essentially unquantifiable human emotions and experiences.

Wilhelm Dilthey (1833-1911) was a metaphysician, historian of ideas, and professor of philosophy at the University of Berlin, who attempted to characterize "human"--as opposed to "natural"--studies, and argued that human beings organize their lives in patterns of interpretive ("hermeneutic") significance--legal codes, religion, myth, art, literature. We have a sense of the "value" of things in the present, he observed, and confront the future with "purpose," but ascribe meaning to human expressions most clearly in our evocations of the past. In one posthumously published essay, "The Understanding of Other Persons and Their Life Expressions," for example, he argued that a kind of "*Verstehen*" ("understanding") enables us to interpret expressions (gestures, works of literature, ...) of other human beings in ways which deepen our own awareness of human identity. Actions can only be observed from the outside, and they express only part of our being. A "spontaneous expression of experience," by contrast, may be perceived directly, for "[a] special relation exists between it, the life from which it comes, and the understanding which grasps it."[2]

More significantly, he held that this "spontaneous expression" ". . . contains more of mental life than can be comprehended by introspection. It lifts mental life out of depths that consciousness cannot illuminate." In other words, projection and identification with the mental and emotional lives of others somehow create higher levels of awareness of our own nature, levels which no simple self-examination could provide. This claim also expresses one of the essential postulates of Victorian historical reconstruction: that we *can* validly project our responses into the past in some way, and that when we do, we extend our own identities as well as mirror them in some infinitely refracting wavefront of widening empathy and mutual awareness. Dilthey correctly observes that such expressive projections are not "true" or "false," "but only sincere or insincere," a criterion one can attempt (with varying degrees of "sincerity") to apply to the intensely interpretive historical recreations of Victorian literature. Moreover, as Dilthey noted, such artistic projections can give rise to meanings *beyond* those which have been present to a given poet's or artist's consciousness, meanings which may acquire a valid aesthetic, psychological, and atemporal "reality" of their own, and become subject to subsequent (re) interpretations in their turn.

Dilthey also expressed another implicit assumption of (most) Victorian literary historical enactments, when he claimed that such "understanding" is ultimately *individual*: "the individual is an object of absolute value, and indeed... the only such object that exists." Note that this claim does not follow in any obvious way from a view that *consciousness* is the principal source and "object" of value, for "consciousness" might in some sense be communal or collective. Dilthey's "individualism"--which should not be identified with political "individualism"--owes much to Kant's view of the ideal integrity of the self and its ("pure") will, and appeals to it help make intelligible the motive force and vivid specificity of recreations found (say) in Browning's *The Ring and the Book* and Morris's *A Dream of John Ball*. One consequence for Dilthey is that philosophical problems and the enduring enigma of other minds (and our own) remain sources of wonder and emergent value:

> The secret of the individual draws us for its own sake, into ever new and more profound attempts to understand it, and it is in such understanding that the individual and mankind in general and its creations are revealed to us. . . . complete empathy is dependent on the possibility of the understanding following the order of the events themselves, on its advancing forward as the course of life itself advances. . . . To relive is to create in the same direction as the original events.

Compare this with the nineteenth century's many narratives of time-travel and historical utopias, among them two of the works we will later examine.

A last passage from Dilthey may help identify another motivation for nineteenth-century historicism-- a desire to *escape* from the constraining "certitudes" of personality and time:

> In this reliving lies an important part of the spiritual gains for which we have to thank the historian and poet. The course of life exercises a determining influence on every man [sic], by which the possibilities which lie within him are narrowed down. His present character determines his further development. In short, whether he is concerned with examining his own situation in life, or contemplating the form of his acquired life-complex, he finds that the prospects of a new outlook on life, or further inner development of his personal character, are limited. But understanding opens to him a whole new realm of possibilities that are not present in his everyday life. The possibility of having religious experience is circumscribed for me, as it is for most people today. . . . But I can relive it. . . . Man, who is bound and determined by the realities of life, is not only liberated by art-- this has often been said--but also by the understanding of history.[3]

None of the authors we will examine could have read Dilthey. But both Carlyle and Morris's narrators are troubled by something like the sense Dilthey describes, of entrapment within a culturally predetermined (and perhaps diminished) time.

Thus "historicism".... But why the Victorian fascination with *medieval* history? In part, at least, in simple reaction to the massive infusion of *classical* history and literature in nineteenth century education. Indoctrination in Greek and Latin literature made inevitable widespread use of mythological and Roman literary motifs, and encouraged attempts to adapt Greek prosody and dramatic structures to other aims. At the same time, however, instruction in the classical languages was specific to upper- and upper-middle class males; its inculcation in the schools was often numbingly brutal, and its cultivation in the universities banal and shallow. By contrast, Mediterranean settings appealed to the Victorian fondness for warmly exotic landscapes; Greek mythology was mildly sensuous, and provided one of the few officially sanctioned alternatives to the puritanical and dogmatic aspects of sabbatarian Christianity. Finally, the *pax romana* seemed to provide a much-praised exemplar for English territorial and imperialist ambitions.

One of the more appealing aspects of Victorian medievalism in its more *historical* (not Arthurian) forms was also its paradoxical mixture of concreteness and immediacy. Many literate Victorians could pursue medieval history informally, prompted and aided not only by their education, but also by vestiges of medieval building and culture which still surrounded them. Druidic and Celtic remains were long since few and hard to interpret, and Roman ones evoked a colonized and provincial past. Medieval remains, by contrast, seemed to offer the Victorians a more authentic record of their "real" origins, and a convenient reinforcement of a sense of patriotic identity as well.

One should also remember that for the Victorians, the "medieval" period began with the fall of Rome, and extended well into what we would now refer to as the Renaissance. The "Middle Ages" seemed to them exactly that--a long stretch of eleven, even twelve centuries, between the "classical" age of Greece and Rome and their own "modern" one. So conceived, the medieval millennium suggested important contrasts with contemporary experiences of urbanization, industrialization, and immiseration, and provided very wide scope for alternate views of history. Systematic study of British antiquities--in such newly formed groups as the Camden Ecclesiastical Historical Society, the Scottish Folio Club, and the Early English Text Society--grew throughout the century, and new historical and critical methods opened exciting prospects for future study.

Medievalism and Victorian Women

Finally, some Victorian intellectuals--Carlyle, for example--may have found medieval history attractive for its avoidance of implicit issues of racial conflict, gradually more and more central to the rationales given for British imperial expansion. Others--among them both Carlyle and Ruskin--may have noticed with tacit approval the degree to which its available sources marginalized and romanticized the lives and social roles of women. In a period when a "reformed" Divorce Law (1857) permitted adultery to men but not women, portrayals of knighthood and chivalric paternalism tended rather obviously to ratify and encourage a patriarchal model of the ideal Victorian family. Most writers concerned with improving the lot of contemporary women looked elsewhere for their models, and even Ruskin's great critiques of the degradation of the worker *never* saw women straight on, as the "workers" they have always been. Morris and Engels were partial exceptions to this pattern, but neither was a feminist in the twentieth-century acceptance of this word.

At best, therefore, male representations of women in medievalist poetry reflected *indirectly* something of women's subordination and discontent within Victorian society: many of its most empathetic and powerful literary evocations are of unhappy or tragically frustrated women. Alternatives to the dreary typology of Tennyson's *Idylls of the King,* with its submissively wifely Enid, conniving harlot Vivien, and destructively adulterous Guenevere, included Arnold's Iseult of Cornwall, Rossetti's Rose Mary, the suddenly-awakened Guenevere of Morris's early "Defence," the indomitable Gudrun of his *Earthly Paradise,* and Swinburne's tragically noble Iseult in *Tristram of Lyonesse.* One of the more sympathetic male Victorian poetic portrayals of a woman in an imagined historical setting is Robert Browning's "Pompilia" in *The Ring and the Book,* and it may not be coincidental that Browning's ideal woman finds no psychological home in the Italian Renaissance. Stabbed by her brutal husband at the age of seventeen, she awaits her early death as she reflects on a platonic ideal of spiritual union: "Marriage on earth seems such a counterfeit,/ Mere imitation of the inimitable:/ In heaven we have the real and true and sure" (II. 1825-27).

Several of the small company of women painters of the period whose works have survived also employed medieval as well as Renaissance subjects to portray gallant or royal women--e.g., Joanna Boyce's "Elgiva" (1854) and "Rowena" (1856); Emma Sandys' "Portrait of a Saxon Princess" (1863); and Mary Newill's "Queen Matilda" (1893).[4] It remains notable, however, that the most important women authors seldom sought medieval settings for their works. Perhaps what they found there simply seemed to them too bleak.

Christina Rossetti, for example, the younger sister of the translator of the *Vita Nuova* who was one of the century's most untiring painters and poets of medieval subjects, generally used contemporary or unspecific romantic and legendary settings for her poems. A few poems about unidentified royal families might have medieval settings, and the sonnet sequence "Monna Innominata" may involve Petrarch's Laura. But the speaker of the sonnets, like the unhappy heroines of Victorian male poets, expresses deep self-abnegation and frustration, and nothing in the sonnets themselves suggests any obvious historical context.

The wryest and most savagely funny satire of the worst aspects of *poetic* medievalism, in fact, was provided by one of the century's more clear-sighted poets, Elizabeth Barrett Browning. Though she herself had included several medieval poems in her *Poems* of 1844 ("The Romaunt of the Page," "Lady Geraldine's Courtship") thirteen years later, in a brilliant passage from Book Five of *Aurora Leigh*, she commented sardonically on "poems made on. . . chivalric bones":

> I do distrust the poet who discerns
> No character or glory in his times,
> And trundles back his soul five hundred years,
> Past moat and drawbridge, into a castle-court,
> To sing--oh, not of lizard or of toad
> Alive i' the ditch there,--'twere excusable,
> But of some black chief, half knight, half sheep-lifter,
> Some beauteous dame, half chattel and half queen,
> As dead as must be, for the greater part,
> The poems made on their chivalric bones;
> And that's no wonder: death inherits death. (II. 1189-99)[5]

The pasts recorded by the great Victorian women *novelists*--the Brontës, Elizabeth Gaskell, George Eliot, were generally within living memory, or extended no farther back than the late eighteenth century, a period which had seen the rise of the novel and of a culture more directed towards literate middle-class women. It may also be revealing that no Victorian woman novelist of greater stature than Charlotte Yonge was prepared to grant the dignity of idealization to "medieval" fiction, and that the major woman novelist who attempted the most radical critique of the Victorian class structure--George Eliot--sought her hero, Daniel Deronda, in a non-European and non-Christian historical tradition. Eliot's narrator describes respectfully the venerable antiquity of Daniel's aristocratic English heritage, but she invokes a quite different historical tradition for her critique of her society--messianic Judaism. Daniel's Zionist mission, like the journeys of Morris's *John Ball* and *News from Nowhere*, forms part of a futurist vision, in this case of a pluralistic and enlightened pan-cultural Jewish state.

Eliot's displaced idealism brought with it its own implicit dangers of sentimentalization and oversimplification, and she avoided painful aspects of Rabbinical tradition (subordination of women, for example, and factionalist bigotry) which she refused to condone in her own British Protestant background. There is nevertheless something powerfully liberating in *Deronda*'s use of a non-contemporary-English, non-Christian ideal as a framework for judgment of her culture. At its best, Eliot's attempt to present a fully developed alternate social, historical, and religious vision is akin to the most successful attempts by male Victorian medievalists to extend their conceptions of human identity and of the future--one of the few models for such attempts, in fact, which is not readily subject to some aspect of Barrett Browning's parody.

A sense of the "medieval" as *alternate culture* (at least for men)--alternative both to contemporary capitalist and imperialist *realpolitik*, and to the unrealities of their conventional classical education--may also have been brought home to the Victorians when they witnessed--before their eyes, in fact--the obliteration of the remains of past centuries, in the swiftest defacement of landscapes, buildings, and folk customs of earlier cultures, "modern" or "medieval," England had ever seen. As late as 1815, seventy per cent of the population of Great Britain lived in rural areas; by the end of the century, nearly three-quarters were crowded into a few enormous, squalid cities (Liverpool, Manchester, Birmingham, London), and the century's growing immiseration and class-oppression were manifest to any honest observer. One of these was the young Friedrich Engels, who composed the following impassioned description of urban alienation--one which would not now seem at all "radical"--in 1844:

> Hundreds of thousands of men and women drawn from all classes and ranks of society pack the streets of London. Are they not all human beings with the same innate characteristics and potentialities?.... Yet they rush past each other as if they had nothing in common....
>
> The more that Londoners are packed into a tiny space, the more repulsive and disgraceful becomes the brutal indifference with which they ignore their neighbours and selfishly concentrate upon their private affairs. We know well enough that this isolation of the individual--this narrow-minded egotism--is everywhere the fundamental principle of modern society. But nowhere is this selfish egoism so blatantly evident as in the frantic bustle of the great city. The disintegration of society into individuals, each guided by his private principles and each pursuing his own aims, has been pushed to its furthest limits in London. Here indeed human society has been split into its component atoms.[6]

A way of life which had arisen in a millennium of incremental growth, in short, had been exploded in three generations. More genteel architectural counterparts of this annihilation took the form of "restoration," which gutted buildings' interiors, and left parts of the facade intact. Such pious mutilation was especially inflicted on older churches, among the most enduring forms of public architecture. In reaction to the phenomenon, William Morris and others founded the Society for the Protection of Ancient Buildings in 1877.

Far from the static period fondly enshrined in twentieth-century folk history, then, the mid-nineteenth century was a period of rapid and ruthless change, and an urgent desire to preserve the remaining artifacts and expressions of a past culture underlay the near-elegiac tone of much Victorian historicism. Disaffected middle-class intellectuals, barely tolerated at the margins of Victorian commercial culture, were most likely to notice its defacement of the historical past, and some of them responded with critical polemics of great rhetorical force and eloquence.

Thomas Carlyle's 1843 *Past and Present*, for example, was his response to the social unrest of the early 1840's. The so-called "Corn Laws" kept food prices so high that ninety-five percent of the population lived in poverty and squalor; those who did not die of starvation struggled to survive in hideous slums which prefigured those of today's Mexico City, Rio de Janeiro, and Calcutta. Several strikes erupted in Manchester and other parts of the Midlands in 1842, the year Chartist petitions for universal manhood suffrage and other reforms also gathered more than three million three hundred thousand signatures in a country of twenty million, many barely able to sign their names. The petition was brought to Parliament, where it was derisively rejected. With most of his class, however, Carlyle opposed any form of worker autonomy, trade unionism, or broadening of the electorate, and in anticipation of a political line the Germans later called "national liberalism," exhorted the English middle-class to lead an industrial army of diligent workers, and seek direction from a heroic future leader and quasi-Hegelian world-historical-individual he called a new "Duke of Weimar."

Like the sarcasm of Karl Kraus or H. L. Mencken in the twentieth century, Carlyle's rhapsodic denunciation often seemed to purge more effectively because it was an unconscious part of what it attacked. His prose explodes in contrasting outbursts of ironic admiration, invective, exhortation, and celebration, and its referents sometimes pass all understanding. Little of the book is susceptible to adequate paraphrase, and much of it is best understood as a kind of lightning rod, in which the tensions of personal restlessness and social discontent ran for a moment to ground.

There had been no 1848 revolution in Britain, and Carlyle's epigrammatic anger and contempt for humbug helped earn him the respect of a generation of restive young middle-class males, who did not necessarily share his obsession with "great men." His urgent exhortations to "work" were also quotable, in part, *because* they prescribed so few details; the socialist William Morris, for example, later acknowledged Carlyle as one of his two Oxford "masters" (the other was Ruskin), whose iconoclasm and sense of purpose gave him hope that some great social change might yet come.

Carlyle's historicist evocations of medieval England in the second book of *Past and Present* fit the political and rhetorical framework just sketched especially well. They provide the work's chief *exemplum* of just government, and are framed and controlled by an unusually careful and directive introduction and exposition, and a peroration which points their message for the present and future. In the introduction, Carlyle presents his narrator as an "Editor," who has discovered the interconnected spiritual meaning within historical process:

> Out of old Books, new Writings, and much Meditation not of yesterday, he will endeavour to select... and from the Past, in a circuitous way, illustrate the Present and the Future. The Past is a dim indubitable fact: the Future too is one, only dimmer; nay properly it is the *same* fact in new dress and development. For the Present holds in it both the whole Past and the whole Future;--as the LIFE-TREE IGDRASIL, wide-waving, many-toned, has its roots down deep in the Death-kingdoms, among

the oldest dead dust of men, and with its boughs reaches always beyond the stars; and in all times and places is one and the same Life-tree! (42)[7]

(Romantic "Organicism," as remarked earlier, could hardly have found a more explicit Metaphor than this!)

Carlyle further devised a fictive medieval chronicler, Jocelin of Brakelond, whose imagined account, *Chronica Jocelini de Brakelonda, de rebus gestis Samsonis Abbatis Monasterii Sancti Edmundi*, is devoted to the administration and character of its similarly fictive Abbot Samson. Liberated from the drossy constraints of "assiduous Pedantry" and the "dry rubbish" of already-known history (53), Carlyle's narrator/"Editor" is free to create fictive but suggestive history, and blur together "representative" persons and events. Only the "Editor" is able to impose such interpretations, however; dry-as-dust cavilers in the audience cannot use the techniques of "assiduous Pedantry" to question the validity of his sources or his methods of appropriation.

The world of Jocelin's chronicle is both remote and paradoxically immediate, and completely subject to Carlyle's authorial control:

... now seven centuries old, how remote is it from us; exotic, extraneous; in all ways, coming from far abroad! The language of it is not foreign only but dead. ... Jocelin of Brakelond cannot be called a conspicuous literary character; indeed few mortals that have left so visible a work, or footmark, behind them can be more obscure. (46)[8]

Jocelin's "obscurity," like a magic mirror which clouds before it reveals its mystery, quickly clears:

The good man, he looks on us so clear and cheery, and in his neighborly soft-smiling eyes we see so well our own shadow,--we have a longing always to cross-question him, to force from him an explanation of much.

A Diltheyan sense of exclusion from the past suddenly closes in, however:
> But no; Jocelin, though he talks with such clear familiarity, like a next-door neighbour, will not answer any question: that is the peculiarity of him, dead these six hundred and fifty years, and quite deaf to us, though still so audible! The good man, he cannot help it, nor can we. (49)

This evocation of Jocelin's kindly, helpless silence becomes an even more poignant displacement of his own hypothetical identity:
> Readers who please to go along with us into this poor *Jocelini Chronica* shall wander inconveniently enough, as in wintry twilight, through some poor strip hazel-grove.... across which, here and there, some real human figure is seen moving: very strange; whom we could hail if he would answer;--and we look into a pair of eyes deep as our own, *imaging* our own, but all unconscious of us; to whom we for the time are become as spirits and invisible! (55)

After this narrative *introit*, the reader's approaches to this desired medieval past become subject to the ambiguous "Editor"'s complete and rather arbitrary control. It should be no more than mildly surprising that this Editor sometimes assumes the persona of his vanished chronicler; that "we Monks of St. Edmundsbury" (73) include him in their number, and that he records answers to several questions he *personally* has asked the Abbot Samson. The narrator also merges with other persons mentioned in the chronicle, however, and at one point admonishes the Abbott in a distinct "Editorial" (authorial?) voice ("... right, Samson; that it [anger] may become in thee as noble central heat,... not blaze out... to scorch and consume!" (96).

Thus ambiguously merged with his no-longer-so-remote band of "brothers," the narrator finally discovers the secret he seeks, when he learns that the deepest experience of Sampson's life--the "culminating point of his existence" (127)--is the latter's identification with *his* deceased predecessor, St. Edmund. In solitude, we see the Abbot worship Edmund's corpse, unwrap his shroud, take its head in his hands, and address to it a solemn prayer.

Carlyle's central tableau is thus a scene of relic-worship, in which a middle-aged man reverently caresses a corpse--a scene which might have seemed somewhat less eccentric to Victorians, accustomed as they were to worship from time to time in cavernous churches filled with elaborate funeral effigies of prelates. Lest we think the Abbott might better have sought his "right man" (125) among those still *living*, the narrator here insists that:

> 'We touch Heaven when we lay our hand on a human Body,'--[the deepest mystery lies in the] Body of one Dead;--a temple where the Hero-soul once was and now is not: Oh, all mystery, all pity, all mute *awe* and wonder; *Super*naturalism brought home to the very dullest; Eternity laid open....

Only such solitary, recurrent spiritual identification with the unappreciated dead, Carlyle claims, can break us free of entrapment in a chaotic and purposeless present. (Anyone who has read Gerard Manley Hopkins's "The Windhover" will recognize in this remarkable passage the cadences and sensations with which Hopkins's speaker addresses "my chevalier"). This strange scene can also be interpreted as another Diltheyan attempt to extend consciousness across a temporal divide, but here the central tableaux of the past have become an absence. In a curious way, the narrator has murdered a living past--narrowed it to a single scene of pious and well-intended necrophilia--in order to render it more amenable to passive appropriation in the present.

All that follows in Samson's life is anticlimax, in any case, and the Editor's record of his life-history concludes with the moral that "The hands of forgotten brave men have made it a World for us. . . ." (134). The real heroes of England, he adds, are those who through all the centuries have worked, "all the men [sic] that ever cut a thistle, drained a puddle out of England, contrived a wise scheme in England, did or said a true and valiant thing in England" (134-35) (Notice the casual sexism and gratuitous nationalism of his otherwise moving refrain.) The narrator's conviction helps assuage his fears that unrecognized work done in the *present* may not matter to the future:

> Work? The quantity of done and forgotten work that lies silent under my feet in this world, and escorts and attends me, and supports and keeps me alive, wheresoever I walk or stand, whatsoever I think or do, gives rise to reflections! Is it not enough, at any rate, to strike the thing called "Fame" into total silence for a wise man? (135)

This near-ecstatic epiphany has one bittersweet quality, however: it actually heightens the sense of dislocation and deprivation he feels in the present. Like Dilthey, Carlyle's narrator especially notes the loss of past religious conviction:

> But, it is said, our religion is gone: we no longer believe in St. Edmund, no longer see the figure of him "on the rim of the sky," minatory or confirmatory! God's absolute Laws. . . have become. . . computations of Profit and Loss. . . It is even so. To speak in the ancient dialect, we 'have forgotten God.' (139)

A moment's reflection suggests that a sense of elegiac estrangement from past beauty neither follows nor entails simplistic dichotomies of "God" vs. "Profit."

Morris expressed his own forms of yearning for lost beauty, but also sought more secular forms of "spiritual" experience in the past, which might provide some benediction for the present and direction for the future.

Past and Present closes with a rhetorically powerful, characteristically ahistorical exhortation to create an obscurely numinous alternative:

> Chaos is dark, deep as Hell; let light be, and there is instead a green flowery world. O, it is great, and there is no other greatness.... The enormous, all-conquering, flame-crowned Host, noble every soldier in it; sacred, and alone noble. Let him who is not of it hide himself; let him tremble for himself.... O Heavens, will he not bethink himself; he too is so needed in the Host! In hope of the Last Partridge, and some Duke of Weimar among our English Dukes, we will be patient yet awhile. (294)

Once again, however, the incantatory surge of Carlyle's biblical rhetoric passes all Diltheyan "understanding." He *has*, however, rhetorically memorialized one fictional attempt to redeem an infinitesimal moment of lost time.

A more reflective and consistant Victorian historicist was William Morris, whose artistic life was devoted to contemporary realization of elements of medieval art and literature. One of his century's most innovative and influential decorative artists, he also created designs for stained glass windows, textiles, and wallpapers from medieval models. As a co-translator with Eiríkur Magnússon of the Icelandic sagas, he made a major medieval literary form available for the first time to English readers; and as the founder of the Kelmscott Press and pioneer of modern book design, he studied the early printed books of Caxton and other late medieval printers for principles which he embodied in his own work. In his writings on art and socialism, Morris was also more preoccupied than other Victorian social thinkers--Engels, Ruskin, Arnold, Mill--with the need to preserve and recreate the past. In many wide-ranging essays--"The Lesser Arts," "Art and Labor," "Gothic Architecture," "The Gothic Revival," "Early England," "The Illuminated Books of the Middle Ages," "The Literature of the North"--he drew on valuable features of medieval culture to praise forms of art and labour which had been blighted by nineteenth century capitalism.

More than other major Victorian poets, even those who used medieval subjects--Tennyson, Browning, Arnold, Rossetti, Swinburne, and Hopkins, among them--Morris also drew extensively on histories, chronicles, and past literature(s) to construct his plots. Much of the poetry for which he is best known--*The Defence of Guenevere* (1858), *The Earthly Paradise* (1867-70), and *Sigurd the Volsung* (1876)--clearly reflected his eclectic use of medieval European history and literatures. *The Defence* recasts incidents from Malory and Froissart; *Sigurd the Volsung* extensively reworks the twelfth-century Norse *Volsunga Saga*; *The Earthly Paradise*'s carefully described fourteenth-century Scandinavian "Wanderers," in flight from the Bubonic Plague, tell medieval tales, and their Greek rescuers and hosts tell medieval versions of classical ones.

Almost all of Morris's many prose romances are set in the Middle Ages, including his earliest tales, written in 1856 for the *Oxford and Cambridge Magazine*. Among the latter is "Lindenborg's Pool," in which a nineteenth-century narrator is temporarily transported into the thirteenth century. Two of Morris's later romances, *The House of the Wolfings* (1888), and *The Roots of the Mountains* (1889), also provide fond but conjectural reconstructions of the economy, kinship patterns, military preparations, music, tribal religion, and burial rituals of Germanic tribal life at the close of the Roman Empire. But one of the nineteenth-century's most complex relationships between a contemporary narrator and medieval subject may be found in Morris's moving historical embodiment of the socialist ideal of "fellowship," the 1889 *A Dream of John Ball*.

Like Carlyle, Morris takes pains to dissociate his love of history from mere antiquarianism and uncritical acceptance of chroniclers' propaganda:

> [This is] a time when history has become so earnest a thing amongst us as to have given us, as it were, a new sense: at a time when we so long to know the reality of all that has happened, and are to be put off no longer with the dull records of the battles and intrigues of kings and scoundrels. ("The Lesser Arts")[9]

Morris even more thoroughly respected the efforts of Carlyle's medieval "workers," but always sought evidence of medieval life he considered more authentic, in sources other than the barren and distorted accounts of progresses and "intrigues" of "kings and scoundrels" he mocks here.

More deeply than for any other Victorian literary figure, Morris's use of medieval history was also motivated by a search for anticipations of the *future* in the past. A *Times Literary Supplement* reviewer correctly observed in 1912 that he was "always concerned with the future even when he seemed most absorbed in the past. He turned to it, not to lose himself in it, but to find what was best worth having and doing now."[10] Morris's fellow utopian socialist Ernst Bloch called historical traces of as-yet-unachieved ideals *novae*, and he asserted--with Morris--that we should try to understand and recreate such "anticipatory designs" in our own present and future. Morris's desire to find such *novae*--concrete realizations in the past of partial alternatives to "the condition of the working class in England"--extended far beyond John Ruskin's reformism and celebrations of the artistic freedoms of Gothic architecture. Morris was as interested in the *conditions* of medieval labour, as he saw them, as in its *results*:

> ... I repeat that *for the workers* life was easier, though in general life was rougher than it is in our days: that there was more approach to real equality of condition... as the distribution of wealth in general was more equal than now, so in particular was that of art or the pleasure of life; all craftsmen had some share in it.... ("Art and Labour")[11]

This hypothetical "*nova*" of medieval life--that it was not only more craft-based, but more communal and egalitarian as well--was the mature realization in Morris's work of an ideal of "fellowship"--mutual love in service to a worthwhile shared cause (compare Peter Kropotkin's "mutual aid"). In his early writings, the conventional personal and sexual nature of these loyalties is more prominent; later configurations of mutual allegiance are wider, and friends and lovers in the later prose romances are often dedicated members of communitarian societies.

Morris's literary descriptions of idealized medieval societies, sketched above, ranged from the early Scandinavian tale "Gertha's Lovers," whose rather self-consciously noble protagonists act to defend their country and a mutually-revered queen, to the already-mentioned *The Roots of the Mountains*, in which a somewhat more historically plausible tribe of "Wolfings" rescues kinspeople from slavery. The fourteenth-century England of *John Ball*, Morris's carefully researched account of the 1381 Peasant's Rebellion, is a better documented and more realistic reconstruction than his Scandinavian and Germanic tales, and his conjectures about it are correspondingly deeper and more reflective. *A Dream* is the most directly polemical and visionary of his historical projections, but it also provides his deepest and most searching analysis of the complex forms of historical sympathy and social consciousness the ideal of communal fellowship will require.

Morris joined England's first socialist party, the Democratic Federation, in 1883; during the next thirteen years of his life he devoted much of his enormous energies to the advocacy of socialism. *A Dream of John Ball* embodied one of Morris's attempts to educate himself and his literate working class audiences about their common history, expose the sources and mechanisms of inhumanity and injustice, and explore historical antecedents which might provide models for pride and emulation. *John Ball* first appeared in 1889, in installments in *Commonweal*, the socialist newspaper Morris edited, interspersed between parts of "Socialism From the Root Up," a brief survey of economic history and the rise of socialism by Morris and his collaborator Ernest Belfort Bax. In context, *A Dream* provided a fuller and much more eloquent literary parallel to the economic arguments with which it was juxtaposed.

The active British socialist movement in the late 1880's was desperately fragmented and small (about 600 members), and worked under constant threat of repression or arrest. This tiny band of socialists and anarchists could not look back on any successful or completed revolutions, and the ruthless suppression of the 1870 Paris Commune loomed as a warning of the likely consequences of isolated revolt. Against this background, *A Dream of John Ball* asked the obvious painful question: "Can there be any hope for future attempts to effect social change, when so many heroic efforts have failed?" In contrast to the directive "Editor" of *Past and Present*, Morris' narrative voice persuades with eloquence and grace; it offers a much clearer and more accessible image of the imagined past; above all, it invites a dialogue between reader and narrator, as both interpret their shared historical epiphany.

John Ball's analogue of Carlyle's Editor is an autobiographical narrator, a struggling nineteenth-century socialist who is "[S]ometimes... rewarded for fretting myself so much about present matters by a quite unasked-for pleasant dream." When his stirring dream ends, he must return to the "row of wretched-looking blue-slated houses," harsh winds, polluted air and river, and "that sense of dirty discomfort which one is never quit of in London," where he hears the factory whistles which call his fellows inexorably to their repellent and underpaid machine labor.

The dream-past of Morris's narrator is a place of apparent peace, beauty and near-preternatural clarity, a much more sensuously appealing environment than the "Editor"'s regulated monastery in *Past and Present*:

> I see some beautiful and noble building new made, as it were for the occasion, as clearly as if I were awake; not vaguely or absurdly, as often happens in dreams, but with all the detail clear and reasonable. (16: 215)
>
> ... [In] the village... I did not see... a single modern building, although many of them were nearly new, notably the church,

> which was large, and quite ravished my heart with its extreme beauty, elegance, and fitness. The chancel... was so new that the dust of the stone still lay white on the midsummer grass beneath the carvings of the windows. (16: 218)

The grace of Morris's careful descriptions of the medieval environment has often been remarked, but equally important in *A Dream* are his descriptions of *people*. The narrator describes the inhabitants of late-fourteenth-century Kent, as first they repair tools, eat and drink, congregate at the marketplace, and greet friends and family; and later as they gather for battle, fight, and mourn their dead.

All his descriptions are suffused with obvious emotion. When the narrator sits with his friend Will Green, and mourns several yeomen who have been killed, he feels again a kinship with the people and scenes around him:

> Thus we sat awhile, and once again came that feeling over me of wonder and pleasure at the strange and beautiful sights, mingled with the sights and sounds and scents beautiful indeed, yet not strange, but rather long familiar to me. (16: 259)

Later, shortly before he leaves, he will take a last look back at the long-vanished Kentish village:

> ... as we passed up the street again I was once again smitten with the great beauty of the scene; the house, the church with its new chancel and tower, snow-white in the moonbeams now; the dresses and arms of people, men and women...; their grave sonorous language, and the quaint and measured forms of speech, were again become a wonder to me and affected me almost to tears. (16: 257)

As the dream begins, Morris's autobiographical narrator shyly approaches his fourteenth-century comrades in the guise of a plainly attired, itinerant Essex "scholar" and poet. His language is tentative, and reflects the double consciousness of his "sending" from the remote future:

> "I knew somehow, but I know not how. . . ." (16: 222)
>
> "My mind was at strain to remember something forgotten, which yet had left its mark on it. . . ." (252)
>
> "I. . . looked back. . . with a grief and longing that I could not give myself a reason for, since I was [presumably] to come back so soon. . . ." (261)
>
> "I felt strangely, as though I had more things to say than the words I knew could make clear: as if I wanted to get from other people a new set of words." (257)

One measure of the townspeople's perceptiveness is the degree to which they recognize his displacement; some recognize that the "scholar" is clearly not from their region, but only John Ball is fully aware that he is a literal *revenant*--a "sending from other times."

The narrator is greeted with cordiality by all the townspeople he meets, but feels closest to two of them: the artisan, Will Green, for whom he comes to feel "no little love" (253); and the revolutionary priest John Ball, whose "face [is] [like Morris's] not very noteworthy but for his grey eyes," which "look as if they were gazing at something a long way off, . . . the eyes of the poet or enthusiast" (228). Together, Morris's nineteenth-century narrator and fourteenth-century visionary will struggle to understand and reconcile the paradoxical patterns of their shared past and future.

Midway through the work, Ball delivers a memorial sermon for his slain "brothers" at the village cross, which is one of the great set pieces of late-nineteenth-century literature:

> Forsooth, brothers. . . fellowship is life, and lack of fellowship is death: and the deeds that ye do upon the earth, it is for fellowship's sake that ye do them, and the life that is in it, that shall live

on and on for ever, and each one of you part of it, while many a man's life upon the earth from the earth shall wane...

Therefore, I tell you that the proud, despiteous rich man, though he knoweth it not, is in hell already, because he hath no fellow; and he hath so hardy a heart that in sorrow he thinketh of fellowship, his sorrow is soon but a story of sorrow.... (230-31)

The book's climax, "Betwixt the Living and the Dead," is a conversation between Ball and the "scholar," set in the village church, which lasts through the night before Ball's departure for London and death. The cadences of their language resonate with echoes of Christ's farewell meal and speech on the road to Emmaus.

Ball asks the strange "sending" what is to happen to him, and to his followers, and the narrator tells him, with sadness and deep respect: "If I know more than thou, I do far less; therefore thou art my captain and I thy minstrel" (268). They have already confronted the difference between the narrator's secular faith and Ball's orthodox Catholic one, in their quiet conversation about those of Ball's comrades who have died:

[John Ball] said, "Yea, forsooth, and that is what the Church meaneth by death, and even that I look for; ... that hereafter I shall see all the deeds that I have done in the body, and what they really were, and what shall come of them; and ever shall I be a member of the Church, and that is the Fellowship; then, even as now."

I sighed as he spoke; then I said, "Yea, somewhat in this fashion have most of men thought, since no man that is can conceive of not being; and I mind me that in those stories of the old Danes, their common word for a man dying is to say, 'He changed his life.'"

"And so deemest thou?"

I shook my head and said nothing.

> "What hast thou to say hereon?" said he, "for there seemeth something betwixt us twain as it were a wall that parteth us."
>
> "This," said I, "that though I die and end, yet mankind yet liveth, therefore I end not, since I am a man... Is the wall betwixt us gone, friend?"
>
> He smiled as he looked at me, kindly, but sadly and shamefast, and shook his head. (265)

Further apprised of his coming death and the bitter failure of his movement, the saddened Ball responds with dignity and courage, confident that the justice of his cause will somehow, eventually, prevail. Harder for him to understand is the stranger's yet-grimmer message from the future, that greater production will someday bring even greater misery and inequity. To the news of successive forms of supposed "progress"--enclosures, industrialism, use of machinery to sequester wealth, "freedom" which brings wage slavery, helplessness of the workers thus "freed"--he responds with a mingled incredulity, anger, and grief which is much more urgent and more intense than his sadness at the "scholar"'s disbelief in the fellowship of the true Church. Morris clearly expects his audience to share the narrator's "shamefast" response to Ball's aggrieved astonishment that workers of 1887, unlike those of 1381, have not yet risen up to rebel against these new, infernally subtle and barely comprehensible forms of oppression and poverty.

When the priest finally learns the ignominy that nineteenth-century capitalists will make a "principle" of setting people against their fellows, he can bear no more:

> "Now am I sorrier than thou hast yet made me," said he; "for when once this is established, how then can it be changed? Strong shall be the tyranny of the latter days.... Woe's me, brother, for thy sad and weary foretelling!... Canst thou yet tell

me, brother, what that remedy shall be, lest the sun rise upon me made hopeless by thy tale of what is to be?" (284)

As the last night of Ball's life wanes, the narrator now struggles to answer Ball's anguished question. Can he offer no adequate comfort to him as he goes to his death, no assurance that the point of his failed uprising will not be doubly dissipated by political and technological changes beyond his comprehension? Does he *himself* truly believe that failed revolutions have served a purpose?

In effect, he must clarify his earlier response to the priest's sermon at the market cross: his insight that

> ... men [sic] fight and lose the battle, and the thing that they fought for comes about in spite of their defeat, and when it comes turns out not to be what they meant, and other men have to fight for what they meant under another name.... (231-32)

He begins with a lyrical image of changing light in the darkened church, which suggests the processive complexity of their shared hopes:

> "Look you, a while ago was the light bright about us; but it was because of the moon, and the night was deep notwithstanding, and when the moonlight waned and died, and there was but a little glimmer in place of the bright light, *yet was the world glad* because all things knew that the glimmer was of day and not of night.... Yet forsooth, it may well be that this... dawn [shall] be cold and grey and surly; and yet by its light shall men see things as they verily are, and no longer enchanted by the gleam of the moon and the glamour of the dream-tide. By such grey light shall wise men and valiant souls see the remedy, and deal with it, a real thing that may be touched and handled, and no glory of the heavens to be worshipped from afar off." (285)

This, then, is the narrator's central response. History is *not* without collective purpose, but that purpose is manifold and contingent, and the victories and defeats of one epoch may be more subtly recapitulated in the next. There will be many dawns and many dusks. The only consolations he can offer are that kindred souls will honor the *memory* of Ball's movement (a self-referential prophecy), struggle toward the essential ideals for which he had died, and preserve their common hope that liberation and social justice will someday prevail: in effect, that "We shall overcome...":

> "The time will come, John Ball, when that dream of thine that this shall one day be, shall be a thing that men shall talk of soberly, and as a thing soon to come about, ... therefore, hast thou done well to hope it; and, if thou heedest this also, as I suppose thou heedest it little, thy name shall abide by thy hope in those days to come, and thou shalt not be forgotten." (285)

Oppression will always win most of the battles. But the spirit of his movement will *not* fail, because it is the resilient spirit of all human beings at their most humane:

> "Yet shall all bring about the end, till thy deeming of folly and ours shall be one, and thy hope and our hope; and then--the Day will have come." (286)

Ultimately, this projection of faith becomes a clear secular counterpart of Ball's hope that he will rejoin his "fellows" in death--the "religion of socialism." As the deeds of future generations have vindicated John Ball's sacrifice, so must nineteenth-century and future audiences redeem that faith. Indeed, the priest finally understands that his visitor maintains a secular counterpart of his own vision--"secular" also in the literal sense of extending across centuries and cultural divides--which he earlier expressed in the hauntingly beautiful analogy of his sermon at the market cross:

> "Yea, forsooth, once again I saw as of old, the great treading down the little, and the strong beating down the weak, and cruel

> men fearing not, and kind men daring not, and wise men caring not; and the saints in heaven forbearing and yet bidding me not to forbear; forsooth I know once more that he who doeth well in fellowship, and because of fellowship, shall not fail though he seems to fail to-day, but in days hereafter shall he and his work yet be alive, and men be holpen by them, to strive again and yet again; and yet indeed even that was little, since, forsooth, to strive was my pleasure and my life." (233)

John Ball's final farewell to his strange friend across the divide of centuries also suggests a "greatness" of shared purpose which is deeper and more genuine than anything Carlyle's "new Duke of Weimar" and his followers might offer:

> "I go to life and death, and leave thee; and scarce do I know whether to wish thee some dream of the days beyond thine to tell what shall be, as thou hast told me [cf. *News from Nowhere*], for I know not if that shall help or hinder thee; but since we have been kind and very friends, I will not leave thee without a wish of goodwill, so at least I wish thee what thou thyself wishest for thyself, and that is hopeful strife and blameless peace, which is to say in one word, life. Farewell, friend." (286)

Earlier in this essay, I remarked on the unconscious omissions and exclusions of all but the best nineteenth-century "medieval" literature--inevitable, perhaps, in historical reconstructions by educated middle-class men for a readership of five percent of the English population. Most Victorian authors of such historical reconstructions (like most Victorian writers of any persuasion) tended, for example, to neglect the poor; Morris was an honorable exception. Most disregarded Jews and non-Europeans; members of sexual minorities; and most conspicuously, women. More realistic studies of the Middle Ages by anthropologists and economic historians have long since undercut any lingering tendency to identify the deeds of Carlyle's "heroes" with Morris's "kings and scoundrels"; a victory there. "History" itself has become a more complex entity in the process. More depressingly, the capacity of twentieth-century militarism and technology to alienate *literate* individuals from their history has also made it more difficult than ever to believe that there may once have existed, 700 years ago, or ever, a world which reflected more cohesively the social, aesthetic, and intellectual capacities of its inhabitants.

In any case, the obvious limitations in inclusion of Victorian historicism need not eclipse its insights into the essential communality and continuity of life. At their best, Victorian searches for historical alternatives to personal and social alienation evoked persuasive models for future integration of aesthetic and social identity, among them Morris's (and John Ball's) regulative ideal of "fellowship."

Most of their future, after all, is ours as well. In a contemporary society which faces *global* economic inequities even greater than the *national* ones Morris condemned, along with the subtle tyranny of military technocracy and catastrophic threats of nuclear destruction, we struggle to preserve some sense of historical continuity, as a ground of conscience and of self-respect. Whether we try to extend Dilthey's *Verstehen* to the past or the future, to repressed or simply foreign cultures, 'historicist' abilities to identify with others across the enclosures of our spatial, temporal, and cultural environments will be essential if we hope to negotiate a future worthy of our past.

The fictive "heroes" of *Past and Present* assured Carlyle that a natural force united his past and future.

Morris's "natural forces" are more social, but also more genuinely historical. *Past and Present*'s medieval "workers" provided a model for Carlyle's conception of future heroism. John Ball and Morris's narrator share a deeper faith, in the continuity of "the life that is in [fellowship], that shall live on and on for ever, and each one of you part of it," (230) a faith which enables his narrator and hero to endure apparent failure and defeat.

A Dream's conclusion is also more participatory and inviting than *Past and Present*'s demanding final exhortation. In Morris's vision, the power to effect social change derives not only from a sense of one's own just cause, but from a loyalty to those who have struggled for other such causes, and may have to struggle again--solidarity, in effect, with a community of secular saints. This is essentially a vision of counterfactual dialogue and invitation, which affirms John Ball's insight that we *should* sustain an ideal of communitarian "fellowship," *because* it may be as remote as Kant's "kingdom of ends." For so we remain human.

More than Abbot Samson's solitary worship of the body of the dead St. Edmund, the meeting of the narrator and John Ball thus reclaims for a secular age some of the images of continuity provided for Ball by his religion. Readers of Carlyle's book cannot really share the experience which forms its central tableau, for its remote and figurative representation of a union of heroes effectively silences its audience. Morris's participatory narrator, by contrast, subtly enacts the central conviction of his life, that history can be rendered meaningful by a counterfactual "friendship" and communion of persons across time. *A Dream of*

John Ball's complexly loving interchange with the past is one of his century's fullest expressions of a genuinely empathetic and imaginative historicism, which witnesses its narrator's belief in the continuity and coherence of human emotions, and his faith in a bonding of often-unrecognized social and artistic saints, across changes of language, culture, and the collective silence of our individual deaths. The priest's sermon once again conveys best Morris's testimony to his audience, and to us:

> ... it is for him that is lonely or in prison to dream of fellowship, but for him that is of a fellowship to do and not to dream. (234)

NOTES

1. "History, Discourse, and Discontinuity," *Salmagundi* 20 (1972): 232.
2. Dilthey, *Collected Works*, Stuttgart: Teubner Verlagsgesellschaft, vol. 7, trans. J. J. Kuehl, in *Theories of History*, ed. Patrick Gardiner, New York: Free Press, 1965, 213-225.
3. Dilthey, *Ibid*, in Gardiner, 219, 221.
4. See Jan Marsh and Pamela Gerrish Nunn, *Women Artists and the Pre-Raphaelite Movement*, London: Virago, 1989.
5. *The Complete Poems of Elizabeth Barrett Browning*, Cambridge, Massachusetts: Houghton Mifflin, 1900.
6. Friedrich Engels, *The Condition of the Working Class in England*, Stanford University Press, 1968, 30-31.
7. *Past and Present*, edited Richard Altick. New York: New York University Press, 1977, 42. Hereafter references to this edition are cited in parentheses after the quotation.
8. Compare G. M. Hopkins, "That Nature Is a Heraclitean Fire": "Squadroned masks and man-marks / treadmire toil there / Footfretted in it."
9. *Collected Works*, 24 vols., edited May Morris, London: Longmans, 1910-15, XX: 8. Subsequent quotations from this edition are referenced in parentheses by volume and page number.
10. *Times Literary Supplement*, 8 August, 1912, 312.
11. *The Unpublished Lectures of William Morris*, edited and compiled by Eugene D. LeMire, Detroit: Wayne State University Press, 1969, 104-105.

Interpreting Victorian Medievalism

Charles Dellheim

"True views on Medievalism," noted W. S. Gilbert in *Patience*, "Time alone will bring."[1] Time, at least scholar's time, has bestowed considerable attention on the Victorian concern with the medieval world. And for good reason: Medievalism--by which I mean the appeal to, and the appeal of, the styles, symbols, and survivals of the Middle Ages--was a striking feature of nineteenth-century art and thought. This essay addresses the critical question of how and why Victorians invoked the Middle Ages. It does so by examining medievalism in its social setting. Although I would hardly offer this essay as the "true view on Medievalism," it does attempt to provide an interpretive framework for analyzing its meanings. I insist on the plural "meanings" because medievalism had no single significance or use in nineteenth-century Britain, or for that matter in the United States or on the Continent. The case I propose to argue is that medievalism was a social language composed of myths, legends, rituals, and symbols that was appropriated by Victorians both to criticize and to affirm their own times.

"True views on medievalism" must consider a wide range of cultural pursuits. In literature one thinks of the Arthurian romances of Alfred Tennyson, Algernon Swinburne, and William Morris; in historiography the political and constitutional studies of William Stubbs, Edward Freeman, and J. R. Green; in painting, the works of Dante Gabriel Rossetti and the Pre-Raphaelite Brotherhood; in social and aesthetic criticism, the essays of A. W. Pugin, Thomas Carlyle, Benjamin Disraeli, John Ruskin, and again William Morris; and in religion the Oxford Movement. Nowhere was the impact of medievalism more striking than in the Victorians' physical environment. Neo-Gothic town halls and law courts, churches and cathedrals changed the face of Britain. Local archeologists and tourists explored the medieval survivals in the modern landscape. The presence of the past was unmistakable in historic towns like York whose skyline was dominated by church spires rather than factory smokestacks. There was also much of historic interest in industrial towns such as Leeds, the site of Kirkstall Abbey. The character of medieval survivals such as Kirkstall Abbey was altered in the Victorian age by the vogue of historic restoration and preservation.[2]

The views on medievalism put forth since W. S. Gilbert's time are largely the work of literary and art historians. The classic works of Charles Eastlake and Kenneth Clark examined medievalism as an episode in the history of taste.[3] Their generalist essays have been followed by a plethora of specialist studies examining individual figures, themes, and movements.[4] For all the interesting work on diverse facets of Victorian medievalism, however, we still have no synthesis on the subject. This is true for several reasons. First of all, it is a subject "everyone knows about. " Second, it is assumed too readily that medievalism was simply a conservative revolt against modernity. Finally, the disciplinary orientation of modern scholarship does not incline, or equip us, to look confidently beyond our own "fields."

II

An historical approach to the question of why Victorians invoked the Middle Ages must consider the nature of nineteenth-century society, the character of medievalism, and the relationship between them. Let me begin with Victorian society. In the first place, Walter Houghton tells us, Victorians saw their era as an age of transition. Uncertain as they may have been as to where they were headed, they knew, or at least thought they knew, what they relinquished. "To Mill and the Victorians the past which they had outgrown was not the Romantic period and not even the eighteenth century. It was the Middle Ages."[5] Seen from this perspective, the Victorian age was an age of destruction and reconstruction. It was also regarded as an age of "decaying feudalism" in which old opinions and ancestral customs were crumbling. Now there is much to criticize in this view of Victorian civilization. Every age can be seen as an age of transition containing the old and the new. Moreover, it was far too late for Victorians to bid farewell to the Middle Ages. It would be more accurate to say that the world radicals hoped to jettison was the post-Restoration social order; the feudal system was, of course, long gone even if certain vestiges remained. Finally, the medieval ideals and institutions that were allegedly dying enjoyed a remarkable recovery in the first decades of the nineteenth century. For our purposes, however, the accuracy of this way of looking, or if you will, not looking at the Victorian world is of secondary importance. What concerns us is that this historical outlook directed attention to the survivals of the Middle Ages and in particular to the relationship between the medieval and modern worlds. So too it encouraged those who opposed the new industrial social order to frame their protests in terms of medieval-modern contrasts. The very pace and depth of change stimulated historical consciousness by dramatizing the widening chasm between past and present.

Medievalism must be understood in the context of a complex social milieu, a milieu that looks far different now than it did in Britain's Victorian heyday. In the traditional Whig and Marxist interpretations, Britain was the most "bourgeois of nations." The passage of the Reform Bill of 1832, and the repeal of the Corn Laws in 1846 signalled the political triumph of the middle class. Industrialism was the foundation of middle-class economic dominion. The cultural values associated with industrialism--self-help and respectability, thrift and determination--shaped the national outlook. Yet revisionist historians suggest that the conventional view of the triumph of the bourgeoisie is more conventional than wise. The aristocracy and gentry retained their hold on the reins of political, and indeed, economic power throughout the nineteenth century. Not only did they dominate the high offices of government, but also they remained the wealthiest social group. The "middle class" was nothing if not a diverse entity whose social, economic, and ideological positions varied considerably. Indeed, there were two middle classes in Victorian Britain: the first composed of Tory Anglicans who were engaged in the old professions, commerce, and finance, and were closely tied to landed society; and the second composed of Nonconformist Liberals involved in industry. Contrary to expectation, commerce and finance were more lucrative pursuits than manufacturing.[6]

Industrialism did not completely transform Britain, Martin Wiener argues, despite its being, or because it was the first industrial nation. According to Wiener, the cultural values of the industrial world were contained by a preindustrial aristocratic-gentry ethos founded on land, status, hierarchy, and deference. Far from subverting the "ancient venerable prejudices" of the old order, many middle-class businessmen sought acceptance in landed society. Ironically, the country gentleman proved a more congenial ideal than the urban entrepreneur. By the late-nineteenth century, the critique of industrialism set forth by Matthew Arnold, Thomas Carlyle, and John Ruskin shaped an anti-industrial conception of the "English way of life." As Britain's industrial dominance was challenged by the United States and Germany, middle-class culture idealized the countryside rather than the city, the past rather than the present.[7] There are problems with this interpretation: it overestimates the extent of the gentrification of the middle class, and it underplays the strength of the industrial spirit, especially in the provinces. This interpretation also assumes that the concern with the past was necessarily an anti-modern force.[8]

Nevertheless, it is tempting to conclude in view of this portrait of the age that medievalism was a traditionalist expression of a traditionalist Britain; or, to put it differently, a symptom of an anti-industrial frame of mind characteristic of a society intent on repudiating industrialism. Indeed, many scholars argue or assume that medievalism was a counter-cultural reaction against the industrial word. For instance, E. P. Thompson contends that medievalism was a "revolt against the Railway Age and the values of Gradgrind."[9]

Medieval ideals and institutions assumed new meanings and uses in the early-Victorian age as the pace of industrialization quickened and its social consequences became visible. Medievalism was, on one level, a response to the social, political, economic, and cultural strains associated with industrialization, notably the birth of a class society, the erosion of aesthetic standards, the creation of squalid cities, and perhaps above all, the condition of the working class.

Three groups turned to the medieval world to frame their protests against the new industrial society. The first was comprised of members of the landed aristocracy and gentry, who experienced what Richard Hofstader called "status-anxiety." What they feared was political and economic displacement from without by the industrial middle class and from within by Sir Robert Peel's New Toryism. The classic example of such a group was Young England, the circle of aristocrats, including Lord John Manners and John Smythe, who gathered around and were manipulated by Disraeli. For Young England, as for the Tory radicals Michael Sadler and Richard Oastler, the paternalist, organic society of traditional England was betrayed by the "abdication of the governors," the refusal of their order to take responsibility for the welfare of the poor. Faced with an increasingly industrial, progressive society, they turned nostalgically to a medieval fantasy-world. They reasserted the feudal ideals of social hierarchy and communal responsibility, calling for an alliance of the aristocracy and people. Genuinely concerned as they may have been with the plight of the working class in industrial cities, they used this issue to discredit the industrial middle class and bolster their own power. These paternalistic medievalists offered security rather than autonomy, charity rather than opportunity, hierarchy rather than equality.[10]

Second, working-class representatives decried the "world they had lost." They framed their protests in terms of lost rights and immemorial liberties, echoing the "Norman yoke" theory of English history. This held that the Norman Conquest destroyed the representative institutions and political liberties of Saxons. By far the most important working-class medievalist was William Cobbett. As the champion of the rural, yeoman England of small landholders and domestic manufacture, he too feared the coming of industry. For Cobbett, the Protestant Reformation was a social calamity because it undermined the medieval Church that served as the defender of the poor. He deflated modern pretensions by arguing that medieval England was more prosperous than modern England. Cobbett's medievalism supported his vision of productive, independent workers in a cooperative society.[11]

Finally, middle-class social critics found much to admire in the Middle Ages. This group included both Ruskin, who hailed from the old middle class, and Morris, whose City stockbroker father used his newly found wealth to set himself up as a country gentleman. Morris, along with several Oxford friends from industrial Birmingham, declared a "Holy War and crusade against the Age" as Edward Burne-Jones called it. The aesthetic critique put forth by Ruskin and Morris focused on the architectural confusion and shoddy workmanship of the "Age of Makeshift." The division of labor that promised efficiency produced the alienation of the laborer. Enslaved by the machine, the worker found neither freedom nor pleasure in work. Not so in the medieval world whose aesthetic achievements were the work of craftsmen who found joy in labor. The recognition that the transformation of art depended on social revolution led Morris from aesthetic criticism to social action, from dreams of Guenevere to dreams of John Ball.[12]

What united these medievalist social critics? First of all, they were opponents of laissez-faire capitalism, economic individualism, utilitarianism, and the belief in progress through technology. In the medieval world they found alternatives to modern art, religion, and society. Second, they projected contemporary ideals into the Middle Ages. Clothing ideological commitments in historic dress lent the authority of the past to their endeavors. Finally, and most important, their discourse was based on a common set of myths and symbols--the manor, the monastery, the knight, the craftsman, and the Gothic style.

No less telling, however, is the fact that the dominant symbols of medievalist language did not translate into the same forms of speech. Here it is necessary to distinguish between "langue" and "parole". Meaning arises from use: The meanings medievalists attached to specific myths and symbols were often as different as the ideological implications they drew from them. It is true, of course, that Lord John Manners and William Morris were both "medievalists." But Manners idealized the hierarchical world of the feudal manor and Morris invoked the egalitarian world of the Icelandic sagas. Manner's medievalism led him to neofeudal reaction, Morris's to revolutionary socialism. A. W. Pugin and John Ruskin agreed that the Gothic style was the highest form of architecture, and agreed too that it was inseparable from the medieval society that created it. This recognition, however, led the convert Pugin along the path to Roman Catholicism that the Protestant Ruskin resolutely rejected. In the medieval guild Ruskin and Morris found an attractive alternative to laissez-faire capitalism and economic individualism. They contrasted the greed and shoddiness of the factory system with the just prices and craftsmanship of the guild system. Yet Ruskin's idealization of the guild became increasingly archaic, not to say pathological: Witness the pathetic, if well-intended spectacle of the Guild of St. George, Ruskin's disastrous attempt to found a modern community along the lines of a late-medieval Florentine guild. The craftsman ideal inspired Morris to build a chair in which Descartes would not have doubted his own existence. There were futuristic as well as archaic elements in Morris' idealization of the guild: aware as he was of the limitations of the guild-system, its example helped spur him to cross the "river of fire" into revolutionary socialism.

III

The Victorians invoked the Middle Ages to criticize their own times. Medievalism was, in part, a reaction against the social, political, economic, and cultural impact of industrialism. But the attention paid to the work of medievalist social critics in revolt against modernity has obscured other uses of medieval symbols. For Victorians also appealed to the Middle Ages to celebrate their own times. I do not mean to imply that all liberals looked back in admiration to the medieval world. Certainly they did not. Jeremy Bentham and the Philosophic Radicals condemned ancient and social arrangements. They rejected the prescriptive power of the past, basing their arguments for radical reform on utilitarian logic rather than historic precedents. In the campaign to repeal the Corn Laws, Radical leaders John Bright and Richard Cobden called for the end of feudality. But at the same time they likened their struggle against aristocratic privilege and inefficiency to the battle of medieval Hanseatic merchants against feudal oppression.

Given the continuing prestige of the past in British society, progressive forces could either repudiate or appropriate history. Both strategies defused the conflict between past and present, medieval and modern. Repudiation denied the value and relevance of the past, thus rendering it powerless. Appropriation lightened the burden of the past by reinterpreting historic myths and symbols or inventing alternatives. "The fundamental character of the mythical concept," Roland Barthes contends, "is to be appropriated." Myth is a "language-robbery" equally useful for justifying old values or legitimizing new values.[13] In a brilliant passage in *The Eighteenth Brumaire of Louis Napoleon* Karl Marx explains why revolutionaries invoke history:

> The traditions of all the dead generations weigh like a nightmare on the brain of the living. And just when they seem engaged in revolutionizing themselves and things, in creating something that has never yet existed, precisely in such periods of revolutionary crisis they anxiously conjure up the spirits of the past to their service and borrow from them names, battle cries, and costumes in order to present the new scene of world history in this time-honored disguise and borrowed language... Thus the awakening of the dead in those revolutions served the purpose of glorifying the new struggles, not of parodying the old; of magnifying the given task in imagination, not of fleeing from its solution in reality; of finding once more the spirit of revolution, not of making its ghost walk about again.[14]

Now let me offer in evidence two examples of the liberal appropriation of the Middle Age: first, a brief sketch of liberal historians' views of the Middle Ages; second, a fuller discussion of the popularity of neo-Gothic architecture in the industrial north.

If conservative medievalists were enraptured by a "dream of order," their liberal counterparts were inspired by a vision of liberty. Well aware as historians were of the despotic elements of medieval law and government, they cultivated an image of the "free" Middle Ages. Here they followed the Whig interpretation of English history that stemmed from Edward Coke and the seventeenth-century common law tradition. In search of the crucible of modern representative institutions, they turned to the "Teutonic" institutions of England. The central symbol was the face-to-face democracy practiced in the "village community."[15] Even Tory historians such as Sharon Turner accepted the myth of Saxon liberty. As he put it in his *History of the Anglo-Saxons*, "Liberty was the spring and principle of their political association; and provided the few civil institutions which their habits required."[16] Historians invoked the Middle Ages because they assumed, as Edward Freeman put it, that early English institutions were "closely connected with our present being." For Freeman, liberals had nothing to fear from the past because "at least as far as our race is concerned, freedom is everywhere older than bondage."[17] This was especially true, J.R. Green demonstrated, of the municipal institutions of medieval towns. The boroughs alone "preserved the full tradition of Teutonic liberty. The rights of self-government, of free speech in free meeting, of equal justice by one's equals were brought safely across the aegis of Norman tyranny by the traders and shopkeepers of the town."[18] Both Freeman and Green used organic metaphors to symbolize the historic continuity of English institutions. They legitimized their reformist politics by picturing democracy as a natural outgrowth of medieval law and government. In so doing, they invented a charter of values for reformers.

The liberal appropriation of the Middle Ages manifested itself in architecture as in historiography. From the 1860s to the 1890s, a spate of neo-Gothic civic buildings were erected in the industrial north. These included the Bradford Wool Exchange (1864), the Bradford Town Hall (1873), the Barrow-In-Furness Town Hall (1882-87), and the Middlesbrough Town Hall (1883-89). Nowhere in the north was the triumph of the neo-Gothic style more complete than in Manchester. A walker in the Manchester of 1900 would have seen a remarkable number of neo-Gothic buildings, including the Assize Court (1859), the Albert Memorial (1862), the Bridgewater Buildings (1864), the Town Hall (1868-77), the Reform Club (1870), the Prudential Assurance

Company (1881), and the John Rylands Library (1890-99).

Why Gothic? One can argue that in choosing the neo-Gothic style, civic leaders simply followed the fashion for neo-Gothic architecture set in large part by the Houses of Parliament. And there is some truth to this notion. But it does not explain why Gothic became a conventional secular style or what this aesthetic convention meant. Or one can argue, as Igor Webb does in his case study of the Bradford Wool Exchange, that industrial Gothic was an imitation of an aristocratic style and an expression of nostalgia for the preindustrial order.[19] Yet this thesis overestimates the gentrification of the middle class and oversimplifies the symbolic meanings of Gothic architecture.

The Manchester Town Hall illustrates the complex "traffic in significant symbols" in Victorian Britain.[20] The triumph of Gothic in Manchester is the perfect emblem of medievalism in modernity. In the 1840s, Manchester was regarded as the laboratory of the new industrial order. Social critics from Friedrich Engels to Matthew Arnold charged that Manchester's middle class was guilty of Philistine materialism and insensitivity to the plight of the working class.[21] The new town hall designed by Alfred Waterhouse was part of a broad cultural program to make Manchester a worthy city. Civic pride inspired the middle-class civic leaders who planned the building. They saw it as an opportunity to put Manchester on the cultural map and to prove that they were not entirely given up to Mammon.

But why was the Gothic style an appropriate vehicle for these aspirations? Surely the city fathers had no intention of evoking the baronial or ecclesiastical connections of Gothic. They hoped to recall the historical associations of Gothic with the free medieval cities of Flanders, Italy, and Germany. It was natural for them to identify with, or at least aspire to, the example of merchant princes distinguished as much by their personal culture and civic commitment as their wealth. As Joseph Chamberlain, the Radical Lord Mayor of Birmingham, put it in 1874:

> We find in the old cities of the Continent--of Belgium, and Germany, and Italy,--the free and independent burghers of the Middle Ages have left behind them magnificent palaces and civic buildings--testimonies to their power and public spirit and munificence, memorials of the time when those communities maintained the liberties and protected the lives of the people against the oppression, and the tyranny, and the rapacity of their rulers.[22]

Now that was a myth to conjure with. Far from being a bourgeois imitation of an aristocratic idiom, Manchester Gothic was, in Barthes' sense, a language-robbery. It reinterpreted the symbolic meanings of Gothic to celebrate the values and achievements of liberal, industrial civilization. The Town Hall demonstrated that Manchester's middle class was not composed of rootless *nouveau riches* lacking culture and tradition. Instead they were heirs of the long and honorable tradition of the merchant princes of the Middle Ages and Renaissance.

The historical iconography of the Manchester Town Hall defined the civic and aesthetic identity of Manchester as a commercial metropolis. It reveals how provincial liberals found in the medieval (and early modern) eras pedigrees for their own values. The elaborate decorations of the building affirmed the political and economic ideals of Manchester liberalism. The political imagery dramatized the origins and development of local self-government and parliamentary rights. For example, a statue of Thomas de Gresley commemorated the Charter of 1301 that made Manchester a free borough. Similarly, the economic imagery depicted the "romance of industry" and the triumph of free trade. For instance, Ford Maddox Brown's mural, "The Establishment of Flemish Weavers in Manchester, A.D. 1363," recalled the local myth which held that the textile industries that accounted for Manchester's success originated with the arrival of Flemish craftsmen in the town.[23]

IV

Throughout this essay I have argued that medievalism was a symbolic language. Why did it flourish in Victorian Britain? The constellation of changes associated with industrialization called into question the traditional order of preindustrial society. The medieval search for usable symbols was part of a larger quest for cultural orientation. In the Middle Ages Victorians found markers that helped them orient themselves in an open-ended, unprecedented world: first, by providing maps of continuity and change; second, by placing the "unfamiliar something" of modernity against familiar medieval myths and symbols. For example, the Gothic style of railway stations such as St. Pancras domesticated the new world of the iron horse by framing it in medieval architecture.

"What is socially determined," Clifford Geertz argues, "is not the nature of conception but the vehicles of conception."[24] Surely this is true of medievalism. Medieval symbols proved suitable vehicles of conception for a wide range of Victorians. Given the fundamental differences in the nature of their conceptions, however, it is not surprising that Victorians drove these vehicles in different directions. To put it differently, they spoke the same language with different accents and inflexions. Liberals, conservatives, and socialists were all able to invoke the Middle Ages because they attached very different meanings and implications to its myths and symbols. Medievalism, then, was nothing if not a plastic language. What unites the diverse uses of medieval symbols is that they may all be seen as part of a quest for identity--provincial, national, aesthetic, religious, and political.

    Let me conclude with some suggestions for future research. Studies in the social history of medieval myths, rituals, and symbols would help illuminate how and why Victorians invoked certain aspects of the Middle Ages. Much remains to be said about how Victorians imagined various aspects of the medieval world and how these images expressed their own fears and aspirations. It would be valuable, for instance, to know how they viewed theologians such as St. Augustine, St. Bernard, and St. Thomas Aquinas; and philosophers such as Peter Abelard, Duns Scotus, and William of Occam. We also know very little about civic rituals based on medieval themes such as the Bishop Blaize festivals in Bradford, the Preston Guild festivals, and the Lord Mayor's show in London. And it would also be useful to have comparative studies of the uses and abuses of medievalism in different times and places. Advancing our knowledge of medievalism is an eminently interdisciplinary project. Its success depends partly on general historians acquiring more sensitivity to the internal logic of art and historians of literature and art showing more concern for the social setting of aesthetic endeavor. In so doing, we may come closer to the "true views on Medievalism" that W. S. Gilbert left to the vagaries of time.

Notes

1. Quoted in Kevin Morris, *The Image of the Middle Ages in Romantic and Victorian Literature* (London: Croom Helm, 1984), 220.
2. On local archeology and tourism and historic preservation see Charles Dellheim, *The Face of the Past: The Preservation of the Medieval Inheritance in Victorian England* (Cambridge: Cambridge University Press, 1982), chs. 2-3.
3. See Charles Eastlake, *A History of the Gothic Revival: An Essay in the History of Taste* (New York: Harper and Row, 1962). See also Sir Kenneth Clark, *The Gothic Revival, An Essay in the History of Taste* (New York: Charles Scribner's Sons, 1929).
4. See Alice Chandler, *A Dream of Order: The Medieval Ideal in Nineteenth Century English Literature* (London: Routledge and Kegan Paul, 1971), and Mark Girouard, *The Return to Camelot* (New Haven: Yale University Press, 1981).
5. Walter Houghton, *The Victorian Frame of Mind* (New Haven: Yale University Press, 1963), 1.
6. W.D. Rubenstein, "Wealth, Elites and the Class Structure of Modern Britian, " *Past and Present* 76 (August 1977): 99-126.
7. Martin Wiener, *English Culture and the Decline of the Industrial Spirit, 1850-1980* (Cambridge: Cambridge University Press, 1981), 1-25.
8. See Charles Dellheim, "Notes on Industrialism and Culture in Nineteenth-Century Britain," *Notebooks in Cultural Analysis* 2 (1985): 227-248.
9. E.P. Thompson, *William Morris: Romantic to Revolutionary* (London: Merlin Press, 1977), 27-39.
10. On the aristocratic ideal see Harold Perkin, *The Origins of Modern English Society 1780-1880*

(London: Routledge and Kegan Paul, 1969), 237-51; and on Disraeli and Young England see Robert Blake, *Disraeli* (London: Eyre and Spottiswoods, 1966), 167-189.
11. See Perkin, *Origins*, 231 and Chandler, *Dream of Order*, 52-82.
12. On Ruskin and Morris see Thompson, *Morris*, chs. 2-3.
13. Roland Barthes, *Mythologies* (London: Jonathan Cape, 1972), 119, 124.
14. Karl Marx and Friedrich Engels, *Basic Writings on Politics and Philosophy*, ed. Lewis S Feuer (Garden City, N.J.: Doubleday/Anchor Books, 1969), 320. 322.
15. See J.W. Burrow, "'The Village Community' and the Uses of History in Late Nineteenth-Century England," in *Historical Perspectives: Studies in English Thought and Society in Honour of J.H. Plumb*, ed. Neil McKendrick (London: Europa Publications, 1975); and Asa Briggs, *Saxons, Normans, and Victorians* (Hastings: Historical Association, 1966).
16. Quoted in Rosemary Jann, "Democratic Myths in Victorian Medievalism," *Browning Institute Studies* 8 (1980): 133.
17. Edward Freeman, *The Growth of the English Constitution from the Earliest Times*, 3rd Edition (London, 1876), 111, x.
18. Quoted in Jann, "Democratic Myths," 151.
19. Igor Webb, "The Bradford Wool Exchange: Industrial Capitalism and the Popularity of Gothic," *Victorian Studies* 20 (Autumn 1976): 45-68.
20. On the "traffic in significant symbols" see Clifford Geertz, *The Interpretation of Cultures* (New York: Basic Books, 1973), 45.
21. On the images of Manchester see Steven Marcus,

Engels, Manchester and the Working Class (New York: Vintage Books, 1974), 28-66.
22. Quoted in *The Idea of the City in Nineteenth-Century Britain*, ed. B.I. Coleman (London: Routledge and Kegan Paul, 1973), 160.
23. For a detailed discussion of the Manchester Town Hall see Dellheim, *Face of the Past*, 131-76.
24. Geertz, *Interpretation*, 212.

The Myth of Merrie England in Victorian Painting

Rebecca Jeffrey Easby

Benjamin Disraeli's novel *Coningsby or the New Generation* (1844) contains an interesting exchange between two characters. "'Henry thinks,' said Lord Everingham, 'that the people are to be fed by dancing around a Maypole.'" He is quickly countered by the young Lord Henry who asks, "But will the people be more fed because they do not. . . ?"[1] On the surface the issue of May-pole dancing seems of little concern, but on a deeper level each character stands as a symbol for the opposing sides of a question raised by Disraeli's political group Young England. Was the life of the people better in "Merrie England," a past age of tradition and social contentment, and if so, could the re-institution of the traditions of the past provide a suitable model for the reform of Victorian society? In both painting and literature a passionate plea for the return of the Maypole was tantamount to a call for social reform.

Those who fostered the myth of "Merrie England," such as Thomas Carlyle, Augustus Welby Pugin, Edward Bulwer-Lytton, Benjamin Disraeli and other members of the Young England group, tended to be both politically members of the Conservative Party and disturbed by the condition of Victorian industrial society. Against such doctrines as Utilitarianism, laissez-faire economics, and the reforms implemented by the Liberal party, particularly the first Reform Bill of 1832, the Conservatives offered a regressive model for contemporary society. Each stressed supposedly "feudal" values; generosity of the upper classes to the lower, loyalty to the crown, a chivalric devotion to duty and honor, and above all faith and reverence for the Church. These aims were in direct response to those values which they believed were lacking in modern society--charity, communication between classes, and a pastoral existence--in short, a simpler, more ordered society based on the patriarchal responsibility of the upper classes.

Fueled by a resurgent interest in popular culture, all images of "Merrie England" share a consistent vision of the better life of the past. Their emphasis is always rural rather than urban and industrial, stressing a more harmonious relationship between the upper and lower classes. Such scenes can be found in both the art and literature of the early Victorian period, and are clearly tinged with a large dose of nostalgia. However, their existence also points to a dissatisfaction with the condition of contemporary society and a desire to return to a simpler time. The myth of "Merrie England" was an example--a method of pointing out the flaws in modern life by comparing it with the more favorable life of the past.

In painting, the ideal of what is often termed the "olden time" usually centers around village festivals and traditional agrarian ceremonies, clearly portraying a more contented lower class, at home with nature and cared for by a benevolent landlord. On some level, the use of the phrase "olden time" implies an awareness of contemporary revivalist criticism and ideas of social reform. Significantly, not one painting using the words "olden time" in its title was exhibited at the Royal Academy until 1834, two years after the passage of the first Reform Bill.[2] It is also important to note that while these images may be "medievalizing" in terms of sentiment, they are not necessarily "medieval" in date. The main aim of the artist was generally not accuracy of time or place, but an attempt to glorify ancient customs which were "medieval" in spirit if not in terms of actual detail. What such images have in common is their attempt to describe a happier existence in the past, whether one hundred or one thousand years ago.

A belief in the value of traditional ways of life led some to celebrate the continuance of ancient rituals in Victorian times. This fusion of social criticism and nostalgia for the old created paintings such as *The English Harvest: A Dream of the Olden Time: Reaping--Midday*, one of a trilogy of similarly titled paintings by the artist J.P. Knight.[3] While the pictures themselves were simple agricultural scenes, their titles imply more than typical pastoral images. Another such painting, George Harvey's *Hop Picking: A Composition of Kentish Scenery* exhibited at the Royal Academy in 1839,[4] is an unspoilt landscape, populated by well-dressed workers in harmony with both their tasks and their environment. In the foreground, peasant children use brooms made from freshly cut hops to dust the shoes of a smartly clad couple, a custom of the area described in the catalogue as "an ancient ceremony performed upon all who pass through a hop field; and the gratuities thereby gained are, at the end of the season, expended on a supper." Another such scene is William Maw Egley's *Hullo Largess! A Harvest Scene in Norfolk of 1862*. Egley depicts an old East Anglian custom where, if the farmer has a visitor during the harvest, the head man among the workers asks for a largess. The workers then form a circle and shout "Hullo Largess" while raising their clasped hands. This is done three times and followed by three successive whoops.[5] In each painting, the contemporary costume worn by the figures celebrates the survival of these ancient customs in a time when many of these rites have been discarded, along with the way of life which had ensured their continuation.

The fact that these paintings are intended to illustrate "ancient" customs points to a relationship between the development of the myth of "Merrie England" and the antiquarian publications of the nineteenth century. Illustrated books such as George Craik and Charles MacFarlane's *The Pictorial History of England* (1837) and Charles Knight's *Old England* (1844) used both copies of manuscripts as well as specially created drawings to provide a graphic picture of the life of the past. Knight, for example, emphasizes the condition of "the people," or the contented and nonthreatening peasant masses who populate "Merrie England." Paintings such as that by Egley illustrate their Victorian counterpart--rural laborers at home with their work and their traditions, and aware of their position within society.

As Peter Burke has pointed out in his *Popular Culture in Early Modern Europe*, a concept of "the people" is difficult to define, but the most pervasive image was that of peasants who lived close to nature and preserved primitive customs.[6] This is an obvious contrast to the realities of the Victorian lower class, where popular movements such as Chartism and the occasional uprisings of agricultural laborers point to a dissatisfaction with social conditions common to urban and rural workers alike. Some would-be reformers basically sought to replace these "new" people with the more pastoral and less threatening version. Towards this end the reintroduction of traditional holidays became a serious suggestion for ending working class discontent made by Young England's Lord John Manners in *A Plea for National Holy-Days* (1843). One can only imagine the reaction of Manchester's industrial laborers to the appearance of a Maypole--an obviously inadequate solution to the problems such as low wages and poor working conditions.

The use of such images can also be related to the literary theorist Mikhail Bakhtin's concept of the "carnivalesque," which has clear parallels in art. According to Bakhtin the carnival plays a critical role, testing all aspects of society and culture and breaking down traditional hierarchies.[7] In this case the carnival serves as a reminder of all that society had lost, particularly the cohesion of "the people" or a happy, contented peasantry. The function of the carnival is also that of a "safety valve," providing a time when social restraints vanish.[8] Without such a "safety valve," relations between the classes were sure to deteriorate, and the continuance of ancient traditions provided, at least to someone like Lord John Manners, a healthy release.

The preservation of tradition in Victorian times can be seen in Jacob Thompson's *The Rush Bearers*, a depiction of a local festival in the artist's native Cumberland. Here both villagers and the landed gentry, in this case members of the Lowther family who were patrons of the artist, take part in an ancient ritual.[9] Another instance can be seen in the engraving identified by *The Illustrated London News* as "from a drawing by an *Irish* artist" of the Harvest Home celebrations. The story states that "many of the old customs ... have fallen into disuse in Ireland, but the Harvest Home is still kept up with much of the vigor of former days."[10] The scene shows the inside of a barn, lavishly decorated with natural greenery, where the workers dance, drink, and generally celebrate the fruits of their labor.

These customs serve to illustrate another concept of great importance to the myth of "Merrie England," the idea of property as friend to the people. *The Illustrated London News* pointed out that in "Harvest Home the master and his family always visit the scene of enjoyment and by their presence ensure the good order as well as the good cheer of the labourers." In both Ireland and Cumberland such rural customs allowed for interaction between the classes, a contrast to urban society where many believed that the breakdown of class relations was the most regrettable result of industrialization. The very nature of the factory system, where the owner spoke to his manager who in turn relayed the orders to the workers, created an ever-widening gulf between rich and poor. The man who owned the factory was much less likely to comprehend, or even be aware of the problems of those who worked for him than was the agricultural landlord who had to live near and often see his tenants.

Jacob Thompson, *The Rush Bearers* (1872), published courtesy of Trafalgar Galleries; *Irish Harvest Home* from *The Illustrated London News* (1849).

This new distance between classes was noted with growing concern by contemporary writers and artists such as Disraeli, whose vivid description of "the two nations" forms the basis of *Sybil*, the second novel of his Young England trilogy, published in 1845. The growing tension between classes was seen as a direct result of the demise of rural life. As a clergyman wrote about Manchester: "There is not a town in the world where the distance between the rich and poor is so great or the barrier between them so difficult to be crossed. There is far less personal communication between the master cotton spinner and his work-men, the calico printer and his blue-handed boys, between the master tailor and his apprentices, than there is between the Duke of Wellington and the humblest labourer on his estate."[11]

Lack of contact between the factory worker and his or her employer was a prominent theme in Victorian literature, highlighting the distance between rich and poor. Elizabeth Gaskell's *Mary Barton*, e.g., contains a scene in which the character Wilson goes to the home of his employer, Mr. Carson, to obtain a note which will allow a fellow employee, who is fatally ill, to recieve immediate medical attention. While Wilson is in rags and virtually starving from lack of food, the Carsons, who live in luxurious surroundings, continue to eat their hearty breakfast in front of the hungry man without noticing his condition. Only the younger Mr. Carson and the family cook perceive Wilson's distress, giving him five shillings and some food respectively. Mr. Carson the elder cannot even comply with Wilson's request, but provides him instead with an outpatient order for the following Monday. His friend dies later that day.[12]

Mrs. Gaskell's story is in sharp contrast to a painting such as William Powell Frith's *Coming of Age in the Olden Time* of 1849. A comparison of the two makes clear the difference between past and present to the Victorian mind. Frith's scene takes place in the courtyard of an Elizabethan manor house in which are assembled both the landed gentry and their tenants to celebrate together this joyous occasion. The heir of the household, who has just attained his majority, takes his place on the steps of the manor, surrounded by his proud parents and grandmother. At the foot of the steps a crier dressed in black reads the formal announcement of the youth's birthday, while the peasants who work on the estate cheer, applaud and offer toasts to the health of their future lord. The celebrations include a great feast of roast oxen, an idea which Frith claimed to have formed when he saw an actual ox roasted at the opening of a cattle market in Islington.[13]

Although there is a clear distinction between the lord of the house and his tenants, the scene celebrates the concern of the lord for those under his protection--there are no Mr. Carsons present here. The clothes of the landowner and his family may be more costly and sumptuous, but all his tenants are cleanly and neatly, albeit simply, dressed. They do not go hungry on this, the day of feasting, or any other day. The tenants' devotion to their lord and master is clearly not just because of the food and the drink he provides; it is obvious that he cares for his laborers as a father cares for his children and they appreciate his concern.

Frith culled the antiquarian details of *Coming of Age in the Olden Time* from many different sources and materials, but none seems to have made such a deep

William Powell Frith, *Coming of Age in the Olden Time* (1849).

impression as Joseph Nash's *Mansions of England in the Olden Time* published between 1839 and 1849. While the manor house can be identified as a mixture of various engravings from Nash,[14] Frith seems to have borrowed more than architecture from his source. In the introduction of his four volume set, Nash explains his motives for such an undertaking: "the artist's object has been to present them in a new and attractive light, not as many of them now appear, gloomy, desolate, and neglected, but furnished with the rude comforts of the early times of 'merry England'... enlivened with the presence of their inmates and guests, enjoying the recreations and pastimes, or celebrating the festivals of our ancestors. Thus, not only the domestic architecture of past ages, but the costumes and habits of England in the 'olden time' are brought before the eye...."[15] Frith's painting is a prime example of this way of thinking, bringing to life a time of contentment, simplicity and order, when relationships and duties were clarified and life was easier and more pleasant.

The underlying message of Frith's painting, that there was more to life than the industrial, money-oriented values of the Victorian age, was obvious to Frith's contemporaries. In a review of an engraving after *Coming of Age in the Olden Time*, the writer asked: "We, in our days of commercial activity and enterprise, can scarcely realise such a scene of festive enjoyment as this, which almost instinctively puts a question to us;-- are we, with all our boasted advancement in science and civilization, really a wiser and happier people than our forefathers of three centuries ago?"[16]

Two years earlier in 1847 Frith had commemorated another event in "Merrie England" in his painting *An English Merry-Making A Hundred Years Ago*. A journal stated that "the picture tells of the simple pleasures of rural life,"[17] and it is an obvious example of the superiority of the past. Members from all factions of the community participate in the dancing and general merriment of the occasion, from the old man being dragged into the dancing by a group of young women and children to the lovers seated under the tree whose future is being told by the gypsy fortune teller.

Another painting at the Royal Academy of 1847 was Frederick Goodall's *The Village Festival*, which likewise portrayed the general merry-making of the past. As in Frith's picture, lively dancers form the background of the scene, while in the foreground, a peddler shows his wares to women and children of various ages and classes. Goodall's view of the past is also apparent in his painting *A Summer Holiday*,[18] where a stately mansion rises behind the scene of dancing and feasting, a reminder of the presence and benevolence of the squire. Goodall was characterized by his contemporaries as an artist who lived in "perpetual sunshine,"[19] and his image of the past is clearly one of peace, harmony, and social contentment.

This festival atmosphere of the past was stressed in a variety of sources. In literature, for example, one finds passages such as Edward Bulwer-Lytton's description from *The Last of the Barons* (1843) of the "greensward before the village (now foul and reeking with the squalid population...)" where "were assembled youth and age; for it was a holiday evening..." and "the merry laughter of the girls, in their gay-coloured kirtles and ribboned hair, rose oft and cheerily to the ears of the cavalcade."[20] Note Bulwer-Lytton's editorial comment,

William Powell Frith, *An English Merry-Making A Hundred Years Ago* (1847), Private Collection, England: photograph Courtauld Institute of Art; Frederick Goodall, *The Village Festival* (1847), The Tate Gallery, London; *Spring in the Olden Time* from *The Illustrated London News* (1843).

Charles Knight, *Maypole Before St. Andrew's Undershaft* from *Old England* (1844); C. Cousens after Joseph Nash, *The Maypole*; George Wilfred Anthony, *May-Day in the Last Century* from *The Illustrated London News* (1844).

which further stresses his meaning. Painting and other forms of visual illustration provided ample proof of the existence of this merry past.

The same year as the publication of Bulwer-Lytton's novel, *The Illustrated London News* ran a story on the history of May Day, where the appended picture of "Spring in the Olden Time--The Maypole," clearly shares this vision of the past. Other illustrations of May celebrations can be found in Charles Knight's *Old England* in his "Maypole before St. Andrew's Undershaft," C. Cousen's engraving after Joseph Nash's *The Maypole*, and in paintings which appeared at the popular London exhibitions, such as *May-Day in the Last Century*, shown at the Society of British Artists in 1845 by the artist George Wilfred Anthony and engraved by *The Illustrated London News*. A well received version of the May festival was Frederick Goodall's *Raising the May-Pole*.[21] The painting depicts the aftermath of Puritan rule when "rose the garlanded pole once more amid the cheers of the assembled villagers."[22] Typically, we see the squire and some of his family, here observing the festivities from horseback. In the foreground are the obligatory rustics, a group of drinking, carousing villagers.

One of the earliest paintings to emphasize the discrepancy between the old and the new is Daniel Maclise's *Merry Christmas in the Baron's Hall*, which was exhibited in 1838. The scene was a situation to which the Victorians could relate, as in many areas traditional Christmas customs were still carried out. Whenever the loss of ancient ceremonies was lamented, they could at least point to Christmas as a time when the old ways were still observed. As Lord John Manners wrote in a book of Young England poetry published in 1841, interesting for its sentiments rather than the brilliance of its verse:

> And now of all our customs rare,
> And good old English ways
> This one of keeping Christmas time,
> Alone has reached our days.[23]

It is this survival of custom that Maclise celebrates in his depiction of Christmas in "Merrie England." The scene itself is that of a Jacobean Christmas, where everyone on a large estate, from the Baron down to the lowliest worker, gathers together in the great hall of a manor house to eat, drink, play games, and celebrate the season. The image of a traditional Christmas was a popular one in literature and engravings; for example, Joseph Nash's depiction of Penshurst, Kent, in *The Mansions of England in the Olden Time,* shows the festivities surrounding Christmas time, wassail, mummers, and morris dancers. The fact that Maclise uses a Jacobean setting for *Merry Christmas in the Baron's Hall* is pure invention on the part of the artist. The subject was taken from a scene in Sir Walter Scott's *Marmion,* a poem set in the Elizabethan age,[24] and was accompanied by an explanatory ballad by Maclise and published in *Fraser's Magazine* in May 1838 which was clearly medieval in spirit.

This discrepancy between the time and place of the source, poem and the painting itself helps to stress the fundamental message behind the picture. Firstly, the subject emphasizes the importance of preserving ancient customs and this festival aspect of the past. More importantly, however, the picture presents an ideal view of class relations. It was probably just such an image as this fanciful Christmas feast that Maclise's

Daniel Maclise, *Merry Christmas in the Baron's Hall* (1838), National Gallery of Ireland; Joseph Nash, *Penshurst Castle, Kent* from *The Mansions of England in the Olden Time* (1839-49); *Christmas Eve* from *The Illustrated London News* (1848); *The Procession of the Wassail Bowl* from *The Illustrated London News* (1849). Photograph courtesy of Christie's, New York.

friend Disraeli had in mind when writing his novel *Coningsby* of 1844. Here Disraeli described the celebrations held on the estate of Eustace Lyle, a paragon of Young England virtue: "Within the hall, too, he holds his revel, and his beauteous bride welcomes their guests, from her noble parents to the faithful tenants of the house. All classes are mingled in the joyous equality that becomes the season."[25]

The underlying social content of *Merry Christmas in the Baron's Hall* was emphasized by Maclise in the poem which accompanies the painting. In it Maclise makes a strong statement about relations between the classes, the importance of ancient traditions and the quality of life in the past as opposed to that of the present. Maclise was himself interested in medievalism, friendly with many Tory reformers such as Disraeli and Bulwer-Lytton, and employed by the Conservative *Fraser's Magazine*. If the content of the painting left any room for doubt as to Maclise's sympathies, the poem makes clear his sentiments:

> An honest mirth flows all around
> Razing distinctions to the ground
> No stateliness is to be seen,
> No chilling distance intervene--
> Good humour flows, and fills between.
> The baron, see, nods to the Squire;
> The serf unto his lord sits nigher:
> And hooded coif, and cap of pride
> Were often seen seated side by side.[26]

The painting itself emphasizes the festival atmosphere of the season in its depiction of a long seventeenth-century hall decorated with pieces of armor and ancestral portraits to stress continuity between past and present. The room is adorned for Christmas with holly, mistletoe, and the traditional yule log and is crowded with figures and activity. The Baron and his family are seated in the rear of the picture observing the general air of gaiety and commotion in the hall. The centerpiece of the feast, a roasted boar's head, is being carried down the side staircase followed by a great procession of hunters, musicians and singers, a fact barely noticed by the bustling groups in the foreground. One group is absorbed in a game of "hunt the slipper," while the other consists of the traditional mummers, entertainers, and the holiday's centerpiece, Father Christmas. The scene is lively, full of fun, and like that of Disraeli, contrasts sharply with that most famous depiction of a Victorian Christmas, *A Christmas Carol* by Charles Dickens. One has only to think of the unreformed Scrooge's definition of Christmas as "a poor excuse for picking a man's pocket every 25th of December,"[27] to see the difference in customs between past and present.

    Attempts to continue the customs of Christmas were celebrated by *The Illustrated London News* in December of 1848 when they wrote that "the Hospitality of the Hall at this festival season is not only a romantic fiction, but a historical fact. All were welcome..."[28] The appended illustration entitled "The Christmas Eve" depicts a group of old and young gathered around a roaring fire while the obligatory dancers twirl in the background. A month later in January 1849, the magazine devoted several pages to a story about a revival of traditional "Christmas gambols" sponsored by the Manchester Mechanics Institute. The festival, captured in illustrations such as "The Procession of the Wassail Bowl," was compared to those engraved by Joseph

Edwin Landseer, *Bolton Abbey in the Olden Time* (1834), Devonshire Collection, Chatsworth. Reproduced by permission of the Chatsworth Settlement Trustees.

Nash, and included mummers, rustic minstrels, and a yule log processional, as well as a gala feast for 3,200 people. The event proved to be so popular that many who applied for tickets had to be turned away.[29] Perhaps the pleas of Lord John Manners had not fallen on deaf ears.

Evocations of "Merrie England" were not merely confined to festivals and holidays, however. Sir Edwin Landseer's *Bolton Abbey in the Olden Time*, exhibited in 1834, also looks to the distant past, this time delving into the relationship between the church and the common people. Aside from this emphasis on the duties of the aristocracy, medievalizing reformers stressed the role of religion in the life of the people.[30] The Church was there to provide many services--as spiritual adviser, to dispense poor relief, and to show hospitality to visitors. In essence, the Church functioned as another benevolent father figure.

Bolton Abbey in the Olden Time is a fanciful reconstruction of a twelfth-century Augustinian priory in Yorkshire which had by Landseer's time dissolved into a picturesque ruin. The abbot, flanked by his assistant, has come to accept tributes from his parishioners. Although it has been argued that the image is ambiguous,[31] Landseer has done nothing to suggest that this system of tributes is unnatural or wrong. It is instead a simple trade, the common people supplying food and the monks spiritual guidance. This image could also be interpreted as an evocation of longing for the old ways when the preindustrial society was based on a system of barter and trade rather than cash and carry. For although the peasants contributed to the abbey stores, they also knew that if hard times befell them they could still depend on the monks to provide food and shelter. To whom could the factory worker turn if the mill closed and he or she had no money?

A similar question about the position of religion in society was raised by J.R. Herbert's 1840 painting, *The Monastery in the 14th Century: Boarhunters Refreshed at St. Augustine's Monastery Canterbury*, a picture which may well have been inspired by Landseer's *Bolton Abbey*.[32] In Herbert's painting, a group of hunters, nobles by their dress, have stopped at the monastery in search of refreshment before continuing their journey. The main focus of the painting, the dispensing of hospitality, also appears in other pictures of the time. Such an action was a clear example of the superiority of the medieval way of life. A review of one such scene, George Cattermole's *Wanderers Entertained* or *Old English Hospitality* (1839) provoked the comment that "the progress of civilisation and the increase of wealth, have not been accompanied by such an exercise in household charity as was a characteristic feature of the social condition of the middle ages."[33] Herbert, who painted *The Monastery* about the time of his conversion to Catholicism, plays up the benevolent and charitable acts of the monastery, stressing the idea that the medieval church not only provided for the spiritual welfare of individuals, but their material needs as well. It has been noted that Herbert's painting contains the germs of popular reforming theory, as the cross prominently displayed on the saddlebag of one of the nobles can be seen as symbolizing the union of the religious and the secular.[34] In common with other "Merrie England" paintings, Herbert's is a vision of a time unfettered by the industrial concerns of productivity and

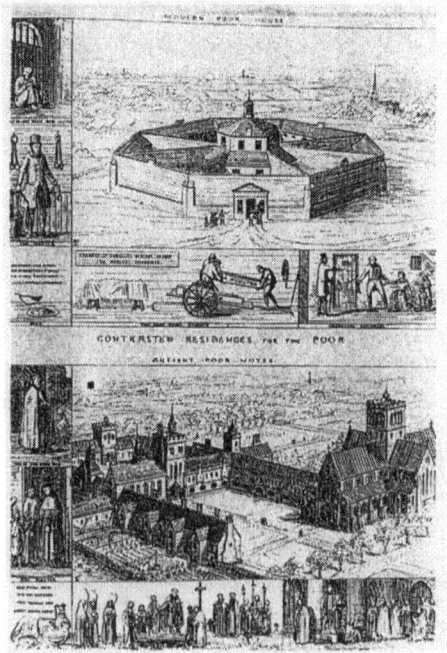

John Rogers Herbert, *The Monastery in the 14th Century: Boar-hunters Refreshed at St. Augustine's Monastery, Canterbury,* The Forbes Magazine Collection, New York; Augustus Welby Pugin, *Contrasted Residences for the Poor* from *Contrasts; or, A Parallel between the Noble Edifices of the Middle Ages and the Corresponding Buildings of the Present Day, showing the Present Decay of Taste* (1841).

wealth. It was a time of much greater concern and welfare for one's fellow man--a concept which obviously had great appeal.

In his 1870 *Contributions to the Literature of the Fine Arts*, Sir Charles Eastlake stated that "the impression which the character of the art receives from causes connected with political relations will open new and interesting sources of inquiry to the cultivated observer."[35] While it is difficult to make hard and fast connections between the political opinions of the artist and their impact on his work, the relation of these images to the myth of "Merrie England" is clear. The restoration of ancient festivals promoted traditional values, emphasizing the increased quality of life in rural as opposed to urban areas, and also promoting the responsibilities of the upper class to the lower. Such concepts had seemingly been lost in the transition to a modern industrial society, and the celebration of the myth of "Merrie England" functions as a contrast to the industrialized reality of the nineteenth century. This type of "contrast" was a favorite device of writers, such as Carlyle in *Past and Present* (1843), in which the author contrasts the moral and saintly atmosphere of the Monastery of Bury St. Edmunds with that of a modern industrial town. Carlyle forces his reader to examine afresh the institutions of his own time, while simultaneously offering his own solutions to the ills of society. A far more visual exercise is Pugin's *Contrasts* of 1836, which provided graphic evidence of the gulf between "Merrie England" and the Victorian present. His illustration of the "past," in which the dead paupers were buried by kindly monks, is in stark contrast to his "present," in which the poor are turned over to medical students for dissection.

The myth of "Merrie England" hinges on a belief in a golden age of the past, when life was intrinsically better than that of the present. The artists and writers of the Victorian age went to great lengths to invent a past tradition, to discover popular culture and transform it into something palatable for general viewing. The historian Eric Hobsbawn has pointed out that this type of "invention" was not uncommon and usually constituted "responses to novel situations which take the form of reference to old situations."[36] Faced with the changes brought on by industrial society, is it any wonder that some wished to return to the days of the Maypole. Although one is forced to wonder when the people of this imagined past did any work, busy as they were with drinking, dancing, and feasting, the festivals of "Merrie England" provided a graphic contrast to tales of the horrors of factory life.

In 1859 Edward McDermott stated in the preface of *The Merrie Days of England*, "How pleasant are the ideas which are associated with the merrie days of England, and how strikingly do they contrast with our experience of the present times."[37] And what a contrast! There are no cold, hungry or miserable people, filthy rat-infested slums, or any huge stacks, belching smoke into an already polluted land. Instead the past was a place inhabited by contented peasants, who are visual examples of Disraeli's assertion that a "mere mechanical mitigation of the material necessities of the humbler classes, a mitigation which must inevitably be limited, can never alone avail sufficiently to ameliorate their condition... the surest means to elevate the character of the people is to appeal to their affections."[38] The emphasis on "Merrie England" in Victorian art and literature points to a dissatisfaction with the present, and a typical Conservative response to the problem--a return to the ways of the past. The reinterpretation of such images in light of Victorian ideas concerning social reform can only add to our understanding of the occurrence of carnival and festival in Victorian art and literature.

    The bulk of this research was given as a paper at the Association of Art Historians Conference held in London in 1991. The author wishes to thank all those who listened to and commented on this research.

Notes

1. Benjamin Disraeli, *Coningsby*, ed. Thom Braun (Harmondsworth, Middlesex, 1983), 159.
2. This painting was Sir Edwin Landseer's *Bolton Abbey in the Olden Time*. Landseer's earlier painting *Hawking in the Olden Time* was originally exhibited at the 1832 Royal Academy (no. 346) as "Hawking," and the phrase "olden time" was added at a later date.
3. Shown at the 1837 Royal Academy nos. 335, 460 and 541.
4. This painting was sold at Christie's London in 1981, but its current whereabouts are unknown.
5. Christopher Wood, *Paradise Lost* (North Pomfret, Vermont, 1989), p. 78.
6. Peter Burke, *Popular Culture in Early Modern Europe* (New York, 1978), p. 22.
7. See Dominick LaCapra, *Rethinking Intellectual History* (Ithaca, 1983), pp. 291-324 for a further discussion of Bakhtin's ideas.
8. Burke, 201-2.
9. Christopher Wood, *Victorian Panorama* (London, 1976), p. 161.
10. *The Illustrated London News*, September 15, 1849, p. 188.
11. Quoted in Eric Hobsbawm, *Industry and Empire* (Harmondsworth, Middlesex, 1972), 87.
12. Elizabeth Gaskell, *Mary Barton*, ed. by Stephen Gill (Harmondsworth, Middlesex, 1972), 109-10.
13. William Powell Frith, *My Autobiography and Reminiscences* (London, 1887-88), I, 187.
14. Roy Strong, *Recreating the Past* (London, 1979), 91.
15. Joseph Nash, *Mansions of England in the Olden Time* (Berlin, 1901, reissued from the original work

published in London, 1839-49), preface.
16. *Art Journal*, 1 Feb. 1855, 67.
17. *The Illustrated London News*, July 3, 1847, 8.
18. Engraved by the *Art Journal* in April 1854.
19. *Art Journal*, April 1855, 109.
20. Edward Bulwer-Lytton, *The Last of the Barons*, ed. by F.C. Romilly (Oxford, 1913), 271.
21. Engraved by the *Art Journal*, January 1854.
22. *Art Journal*, January 1854, 5.
23. Lord John Manners, *England's Trust and Other Poems* (London, 1841), 97.
24. Mark Girouard, *The Return to Camelot* (New Haven, 1981), 80.
25. Disraeli, *Coningsby*, 459.
26. *Fraser's Magazine*, May 1838, 635.
27. Charles Dickens, *A Christmas Carol* in *The Christmas Books*, Vol, I, edited by Michael Slater (Harmondsworth, Middlesex, 1971), 53.
28. *The Illustrated London News*, Suppliment, 1848, 411.
29. *The Illustrated London News*, January 13, 1849, 27-28.
30. Alice Chandler, *A Dream of Order* (Lincoln, Nebraska, 1970), 155-63.
31. See Richard Ormond, *Sir Edwin Landseer* (London, 1982), 121-22, who views the picture as simply an evocation of monastic life in the Middle Ages, and Joanna Banham, "Past and Present" in *William Morris and the Middle Ages*, edited by Joanna Banham and Jennifer Harris (Manchester, 1984), 22, who interprets the picture as an illustration of the corruption of the medieval church. This latter interpretation is based on the cynical approach to monasticism taken by Whig historian Henry Hallam in his *View of the State of Europe in the Middle Ages* (1818). Hallam's view is an essentially Liberal position, adverse to both feudalism and Catholicism,

and clearly different from a more Conservative interpretation.
32. Christopher Forbes, *The Royal Academy Revisited 1837-1901: Victorian Painting from the Forbes Magazine Collection* (Princeton, 1975), 64.
33. *Art Journal*, 1 July, 1857, 210.
34. Banham, "Past and Present," 23.
35. Sir Charles Eastlake, *Contributions to the Literature of the Fine Arts* (London, 1879), I, 237.
36. Eric Hobsbawm, "Introduction: Inventing Traditions" in *The Invention of Tradition*, ed. by Eric Hobsbawm and Terence Ranger (Cambridge, 1984), 2.
37. Edward McDermott, *The Merrie Days of England* (London, 1895), p. iii.
38. Disraeli, *Coningsby*, 459-60.

Tennyson's Hierarchy of Women in *Idylls of the King*

Rebecca Cochran

In *Idylls of the King*, Tennyson's Arthur earns the epithet of "the blameless king." He is a Carlylean leader with a vision of a perfect society. To some extent, Arthur fails to achieve this vision because his knights refuse to follow Carlyle's dictate to "treat him with an obedience that knows no bounds."[1] In his presentation of Arthur as the ideal ruler, Tennyson reflects the Victorian compulsion for order under the auspices of inspired leadership, and the value of subordinating private desire to the public good. However, intimately connected with the failure of Arthur's mission is the moral character of the women in the *Idylls*. As guardians of the public good, Tennyson's Arthurian women should inspire their partners to perform noble deeds in accordance with the king's dictates. In order to do so, the female figures must comply with the Victorian prototype of the perfect woman, who is sexually pure and is both a submissive wife and selfless mother. As J. Phillip Eggers remarks:

> Tennyson believed in what John Kilham in *Tennyson and "The Princess"* calls "the doctrine of Female Influence," a tenet that woman's destiny is to exert moral influence through her role in Christian marriage.[2]

In the *Idylls*, Tennyson establishes a hierarchy of women to illustrate precisely this principle: he presents in detail seven women who may be assessed by the degree to which their moral conduct either aids or hinders Arthur's cause.

I shall examine these female figures by order of their appearance in the completed *Idylls*, with the exception of Guinevere, whom Tennyson depicts throughout the work. She is his most complex and compelling figure, and the poet uses his hierarchy to illuminate her character, and her role in the downfall of Arthur's kingdom. Therefore, it is most beneficial to discuss Guinevere in relation to the other female figures in the *Idylls*.

In "The Coming of Arthur" Tennyson provides us with only a brief introduction to Igraine, Bellicent, and Guinevere. The first in-depth depiction of an Arthurian woman is of the haughty Lynette, who arrives at court to beg for Lancelot's assistance in rescuing her sister, Lyonors. When Arthur grants this quest to Gareth, Lynette rashly assesses him by his appearance and his lowly position in the king's court. She then spurns the young knight with unrelenting mockery. Not only is Gareth undaunted by her behavior, he is inspired to perform courageous deeds, exemplified by his victory over each of the wicked knights who pose a threat to him. After Gareth proves his worth in combat, Lynette recognizes his nobility and repents of her cruel treatment of him. In Tennyson's source for this episode, Malory, it is Gareth's brother, Gaheris, who then weds Lynette, while Gareth marries Lyonors, the lady of highest rank whom he has rescued. Tennyson alters this ending, directly contradicting Malory: "And he that told the tale in older times / Says that Sir Gareth wedded Lyonors, / But he, that told it later, says Lynette" ("Gareth and Lynette" 1392-94). Thus, at the poem's conclusion, the "shrew" is tamed, and the result is the best of all possible endings: matrimony.

Because of her pride and temerity, Lynette's initial judgment of Gareth results in her rude behavior. In spite of this, she is not depicted as an evil character, but rather as one who merely displays a mistake in judgment, a defect which she corrects. Like Tennyson's Princess Ida, Lynette redeems herself when her fault becomes apparent to her. Furthermore, her cruelty to Gareth encourages him, ironically, to prove his worth, and her scorn serves as a test of the knight's youthful enthusiasm for the vows of the Round Table. As he proves his prowess, Gareth performs a service for the community by defeating the wicked knights; he also fulfills his private duty when he forms a fruitful union with Lynette. It is significant that Gareth's heroism is inspired by love, since "the maiden passion for a maid" is one of the values Arthur espouses when, during his final interview with Guinevere, he defines the virtuous life.

Enid, the only female character to whom Tennyson devotes two idylls, embodies those virtues the poet values most in woman. We witness Enid's courtship by and marriage to Geraint, and her final test and reward. A faultless wife, Enid is willing to suffer endless humiliation for her husband. In this respect, she is a "patient Griselda" figure. Tennyson's special interest in the theme of the perfect wife is also suggested by the fact that this is the only episode for which he failed to rely upon Malory as a source. Here, he turned to

"Geraint, Son of Erbin" from the *Mabinogion*, and may have been influenced by Chrétien de Troyes' *Erec and Enide*.[3]

In Tennyson's account, Enid is a noble woman whose family has been reduced to destitution by a wicked knight, Edryn. By contrast, in Chrétien's romance, Enid's father is impoverished because of his involvement in a lengthy war, and in the *Mabinogion*, it is the earl who has tried to cheat Edryn out of his inheritance. Tennyson alters his sources in order to emphasize the nobility of Enid's family and their perseverance under such unfortunate circumstances. It is significant that Geraint falls in love with Enid as she sings a song which expresses her Boethian attitude towards fortune. At the opening of "The Marriage of Geraint," Geraint had promised Guinevere that he would avenge an insult which Edryn had given to her handmaiden; thus, when he defeats Edryn in a tournament, he accomplishes this and wins Enid's hand in marriage by restoring her father to his rightful position.

Guinevere had pledged that, in return for this favor, she would clothe Geraint's bride in rich attire. Therefore, when Geraint and Enid prepare to depart for Camelot, where they will be wed, Geraint insists that Enid wear her old rags. Tennyson expands this episode from the *Mabinogion* when, on the eve of their departure, a dress Enid had adored from childhood is returned to her, and she dreams of wearing it to court the next day. In this way, Tennyson heightens the discrepancy between Enid's own desire and Geraint's demand, thereby increasing the extent of her sacrifice. Like Griselda, Enid remains unspoiled by luxury.

This story of their courtship and marriage is told in a flashback that serves as both a testimony to Enid's virtue and as a means to heighten our sympathy for her in the events recounted in "Geraint and Enid." In this *Idyll*, Geraint grows suspicious of his wife when he hears rumors of Guinevere's adultery, a detail intended to emphasize that the queen's behavior, early in the *Idylls*, has begun to corrupt the court. By contrast, in Chrétien's account, Erec had merely grown uxorious, while in the *Mabinogion* Geraint's suspicion of Enid is unrelated to any rumors of the queen's adultery.

Geraint returns with Enid to his own kingdom, where he neglects his duties and becomes more convinced of his wife's infidelity. By doing so, he subjects himself to ridicule and mistakenly attributes his wife's concern about his honor for the pain of an adulterous love. In his jealous state, Geraint decides to test Enid's fidelity: he orders her to prepare for a journey and commands her not to speak to him, a rash decision that endangers them both.

Since Geraint has commanded Enid to ride ahead of him, she perceives each perilous situation before them, and is thus placed in a seemingly impossible dilemma: she must either disobey her husband by alerting him or allow Geraint to be assailed, unwarned, by outlaws. Each time, Enid breaks her promise of silence in order to protect her husband, and each time her loyalty is repaid with an angry reproach. In spite of the fact that Enid remains ignorant of Geraint's suspicions and therefore finds his harsh treatment puzzling, she never falters in her love for him.

The climax of the adventure/test occurs when the two are captured by the beastly Earl Doorm. The wounded Geraint witnesses Enid's loyalty as the earl commands her to obey him, but she refuses, claiming that she would rather die than live without her husband. Finally convinced of his wife's fidelity, Geraint regains his failing strength, kills Doorm, and scatters his evil followers. Once again, Tennyson illustrates the beneficial effects of a worthy woman.

Both *Erec and Enide* and the *Mabinogion* recount additional adventures for the hero, but Tennyson concludes this story almost immediately following Doorm's death. In the medieval works, the main point is to prove the hero's worth, but Tennyson wishes to demonstrate the virtue of his heroine, Enid. Once he has accomplished this he quickly terminates her narrative. Tennyson views Enid's behavior throughout her trial as exemplary and heroic. She exhibits those ideal qualities of the perfect Victorian woman: modesty, obedience, patience in adversity, and fidelity to her husband at the expense of great personal suffering. And according to Tennyson, although Geraint's jealousy is foolish, it is mitigated by the fact that it was motivated by his horror of the queen's adultery. In addition, in his jealousy Geraint slays several bandits, thereby performing a service to the public and fulfilling his knightly mission.

At the conclusion of the poem, we are told that from this point Geraint "kept the justice of the King / So vigorously yet mildly, that all hearts / Applauded, and the spiteful whisper died away" (955-57). However, it is of Enid that we hear the most praise:

> But Enid, who her ladies loved to call
> Enid the Fair, a grateful people named
> Enid the Good; and in their halls arose
> The cry of children, Enids and Geraints

>   Of times to be, nor did he doubt her more
>   But rested in her fealty, till he crowned
>   A happy life with a fair death, and fell
>   Against the heathen of the Northern Sea
>   In battle, fighting for the blameless king. (961-69)

The fruit of Enid's patience and virtue is a happy marriage, a fair name, and healthy children. The Victorian belief that offspring testify to a virtuous marital union is implied by Arthur's remark that he and Guinevere are fortunate for having had no children: "Well it is that no child is born of thee. / The children born of thee are sword and fire, / Red ruin, and the breaking up of laws" ("Guinevere" 421-23). The queen's inability to produce children and her failed attempt to be a foster mother at the opening of "The Last Tournament" suggest that, because of her sin, Guinevere is unfit to perform her roles as wife and mother.

Enid is so saintly she scarcely seems real, but rather the embodiment of all that Tennyson values in a woman. Therefore, it is Enid against whom all the other female characters must be measured. Tennyson emphasizes his approbation of Enid by juxtaposing her to Vivien, the next woman presented in the *Idylls*, and the one who serves as the antithesis of Enid. If the latter represents the nineteenth-century "Angel of the House," Vivien serves as an example of the "other" Victorian woman: the whore. Vivien first appears in "Balin and Balen." Her destructive role is immediately obvious when, by repeating the rumor of Guinevere's adultery to the already unstable, hot-tempered Balin, she causes the mutual fratricide of Balin and Balen that concludes the idyll.

Vivien's malignant deeds continue when she arrives at Arthur's court. She and the evil King Mark had formed a pact to sow the seeds of discord at Camelot. Here, Vivien uses flattery and malicious rumors to accomplish this purpose. Most important about her, however, is her motivation to commit evil. Because she has a twisted mind, she is incapable of perceiving good; she feeds on destruction and death, and finds satisfaction only in the grief of others. Her baseness infects the court and causes Merlin's demise as well. Vivien inverts the association of truth with goodness, equating truth with evil, evinced by her conversation with Mark before she departs for Camelot:

> "As Love, if Love be perfect, casts out fear,
> So Hate, if Hate be perfect, casts out fear,
> My father died in battle against the King,
> My mother on his corpse in open field;
> She bore me there, for born from death was I
> Among the dead and sown upon the wind--
> And then on thee! and shown the truth betimes,
> That old true filth, and bottom of the well,
> Where truth is hidden." ("Merlin and Vivien" 40-48)

Truth, at the "bottom of the well" for Vivien, is "filth," while for Arthur the "great deep" is the mystery from which he springs, and to which he will return. It is Vivien's sullied mind which obscures her moral vision and prevents her from seeing truth and goodness in the world.

In her relationship with Merlin, Vivien displays those qualities that Tennyson condemns in a woman. Just as Enid, modelled on Griselda, is the epitome of virtue, Vivien, her vice-ridden opposite, is modelled on the archetypes of Lilith and Delilah. As Lilith, she acts as the evil temptress, as Delilah, the seductive diviner of secrets for personal gain. In both cases, the feminine desire for knowledge is destructive. Thus, Vivien flatters Merlin in order to attain personal power and fame. Tennyson comments on Merlin's entrapment: "Some even among the highest intellects, become slaves of the evil which is at first half-disdained."[4]

If Merlin represents the intellect, Vivien deliberately abuses intellectual power, which becomes enslaved by the flesh. Hallam Tennyson remarks on this: "My father created the character of Vivien with much care--as the evil genius of the Round Table--who in her lustfulness of the flesh could not believe in anything either good or great"[5]. This fear of female sexual potency is, of course, very Victorian, and the ensuing depiction of Merlin's seduction by Vivien is predictably one of the most revolting scenes in the *Idylls*.

In "Merlin and Vivien" snake and serpent imagery abound, in order to draw the parallel between Vivien and the archetypal temptress on which she is modelled: "And lissome Vivien, holding by his heel, / Writhed toward him, slided up his knee and sat, / Behind his ankles twined her hollow feet / Together, curved an arm about his neck, / Clung like a snake" (236-40). As she successfully manipulates him, Vivien becomes transformed, in Merlin's eyes, from a brilliantly agile and beautiful, but dangerous, snake to one who is "Stiff as a viper, loathsome sight" (843). Merlin's desire, on the one hand, to be beguiled, and his altered perception of Vivien, suggest a more puritanical version of Keats' "Lamia." Too late the mage recognizes Vivien for what she really is when he calls her a "harlot" (840). Too late he learns the enormity of his error: "Too much I trusted when I told you that / And stirred this vice in

you which ruined man / Through woman the first hour"
(359-61).

Vivien's selfish behavior might be judged as vicious in any age, but the Victorians would have found particularly unattractive her pursuit of knowledge, her aggressiveness, and her seductive powers, which she uses to destabilize the male intellect. Tennyson's women who compete with men are condemned; the 'separate but equal' philosophy the poet espouses at the conclusion of *The Princess* and which he repeats here does not include shared endeavors with men, but instead advocates complementary activities for women in the domestic realm. Clearly, in the *Idylls*, woman's duty is to be passively virtuous and to inspire her partner to fulfill his obligation to the King. She must subordinate her own ambitions and desires to those of her spouse or lover.

By fusing two of Malory's characters, Tennyson presents Vivien as the antithesis of his feminine ideal, while sharpening and modernizing his portrayal of her. The poet conflates Malory's Morgan le Fay and his Nimuë, the Lady of the Lake. In the medieval work, Nimuë fears Merlin, who aggressively attempts to seduce her:

> And alwaies Merlin lay about the lady for to have her maidenhead, and she was ever passing wery of him, and faine would have been delivered of him, for she was afraid of him.[6]

Furthermore, in Malory, after she entraps Merlin in self-defense, Nimuë performs many beneficial deeds with the magic she has learned: several times she saves Arthur's life when he is threatened by the guile of Morgan le Fay, and it is Nimuë who marries Pelleas. Tennyson fuses this Malorian figure with her temperamental and moral opposite. He uses most of the evil tendencies of Morgan le Fay for his depiction of Vivien, but retains only Nimuë's entrapment of Merlin. In Malory's narrative, it is Morgan who works continually to undermine Arthur. Always in search of a paramour, Morgan's lustfulness in Malory is transposed onto Tennyson's Vivien. In his conflation of these two characters from the medieval work, Tennyson unifies his poem by creating a female figure who is both purely evil in her opposition to Arthur and who is also responsible for Merlin's demise.

The next woman presented in the *Idylls*, Elaine, is also aggressive and willful, but less so than Vivien. Unlike the latter, Elaine does not wish to usurp the power of men or destroy the knight she loves: her main fault is her insistence on living in fantasy. Elaine wrongfully worships Lancelot with an intensity akin to religious fervor, she deceives herself by idealizing him, and she daydreams instead of accepting her duty in life. We are told at the opening of "Lancelot and Elaine" that she "made a pretty history to herself" about Lancelot, and "so she lived in fantasy" (18, 27). Even though Lancelot discourages her affection, Elaine refuses to forget him, and foolishly wills her own death. Tennyson believes this is a waste and a sin, evinced by the following passage in which Elaine recalls her father's words that foretell her own end:

> Her father's latest word hummed in her ear,
> "Being so very wilful you must go,"
> And changed itself and echoed in her heart,
> "Being so very wilful you must die." (775-78)

Tennyson believes that only men should woo; this is the pattern of courtship in every other case in the *Idylls*, with the exception of Vivien's seduction of Merlin. Since Elaine refuses to recognize and amend her error, she must be placed beneath Lynette in Tennyson's hierarchy. While Lynette's idyll concludes with matrimony, Elaine's ends with her death. Her self-sacrifice is a kind of self-indulgence which prevents her from meeting a suitable partner with whom she can fulfill her duty in life as virtuous wife and mother. Elaine is pure, but her purity does not serve Arthur and his realm.

Just as the young Elaine falls in love with the mature Lancelot, the youthful knight, Pelleas, conceives an inappropriate passion for an older woman, Ettarre. However, this "love" turns out to be nothing more than lust, for which Pelleas eventually castigates himself. Towards the opening of "Pelleas and Ettarre" we are told:

> The beauty of her flesh abashed the boy,
> As though it were the beauty of her soul:
> For as the base man, judging of the good,
> Puts his own baseness in him by default
> Of will and nature, so did Pelleas lend
> All the young beauty of his own soul to hers. (74-79)

This is a reversal of Vivien's problem: she sees filth and evil in everyone because of her own sullied mind, while Pelleas perceives virtue and beauty where none exists, owing to his innocence. Ettarre's beauty, then, is superficial and is largely projected upon her by Pelleas, who eventually suffers disillusionment as a result of this misplaced affection.

Ettarre encourages Pelleas' adulation in order to feed her own vanity. After Pelleas wins a tournament and presents Ettarre with the prize, "the heat / Of pride and glory filled her face" (164-65). When the feckless Gawain, who has pledged to help Pelleas attain his love, betrays this trust and sleeps with Ettarre himself, Pelleas realizes how base his passion for her has been:

> "Fool, beast--he, she, or I? myself most fool;
> Beast too, as lacking human wit--disgraced, . . .
> For why should I have loved her to my shame?
> I loathe her, as I loved her to my shame.
> I never loved her, I but lusted for her --" (466-67, 473-75)

Pelleas views himself, Gawain, and Ettarre as "beasts" because of their ignoble lust. His fear of this aspect of his own character and its presence in that of Ettarre, is reflected in the landscape, as John D. Rosenberg so astutely points out:

> Ettarre's too-easy accessibility is more than hinted at by the "wide open" gates of her castle (405) and the "yawning" entrance leading to her private grounds (412). After discovering Ettarre asleep with Gawain, Pelleas rides in fury from her castle, whose towers silhouetted against the moon loom up as a kind of distorted enlargement of her body. Ettare and the landscape merge in Pelleas' disordered mind into a composite image of sexual menace.[7]

Pelleas' only consolation is the belief that Arthur and his court are noble, even if he and Gawain are not. However, when Percivale meets Pelleas and accidentally repeats the rumor of Guinevere's adultery, Pelleas' belief in Camelot and its ideals is totally destroyed. This knowledge creates in the young knight a horrible resentment and despair: "Black nest of rats. . . ye build too high" (544). Moreover, Pelleas' disillusionment here parallels the earlier scene in which Balin is driven mad when Vivien forces the same knowledge upon him. For both knights, this rumor is revealed to them at a moment when they are most vulnerable. Pelleas, filled with self-loathing, becomes suicidal, as shown by his random encounter with Lancelot, in which he shrieks hysterically, "Slay then... my will is to be slain" (567). While Balin's madness causes his own death and that of his brother, Pelleas' prompts him to found a Round Table which espouses values antithetical to Arthur and his cause. This opposition creates a schism in the kingdom that ultimately allows Modred to usurp the throne.

Tennyson alters Malory's conclusion to this tale. In the latter, Ettarre is punished for her cruelty when Nimuë casts a spell upon her which causes her to die for unrequited love of Pelleas. At the same time, Malory's Pelleas falls in love with Nimuë. By contrast, Tennyson omits this incident in order to use Pelleas' disillusionment to forward the impending disaster of the Round Table's demise. Thus, Ettarre's behavior, along with the queen's sin, produces more serious consequences and larger ramifications than in Malory's narrative. Furthermore, Tennyson undercuts any sympathy the reader may feel for Ettarre:

> ... And he that tells the tale
> Says that her ever-veering fancy turned
> To Pelleas, as the one true knight on earth,
> And only lover; and through her love her life
> Wasted and pined, desiring him in vain. (482-86)

While Malory's Ettarre is afflicted by Nimuë's spell, her counterpart in the *Idylls* is the victim of her own "ever-veering fancy." Thus, because of her own immoral conduct, poetic justice is achieved.

Tennyson emphasizes Ettarre's destructive sexual power while Malory, by contrast, underscores Pelleas' shameful willingness to lose his honor for an unworthy woman. Malory also disapproves of Gawain's betrayal of Pelleas, but Tennyson remains surprisingly silent about Gawain's actions in this episode, probably because he does not wish to mitigate Ettarre's role in Pelleas' destruction. Thus, Malory condemns the abandonment of the knightly code, but in the *Idylls* it is female immorality that receives the greatest condemnation. The fact that Tennyson points to Gawain's flaws in other idylls, especially in "Lancelot and Elaine" and "The Holy Grail," suggests that this is why he minimizes Gawain's culpability here. He wishes to stress that the main corrupting forces are Ettarre's promiscuity and Guinevere's adultery.

The presentation of Tristram and Isolt in "The Last Tournament" reveals a further disintegration of Arthur's order. In "Pelleas and Ettarre," lust mistaken for love turns to hatred and cynicism, but here, in the "autumn" of the Round Table, we see the degree to which shallow lust results in evil consequences. In this idyll, the love between Tristram and Isolt is carnal, fickle, and selfish. Tennyson depicts Isolt as vain and petty, and Tristram as a bored, calculating suitor.

As "The Last Tournament" opens, Arthur departs to crush the Red Knight (Pelleas), leaving Lancelot in charge of the "Tournament of the Dead Innocence." Tristram, who can create only "broken music" on his harp, wins the jousting tournament but discourteously refuses to offer the prize to any lady present. Instead, he keeps the ruby carcanet because he hopes to offer it to Isolt, and thereby "smoothe / And sleek his marriage over to the Queen" (389-90), a cold and calculating thought.

On his journey to Cornwall, Tristram stops to rest, and dreams that the two Isolts in his life quarrel over the prize. Isolt of Ireland, his long-time mistress, is the victor, but the ruby turns to blood in her hands--a symbol of her iniquitous passion. Isolt of Brittany's hands remain white and pure. This contrast between the two Isolts is amplified later: one Isolt is predatory and destructive, the other an innocent, victimized wife.

Before he arrives in Ireland, Tristram once again displays his unknightly behavior. While riding through the forest, he encounters a weeping woman:

> 'Why weep ye?' 'Lord,' she said, 'my man
> Hath left me or is dead;' whereon he thought --
> 'What, if she hate me now? I would not this.
> What, if she love me still? I would not that.
> I know not what I would'--but said to her,
> 'Yet weep not thou, lest, if thy mate return,
> He find thy favour changed and love thee not.' (493-99)

Instead of offering his protection to this abandoned woman, Tristram advises her to guard her beauty, for him the measure of woman's worth. He should have volunteered to search for the missing knight or at least protect the damsel, both stock situations in Malory. But Tristram is so preoccupied with his own fickle emotions that he cannot think of another's needs. We also witness his ambivalent attitude towards Isolt of Ireland, whom he plans to seduce when he arrives in Cornwall.

Isolt of Ireland greets Tristram and remarks that, as he approached, she had received a premonition of his arrival: "My soul, I felt my hatred for my Mark / Quicken within me, and knew that thou wert nigh" (517-18). This perversion of good is emphasized again, a few lines later: "My God, the measure of my hate for Mark / Is as the measure of my love for thee" (535-36). Here we witness not only love turning to hate, as in "Pelleas and

Ettarre," but the generation of hate by love, since Isolt's loathing for her husband results partly from her lust for Tristram. The quality of Isolt's speech is also worthy of comment. Even though she despises her husband, Isolt uses the possessive when she refers to him ("my Mark"), which reveals her selfish nature. She frequently degrades spiritual words; her interjections of "my God" and "my Soul" are ironic since Isolt cares only for worldly pleasures.

When Isolt questions Tristram about his bride in Brittany, the knight has only praise for her: "patient, and prayerful, meek, / Pale-blooded, she will yield herself to God" (602-03). This description of Isolt of Brittany contrasts dramatically with that of Isolt of Ireland, a passionate woman. Isolt then asks Tristram to flatter her, an indication of her vanity:

"Flatter me rather, seeing me so weak,
Broken with Mark and hate and solitude,
Thy marriage and mine own, that I should suck
Lies like sweet wines: lie to me: I believe." (637-40)

Although she has made a religion of profane love, such passion does not last, and Isolt despairs because she has placed her trust in transient pleasures. In spite of her pleading, Tristram refuses to tell her a direct lie, but chooses to skirt the issue of her beauty. He also values love for its physical enjoyment, and the only consolation he can offer his aging mistress is cloaked in the form of a covert insult: "May God be with thee, sweet, when old and gray / And past desire..." (622-23). As one might predict, this comment troubles Isolt even more, and she implores Tristram to swear that he will love her when she is "gray-haired, and past desire, and in despair"

(648). In this expansive conversation, we see that both characters equate sexual pleasure with happiness.

If Tristram is bored with Isolt, she too has become disillusioned with their affair: "O were I not my Mark's, by whom all men / Are noble, I should hate thee more than love . . ." (594-95). At last, weary of this talk and impatient to satisfy his sexual appetite, Tristram produces the ruby that he hopes will appease Isolt's anger. The repugnant nature of their love is disclosed in the following lines:

"Press this a little closer, sweet, until --
Come, I am hungered and half-angered-meat,
Wine, wine--and I will love thee to the death,
And out beyond into the dream to come." (712-15)

Tristram's association of sex with the other physical urges of food and drink underscores his gross sensuality, to which Isolt readily responds.

Throughout the idyll, Tennyson's irony undercuts the notion that the two are noble lovers. The petty, possessive nature of Isolt and the cynicism of Tristram reinforce this point. The poem's conclusion, however, serves as the crowning irony. First, in an effort to seduce Isolt, Tristram sings a lyric about his love for two stars:

"Ay, ay, O ay--the winds that bend the brier!
A star in heaven, a star within the mere!
Ay, ay, O ay--a star was my desire,
And one was far apart, and one was near:
Ay, ay, O ay--the winds that bow the grass!
And one was water and one star was fire,
And one will ever shine and one will pass.
Ay, ay, O ay--the winds that move the mere." (725-31)

Clyde Ryals comments: "Clearly if this lyric has any relevance at all to the meaning of the poem, we must understand the water as Arthur, or Arthur's ideals, and the fire as illicit passion"[8]. I believe this verse serves as a compressed history of Tristram's amorous adventures, characterized by his feckless nature. Because one star was absent, he loved the one that was readily available. In other words, Tristram pledges his love to whichever Isolt is close at hand. His inconstancy in love, however, is not the most ironic aspect of the song.

When Tristram asserts that one star will shine forever while the other will fade, it is clear that the fading star represents Isolt of Ireland, since he has already told her that she will one day be "old and gray and past desire." Isolt of Brittany, on the other hand, will "ever shine," as Tristram suggested earlier when he associated her with the permanent spiritual realm. Isolt of Ireland's external beauty will vanish, but the beauty of Tristram's wife is spiritual and will therefore remain untouched by time. Isolt appears to be unaware of the significance of this song--an insult cloaked as a traditional love lyric intended to woo her. Or perhaps she chooses to believe the soft lie instead of acknowledging the underlying meaning of the lyric: her own version of cynicism.

The final irony and condemnation of the lovers is Mark's cowardly and shameful slaying of Tristram; he stealthily approaches the lovers as they embrace and stabs Tristram in the back. Thus, all three characters are portrayed in their baseness as the idyll concludes. Their ignoble actions condemn them: adultery, deception, and murder.

Tennyson selects as his source the less romantic prose version of the medieval Tristram legend as it appears in Malory, and he alters this source for the worse. First, the poet omits the incident in which the lovers consume the aphrodisiac which causes them, through no fault of their own, to conceive an undying love for one another. By eliminating this most essential element of the medieval narrative, Tennyson places the blame for the illicit passion squarely on the shoulders of Tristram and Isolt. He focuses solely on the sordid end of the prose legend, and, when he transforms their adultery into an act of free will, the poet undercuts the reader's sympathy for the lovers.

Even though Mark is a despicable character, Tennyson suggests that Tristram and Isolt are wrong to engage in an adulterous affair. Moreover, the poet introduces the lovers during the "autumn" of the Round Table to use them as symbols of the corruption that has permeated Arthur's realm.

Tennyson employs the Tristram and Isolt episode to serve as a parallel and contrast to the adulterous love of Lancelot and Guinevere. The queen is the only major female figure to appear throughout the *Idylls*, and Tennyson's depiction of her is extremely complex. Her position in Arthur's world is evident from the following passage from "Guinevere," in which she is seated "betwixt her best / Enid, and lissome Vivien, of her court / The wiliest and the worst" (27-29). As David Staines observes, however, Guinevere is depicted more fully than her female counterparts because "she is aware of the powers of good and evil that exist within her own being." Moreover:

> She alone has the full perspective, since she is conscious of the two other positions struggling within her soul; not capable of the simplistic obedience of Enid, yet capable of having the same ennobling effect upon those around her, capable of basking in sensuality as Vivien does, but capable also of realizing its base and ignoble aspects, she stands in the centre of the world, a

microcosm of the problems that confront human nature and an example of its folly and frailty.[9] (49-50)

The similarities between Tristram and Isolt and Lancelot and Guinevere are largely superficial and external. The latter enjoy a more sincere love than their shallow counterparts. As Clyde Ryals points out, Tristram is "a Lancelot in strength and daring and, to put it baldly, in adultery, but the opposite of Lancelot in grace and courtesy and conscience" (126-27). Likewise, both Isolt and Guinevere "look upon love as an escape--Guinevere from almost absolute goodness, Isolt from almost absolute evil" (129). Thus, while the triangle formed by Tristram, Isolt, and Mark is paralleled by that of Lancelot, Guinevere, and Arthur, it is a parallel for contrast. However, Guinevere's transgression seems even less excusable than Isolt's, since Arthur is the best of men, Mark the most despicable.

Throughout the *Idylls*, Guinevere is an essentially noble character who possesses one tragic flaw: initially, she does not "recognize the highest" when she sees it. This is apparent from the opening idyll, in which the queen mistakes the colorful Lancelot for Arthur. But because she is fundamentally noble, Guinevere eventually repents of her error, albeit too late to aid Arthur in his cause. She finally realizes Carlyle's assertion that "No nobler feeling than this of admiration for one higher than himself [or herself] dwells in the breast of man [or woman]."[10]

In spite of her adultery, Tennyson attempts to present Guinevere as a woman who is worthy of Arthur's love. The queen's graciousness towards the knights is witnessed by her willingness to grant Balin's request to wear her favor on his shield, by her generosity to Geraint and Enid on their wedding day, and by the fact that she loves Enid best of all the ladies at court. In her own gender, at least, Guinevere *does* recognize the highest when she sees it.

Tennyson holds the queen responsible for the destruction of the Round Table. Her adultery is doubly evil, because she betrays her husband and ignores the responsibility which comes with her high position in society. As J. Philip Eggers remarks, Guinevere "helps to prove the powers of Female Influence in a negative way: by thinking only of her feelings and ignoring her influence on society, she gains unintended revenge upon the Round Table for its violation of her emotions."[11] The devastating rumor of her sin serves as a disruptive force in the lives of Geraint and Enid, Balin and Balen, and Pelleas. Thus, both Tennyson and Arthur hold her directly responsible for the demise of the Round Table.

The tragedy of Guinevere's life, then, is that she realizes--too late for earthly reparation--that she has betrayed the love of the "highest and the best" of men, Arthur. She must confront the guilt that results from this deception, and she pitifully acknowledges her destructive role. While in Malory's work it is the terrible, vengeful feuds and the spite of Aggravaine and Mordred which play the largest part in the demise of Arthur's realm, in the *Idylls* it is the rumor and bad example set by the adultery of Lancelot and Guinevere that corrupt Camelot. This emphasis upon the guilty lovers throws into relief Tennyson's view of Arthur as "the blameless king."

The presentation of marriage and the importance of domestic harmony in the *Idylls* demonstrate that Arthur's ability to create and sustain an ideal realm depends directly upon the morality, especially the sexual conduct, of the female characters. For Tennyson, woman's role, as the emotional and spiritual center of the domestic sphere, is to act as the inspirer and guardian of virtue. Therefore, the best woman is one who is willing to make any sacrifice for her husband or suitor. She is humble, meek, selfless, and obedient--she is Enid. In return for her virtuous influence, she will be blessed with a fair name, righteous progeny, and a partner who will win honor for his service to an ideal leader. Thus, Tennyson's hierarchy points to those characters who should be either emulated or condemned by female readers. Because of the complexity of her character, Guinevere alone stands outside this moral hierarchy, although Tennyson employs it to shed light on her role in the *Idylls*.

After Enid, Lynette is Tennyson's second choice because she is able to recognize and correct her flaw. At first she is haughty and rude, but she inspires Gareth and, like Enid, she marries a worthy mate: the conventional stamp of approval for women in the *Idylls*.

Tennyson's Elaine follows Lynette in virtue. The poet opens her idyll with praise, "Elaine the fair, Elaine the loveable, / Elaine the lily maid of Astolat" (1-2), but she must be placed beneath Lynette because of her unrelenting desire to win Lancelot's love. Elaine lives in fantasy, and is too aggressive to win Tennyson's unqualified approval. By refusing to accept reality, she lives a futile, self-indulgent life, and her purity is wasted. Thus, her spirituality is similar to Galahad's purity, which Arthur criticizes because it is not used to benefit the kingdom.[12]

With Ettarre, Isolt, and Vivien, Tennyson presents characters who lack redeeming qualities to balance their vices. Like Vivien, Ettarre uses her beauty for destructive ends. Instead of loving one man, she is shallow, vain, and spiritually bankrupt. The young Pelleas might have become another Gareth, had he loved a worthy woman; instead, he ends as a cynical madman who threatens Arthur's realm. Finally, Ettarre is promiscuous, as shown when she sleeps with Gawain.

Isolt is even worse than Ettarre because she is an adulteress, and because she fails to acknowledge her own baseness.[13] Her love for Tristram is simply a form of cupidity. She intensifies Mark's hatred when she retaliates against his spite, ultimately provoking him to murder. Moreover, Isolt's affair with Tristram obstructs his chances of happiness with his wife, who possesses the Enid-like virtues of purity, patience, and godliness. Isolt's transgression is, in one manner, worse than Guinevere's, since her adultery is "double": Lancelot is not married, as is Tristram, even though Tennyson suggests that he might have found happiness with Elaine had his illicit affair with the queen not impeded it. Unlike Guinevere, Isolt possesses no redeeming qualities and remains unrepentant of her adultery.

Vivien serves as the antithesis of all that Tennyson values in a woman. She seeks power to advance her own reputation and to work her evil ends. She also uses her sexuality to destabilize the male intellect. Her aggressive schemes undermine Arthur's cause: the rumors she spreads, coupled with her entrapment of Merlin, contribute to the corruption of the Round Table. Guinevere fails to achieve Enid's purity, but she rises above the evil women by virtue of her complex sensibility and her capacity for repentance. Since her position in society is an exalted one, her sin is amplified and carries more destructive power than it would have had she been of lower rank. Her stature and her inherently noble nature assure her of a tragic dimension in the *Idylls*.

Tennyson's depiction of his female characters and their role in Arthur's inability to realize his vision of an ideal society is one of the factors that contributes to the innovative quality of *Idylls of the King*. The creation of a hierarchy of women who are assessed according to the values of Tennyson's audience reveals the extent to which the poet transformed the medieval legend to suit Victorian sensibilities.

Notes

1. In his chapter entitled, "The Hero as King," Carlyle asserts that the king "is practically the summary for us of *all* the various forms of heroism." However, his two most important functions are "to command over us... to tell us for the day and hour what we are to do," and "to make what was disorderly, chaotic, into a thing ruled, regular. He is the missionary of Order." Arthur's ability to make order out of the bestial wilderness and his commitment to uphold the law are well-established in the *Idylls*. Moreover, Carlyle's remark that the hero is "God-inspired," and "A messenger sent from the Infinite Unknown with tidings to us" is echoed in Tennyson's invention of Arthur's birth in the opening poem.
2. Eggers, J. Phillip, *King Arthur's Laureate: A Study of Tennyson's "Idylls of the King"* (New York, New York University Press, 1971), 145-46.
3. Hallam Tennyson comments: "My father had also read *Erec and Enide*, by Chrestien de Troyes" (Christopher Ricks, ed., *Poems of Tennyson*, London: Longmans, 1969, section 486, 1525). However, there are many more contrasts than comparisons between Tennyson's Geraint and Enid story and Chrétien's romance. Clearly, the *Mabinogion* served as his main source.
4. Tennyson, Hallam, *Alfred Lord Tennyson: A Memoir*. 2 vols. (London, 1897, Rpt. New York: Greenwood, 1969).
5. Tennyson, Alfred, *Poems of Tennyson*, ed. Christopher Ricks (London, Longmans, 1969), section 469, 1593.
6. Malory, Thomas, *The History of King Arthur and the Knights of the Round Table*, ed. Thomas Wright, 3

vols. (London, 1858, Rpt. John Russel Smith, 1866), I, 117.
7. Rosenberg, John D., *The Fall of Camelot: a Study of Tennyson's "Idylls of the King."* (Cambridge, Harvard University Press, 1973), 71).
8. Ryals, Clyde, *From the Great Deep: Essays on "Idylls of the King"* (Ohio University Press, 1967), 63.
9. Staines, David, *Tennyson's Camelot: The "Idylls of the King" and Its Medieval Sources* (Wilfred Laurier University Press, 1982), 45, 49-50.
10. Carlyle, Thomas, *On Heroes, Hero-Worship and the Heroic in History* (London, 1841, Rpt. Lincoln, University of Nebraska Press, 1966), 11.
11. Eggers, J. Phillip, *King Arthur's Laureate: A Study of Tennyson's "Idylls of the King"* (New York, New York University Press, 1971), 149.
12. In "The Holy Grail," Arthur criticizes each of his knights who had undertaken the quest, including those with various degrees of success. He remarks of Galahad: "And one hath had the vision face to face, / And now his chair desires him here in vain, / However they may crown him otherwhere" (896-98). Like that of Percivale's sister, Galahad's calling is genuine, and his motives to undertake the quest are pure, but the emphasis upon the importance of active service in the public realm as the highest good prevents Galahad from being viewed as an entirely fautless character.
13. Ettarre confesses that Pelleas is a noble knight when she states, "He is not of my kind. / He could not love me, did he know me well" (297-98).

William Morris's Late Romances: The Struggle Against Closure

Hartley S. Spatt

William Morris was not an ideal Socialist. Arrested in 1885 for preaching anarchism on a London street corner and haled before a magistrate, he identified himself not as a Socialist theoretician and member of the masses but as "a literary man, pretty well known, I think, throughout Europe."[1] The last decades of Morris's career were characterized by what most people would consider a contradictory combination: Socialist didacticism, written into the pages of *Justice* and *Commonweal*, alongside of medievalist escapism, filling the pages of his prose romances. But that is not to say, as English utopians of a generation past did, that Morris's Socialism was a romanticized, merely literary ideology; on the contrary, he had seen too clearly the brutality which lay at the heart of contemporary society to foresee anything but violent revolution in England's future. Nor is it to say that Morris's late romances are nothing more than "therapeutic dreams,"[2] for, as this essay will show, they stem from the same deep well of Romantic trope that his best early work had drawn upon. Rather, it is to claim that Morris searched, during his last decades, for some synthesis that would bridge the seeming gap between the Socialist, "the voice through which the poetry of mankind speaks," and the artist, free "to express [that poetry] in his own way."[3] That synthesis Morris found in a concept crucial to Marx's vision of Socialism, as to his own: dialectic.

The method of antitheses was not new to Morris in 1877, when he became a Socialist. His greatest poem, *Sigurd the Volsung* (1876), had been framed by a symbol of vibrant, noble life on the one hand, and a symbol of consuming, apocalyptic destruction on the other, the Holy Tree and the Holy Fire, imaged in the engravings set at the beginning and end of the epic. According to Morris, the Tree and Fire "represent[ed] the opposing powers of good and evil" (XXII, 228).[4] Numerous religions, Morris claimed, had attempted "to fuse the two symbols into one" and thus achieve a transcendence of antithesis; what that "one" might be, however, Morris never ventured to say, either in poems or lectures. I do not believe that Morris refused to name a symbol of transcendence simply because he did not know one; I would argue that he rejected the very assumption, essential both to ancient religions and to Socialism as well, that transcendence was the ultimate goal. To transcend dialectic, Morris believed, would be to leave behind the very conditions that make us human--our "hopes and fears," whether for art or for ourselves.

Socialism, however, did offer Morris a perspective more reflective and historical than his aesthetic one, which thereby let him view his own time as an objective entity. Unfortunately, it simultaneously tended to lead him, via Marx's doctrine of dialectical materialism, towards the uncongenial aesthetic of socialist realism. The paradox is best expressed by

Christopher Caudwell, himself an inheritor of the "socialist idealism" Morris helped to create: "A novel is self-determined and self-driving... contained within itself... [But] the solid little world of the novel is not real or historical; it is created within the author's mind... like a self-contained, walled-in peepshow... projected into the social world."[5] Morris, in both his Socialist writings and his romances, searched for a world "reflecting society and yet completely self-determined"--an attitude that may appear "self-contradictory," yet which is characterized in both pursuits by a justified contempt for the restrictions of the literal. Hence his well-known outburst when, having written his first two romances, Morris received an inquiry about his sources from a solemn German scholar. "Doesn't the fool realize," Morris exploded, "that it's a romance, a work of fiction--that it's all LIES!"[6] Morris's worlds may be no more than "projections" of reality, but they have the same palpable presence as the driven world of history. Morris insists that one must maintain sufficient distance from the story one is telling to perceive it as "LIES" as well as truth, suspended in an energizing dialectic; if one does not, then the dialogue collapses into propaganda or fairy tale. In the worst case, failure to acknowledge the crafted nature of historical tales leads to enthrallment by their misprisions of social or individual identity; only the most heroic effort can break such a spell.

It is for this reason above all that Morris cherishes the oral tradition. The spoken tale and the political speech are equally "LIES"--historicist constructs that reveal the speaker's "own way" towards the communal goal, and truths--the products of perceptions that reify "the poetry of mankind." In fact, it is an uneasy balance. As many of the speeches of Morris's contemporaries demonstrate, "the poetry of mankind" can become awfully prosaic, failing either to rouse the spirit of its listeners or to articulate it. Correspondingly, as Morris's late romances show, if the teller does not succeed in blazing a new trail to poetry, the tale can become a trap for the teller, imprisoned in the "walled-in peepshow" of his/her lies. The oral narrative, and the very memory upon which that narrative is based, are simultaneously blessing and curse: they give cohesion to the race, yet they can submerge the people into stagnation. Not until Morris mastered the autobiographical tale would he achieve a balance between these antithetical forces.

The deadly double-bind is confronted in Morris's very first romance, *A Dream of John Ball* (1886). In this, one of his best-known Socialist pieces, Morris "awakens" into a dream of 1381, the year of the Kentish uprising; he spends the night conversing with John Ball--himself a dreamer, because he envisions a world of Fellowship supplanting centuries' worth of class and custom, yet a realist who knows he will wake from that dream only on the scaffold. When dawn comes Morris finds himself back in his "familiar bed," listening to "the frightful noise of the 'hooters,' one after another, that call the workmen to the factories" (CW, XVI, 287-8). On the one side is "the glamour of the dream-tide," now reduced to "day-dream"; on the other is the "cold and grey and surly" light of dawn, "a real thing" (285). It is the man in Morris's memory whose dream abides, not the resident of the Great Wen; yet if John Ball's dream is to be realized, we must look beyond our own time into the "tales of old time" on the one side, and the "times to come" (286) on the other.

Morris perceives both a promise and a threat in this dialectic. On the one hand, there is the objective struggle towards material progress, which never attains its ideal; on the other, there is the dream which, by seeking to establish an alternative model, threatens to supplant reality: on one side failure, on the other phantasm. In the failure of the two modes to connect lies the potential for tragedy, reified in Morris's "peep-show" of the future, *News from Nowhere* (1891). Once again Morris's persona is a dreamer, like John Ball dreaming of a future that has fulfilled the "longing" of the past (Morris's own present). But their conjunction can be achieved only for a single extended moment, "a day of it." Nowhere has successfully transformed its inheritance--Parliament has been turned into a Dung Market, for example; but its people settle for self-congratulation rather than seek further progress: "Once a year, on May-day, we... have music and dancing... where of old time... the men and women lived packed amongst the filth" (XVI, 66). On May-day young girls sing old revolutionary songs, totally "unconscious of their real meaning." When they cry, "How glorious life is!" the claim rings hollow. Strongly implied in such exchanges is the inability of this new world to define itself other than by inversion of the old; the people of Nowhere have not triumphed over the past, they have become enmeshed in it.

That absorption of the present by its past is typical of the people's relations with nature and one another as well; they are uniformly characterized by a subjectivity that masquerades as objectivity. The nar-

rator wonders, for example, why his guide sounds melancholy over the approach of winter:
> If you look upon the course of the year as a beautiful and interesting drama... you should be as much pleased and interested with the winter... as with this wonderful summer luxury. (206-7)

But the guide deliberately misinterprets the dreamer's speech, seizing upon the trope of the drama:
> I can't look upon it as if I were sitting in a theatre seeing the play going on before me, myself taking no part.... I am part of it all, and feel the pain as well as the pleasure in my own person. (*Ibid.*)

And it is the same with any reference to life as something which can be observed, rather than experienced-- the presumption that one can achieve aesthetic distance from any segment of the material world is hotly denied:
> Your books... were well enough for times [past, but]... it is the world we live in which interests us: the world of which we are a part. (150-1)

So powerful is the subjective experience that Morris's utopia truly does verge on being "nowhere," a realm whose inhabitants exist on the verge of that personal nonentity Wordsworth called "the abyss of idealism."[7] Perhaps the purest example of Nowhere's hegemony over its inhabitants, a hegemony the people have consciously chosen and continually endorse, is the fatal love-triangle reported near the beginning of Morris's tale, but not elucidated until near the end. Two rivals have fought over a girl, and one has accidentally killed the other; the survivor "is so upset that he is like to kill himself; and if he does, the girl will do as much." The guide comments on the situation, fraught with a "sentiment and sensibility" called "criminal" earlier in *Nowhere* (58):

> I cannot for the life of me see why he shouldn't get over it before long. Besides, it was the right man that was killed [the rejected suitor, who started the fight] and not the wrong... Of course he *must* soon look upon the affair from a reasonable point of view. (166-7)

When people fail to see themselves as actors and spectators, subjectivized projections of their milieux but simultaneously objective projectors, society as we know it disintegrates. Having given up their individuality in favor of the universal, prescribed code of "reasonableness," such people give up their right to individual hopes, individual passions, individual lives; they lay down what life is left them almost wearily--"thinking of nothing," save that "beginning again, even in a small way, is a kind of pain" (190). It is therefore inevitable that the dreamer should find himself ultimately expelled from Nowhere; in his insistence on a permanent, ongoing dialectical process he represents a threat to that sense of permanent resolution which the people of Nowhere cultivate. At the end, they literally cannot see his point of view, or his identity as the last individual.

Nowhere has totally fulfilled its dreams, and as a result has nowhere to go. Like the men of the Renaissance Morris condemned over and over in his lectures, so blinded by the glories of classical art that they could create only perfect imitations, the people of Nowhere have achieved a world outside of time and change. To seek to transcend the world's imperfections is a grand ideal; but it is disastrous to succeed. As Morris declared in "The Prospects of Architecture," art must be "fed not by knowledge but by hope" (XXII, 136). When hope disappears, the "era of rest" that ensues is but a simulacrum of death. As Morris would put it some years later,

> What all men are to-day sure is that an end turns out only to have been some halting-place on the road, which when we have reached it shows us the road stretching along toward the new perspective blue in the distance.[8]

The "News" Morris brings back from his mythical realm is not that people occasionally attain their hearts' desires; it is that the attainment is a trap. As a Socialist, Morris needed to believe in the potentiality of a material utopia; as an artist, he could not help but recognize its potentiality for spiritual imprisonment. It is for this reason most of all that Morris gradually turned away from Socialist romances to the historical romance--from propaganda to "LIES."

II

The House of the Wolfings and *The Roots of the Mountains* were written during the same four-year period which saw Morris compose *A Dream of John Ball* and *News from Nowhere*. On the surface, the two sets of works have nothing in common. The latter are avowedly Socialist, conversational, and contemporary, whereas the romances are none of the above; their language, with its deliberate archaisms and alternations of prose and poetry, would have been quite illegible to the readers of *Commonweal*. Yet the underlying subject of all four works is consistent: the working out of the dialectical process, and the fate of the individual caught up within that process.

Morris's "new perspective" embodies a series of antitheses common to the two books: the dialectic of Wolf and Dale, Markmen and invaders, ritual speech and colloquial rejoinders, "words spoken in days long ago" versus a "tale now fashioned" (XV, 123; XIV, 188);

and the even more intriguing dialectic between two very different ways of reading--not merely the differing languages of Wardour Street and Camden Town, or the differing expectations we bring to political prose and poetic romance, but a dialectic between logic and vision, which Morris dedicates the rest of his literary career to resolving.

The House of the Wolfings centers on the problems associated with "the merging of the individual in the community." Thiodolf, hero of the Wolfings, must give up his life and love to save his people; he must choose between "death in life,/Or life in death victorious" (XIV, 165). The Valkyrie who loves him begs him to wear a magic hauberk, and save himself, lest

A few bones white in their war-gear that have no help or thought
Shall be Thiodolf the mighty, so nigh, so dear--and nought. (108)

Wood-Sun's perspective is the converse of Dick's in *News from Nowhere*; each sees life in but one form, rather than as a vibratory fusion of individual and community identity. Thiodolf responds by affirming his part in the larger "tale of the Wolfings," in which he will live "ever reborn and yet reborn" (109). And Hall-Sun, their daughter, is granted the final word on the delights of process and interchange:

Many a deed had he done as he lay in the dark of the mound;
As the seed-wheat plotteth of spring, laid under the face of the ground...
That the turbid cold flood hideth from the constant hope of the years. (164)

Linked to the land in a visionary symbiosis, the people of the Mark can view themselves as living forever in the cycle of the seasons--"between the plough-stilts... smiting down the ripe wheat... wending the windless woods in the first frosts" (105-6)--what the narrator calls being "wedded to the seasons" (29). The only alternative to this "eternal recurrence of lovely changes" (XXII, 11) is to armor oneself against process; Thiodolf puts on the magic armor, which protects him against death, and finds that it also protects against life: "he felt as if he also were stiffening into stone" (XIV, 150). Only by taking off the armor can Thiodolf risk his individual life for the sake of his people's existence, and gain new life in "the tale now fashioned... [so] that we that have lived in the story shall be born again and again" (188).

But at the same time *The House of the Wolfings* presents the darker side of oral tradition. The tribal elders fear that if the Wolfings are defeated by the invading Roman legions they will be forced into exile, where they will "call new places by old names, and worship new Gods with the ancient worship" (30); they will then be prisoners of their tradition and their narratives, no longer "plotters" of them. And when the invasion takes place, these fears seem to come true; describing his people's burned-out house, a messenger laments: "O wide were grown the windows, and the roof exceeding high!" (141). Only the final triumph of the Wolfings, gained through Thiodolf's sacrifice, prevents this usurpation of the people's imaginative existence.

But it is a triumph which must be repeated with every generation; each moment, each individual, must add its unique perception and experience to the common tale, or fall victim to its ever-strengthening bonds. Such is in fact the case in Morris's second romance, *The Roots of the Mountains*. In this romance Morris presents the direct descendants of Thiodolf's people, who (as feared by the elders in the earlier work) have been forced out of their ancestral Mark. Struggling to retain their heritage, these Woodlanders, as they are now called, live apart from their neighbors and protectors, the Dalesmen; but the more they struggle to preserve their past, the more they jeopardize their future. Where the first work traced a need for "the merging of the individual into the community," Morris's second tale depicts the necessity for merging two communities into a greater whole.

Interestingly, the world of the Dalesmen is almost identical to the world of Nowhere: a cashless society, in which all people freely labor at all tasks, ornamenting their lives with the products of their work and with social rituals commemorating their past and invoking their future: "tomorrow was not a burden to them, nor yesterday a thing which they would fain forget" (XV, 11). But it remains a world of pain and threat, not only from the same Huns who have pushed the Woodlanders off their ancestral land but from within; indeed, it is precisely because the Dale faces such dialectical resistance that it has avoided the stagnation of Nowhere.

The threat is embodied in the subordinate status of the Woodlanders; they are "well nigh servants" to the Dalesmen. How could the socialist prototype, the Mark, have degenerated into the base of a stratified class system? Ironically, the very success of the first Wolfings has trapped their descendants. Just as Nowhere's success took away its vitalizing "hopes and fears," leaving them with neither aims to strive for nor adversaries to perpetuate the dialectical process, so have the people of the Mark been trapped by "the old story-lays," the "tales of old time." They still use the obsolete anapestic hexameter poetry introduced by Thiodolf and his contemporaries, a form into which the achievements of the present cannot be cast. Face-of-God, the Dalesman hero, recognizes the potential harm these tales and traditions pose to his own people as well; because he is courting a Woodlander, he can see how they represent a pathological reliance on outworn forms, rather than a freely willed resolution. Meeting Sun-Beam in the ancient Wolfing hall, he draws her outside before embracing her: "There are words crossing in the air about us--words spoken in days long ago, and tales of old time, that... I would not hearken to, for in this hour I have no will to die" (123). Woodlander traditions have become so ritualized, so irrelevant, that any individual effort to direct a future course is stifled; and without hope they sink into vassaldom.

Exorcism is their only hope; they must renounce not only their rituals but also their sense of inevitable powerlessness. Morris accomplishes this exorcism in three ways. First, the Woodlanders must exorcise the spectre of their identity, by acknowledging kinship with the Dalesmen and proclaiming themselves to be more than merely descendants of the Mark. Secondly, they must join the coming fight against the Huns and, by achieving a victory equivalent to that of their ancestors over the Romans, justify its supercession. Finally, and perhaps most importantly, they must recite "the ancient story" one last time (288-9) and then synthesize it with the prose art of the Dale, achieving a new tetrameter form that looks not to the glories of the past but to the uniqueness of the present. "To-day hath no brother in yesterday's tide," they exult; but the future will not be enthralled by its glories: "This eve of our earning comes once and no more... To-morrow no other alike it doth hide" (400-1). *Carpe diem*, these restored men and women exult--not in despair of the latter days, but in hope, "determined to be free" (XV, 285) of the illusory resolution offered by the past.

Morris's model for the future's enthrallment by the successful narratives of the past is Icelandic. Morris was a great popularizer of the sagas, translating several and basing his greatest narrative poem, *Sigurd the Volsung* (1876), on the *Volsunga Saga* rather than its more literary descendant, the *Nibelungenlied*. In Icelandic tale-telling, and especially in the religious code he found in the sagas, Morris found what to his own agnostic eyes was a deep discontinuity. On the one hand, the purpose of heroic action is to prove the hero's fitness to join the army of Odin's warriors, who will fight their greatest battle during *ragna rok*, the end of the gods. On the other hand, the hero's deeds are equally necessary as raw material for a tale of heroic action, which will provide a paradigm of heroism for the next generation and so perpetuate the desire to do great deeds and be initiated into Odin's army. But to Morris, and any contemporary, the tale is also the only evidence we have that Odin and the *ragna rok* exist. Heroes "fashion a tale" (XII, 22) out of their own lives, from which we infer the larger tale of Odin, the great battle, and divinity itself.[9] The two creators join, blurring the definition of divinity: one god (Odin) future generations are to worship, while another (the hero) is creator of the first. Thus the gap between humanity and the gods is bridged by the fashioners of tales. In the last lines of *Sigurd the Volsung*, Odin and the heroes of the poem fuse: none of them is a god; each is merely a "Goth"

(306). In the Norse sagas, in other words, Morris found a pattern by which the future may be rendered safe from the exaltation of the past, through self-effacement and identification. But the question remains: who, once the tale has been exalted by the assent of generations, would dare to aspire to either state?

Morris's recognition of this seemingly unresolvable dialectic was sharpened by his own experiences. To the Icelandic singer, the recruitment of new heroes for Odin's army was a goal worth the risk of distorting the hero's individuality or imposing the standards of the past on a changing present. The result was a tale impervious even to the arrival of Christianity; to the people of Iceland, the Day of Judgment co-existed for generations with the *ragna rok*, even though their paradigms are almost antithetical. Morris, however, encountered radically different conditions during the 1880s and 1890s, when he joined the ranks of a new species of story-teller, the sidewalk Socialist. As we have already seen in the case of *A Dream of John Ball*, Morris discovered that his greatest challenge was not preaching the word, but jarring his readers loose from their adherence to past words. Speaking of art and "The Socialist Ideal" in 1891, for example, Morris asserted: "I use the word *art* in a wider sense than is commonly used among us... The Commercialist sees... no pretense to art, and thinks that this is natural, inevitable, and on the whole desirable. The Socialist, on the contrary, sees in this obvious lack of art a *disease* peculiar to modern civilization.... Or, to put it very bluntly and shortly, under the present state of society happiness is only possible to artists and thieves" (XXIII, 255-6). But the adages of Samuel Smiles were far too deeply rooted in the psyches of his listeners for Morris to be successful with such witticisms; and it was in reaction to his failures of preachment that he turned more and more to the romance. Only in fiction could he create an artist (or a thief) of socialism, one who could achieve mastery over the world of commercial transactions and the world of subjective artistry alike--bow to the forms of social art, yet subsume them within new, self-generated forms of art.

III

It is because *The Water of the Wondrous Isles* (1896), completed in the year of Morris's death, presents this synthetic hero that it stands out as the greatest achievement of his final years. The skeleton of the story, as Morris recognized, "falls very flat"[10] when schematized; it revolves around three knights, three ladies, and the efforts of Birdalone, the heroine, to create a permanent "fellowship" with them which will simultaneously allow her to achieve a personal bond with the knight she loves, Arthur. The action includes several encounters with evil witches, the intercession of a Faery Godmother, and assorted miraculous coincidences and conveyances--it is, after all, a romance. Most importantly, the romance depends, at its most crucial moments, on the telling--or the refusal to tell--of the personal narratives of each of the main characters. By solving the dialectic inherent in personal autobiography, Morris at last comes to terms with the tensions of the social narrative, and learns how to articulate "the poetry of mankind." It is, in fact, Birdalone's success as a verbal and mythic artist which enables her to become a heroic worker of romantic magic: by becoming tale-teller to her world, Birdalone becomes its maker.

This process begins quite early, with Birdalone's arrival at the castle where the knights are awaiting word of the ladies; she has just escaped from the island where the ladies are being held captive. Her mission is merely to assure the knights of their ladies' safety: "Those who sent me... bade me do mine errand" (XX, 119). When Arthur kisses her hand in formal greeting, he seems to embrace not Birdalone but some autonomous appendage: "the dear hands suffered it all, and consented to the embracing" (116). But during the course of her imposed tale Birdalone is asked by the curious knights how she came to find the ladies; pressed by them, she finally takes "heart... to tell them all the story of her... crossing of the water." And the result is an explosive recognition of Birdalone not as agent but as actor; meeting her later, Arthur exclaims: "After what thou hast told us today, I seem to know thee what thou art" (128-29). The two exchange names (since such tokens of individuality have been unnecessary when she was simply "the kind maiden do[ing] her errand"), and this acknowledgement binds them permanently. There is a complex social deconditioning in Morris's tale-telling paradigm: in antithesis to English convention, where introductions are simple but one's personal history is guarded even from one's closest friends and family, here autobiography is a prerequisite to acquaintance. Later, when Birdalone is aided by the Black Knight, the same ritual is followed; before the two exchange names, Birdalone "without more ado" falls "to telling him of her life" (183).

The Black Knight is killed by the evil Red Knight before any higher level of intimacy can be reached; Birdalone survives only because the three original knights return providentially. One more knight is killed attempting to save Birdalone, and Arthur is maddened to see her grieve over the Black Knight's body rather than rushing to embrace him. With this derangement of the social balance, it seems that "the breaking up our fellowship" (201) is at hand. Under the stress of this immanent disintegration, autobiography assumes an active role in determining the characters' destinies. Afraid that she will be unable to convince Arthur of her purity, and stricken with guilt over being the unwitting cause of the Black Knight's death, Birdalone begs one of the ladies to explain the circumstances of her abduction to the rest of the fellowship, but the latter refuses: "Nay, nay... never shall I be able to tell it so that they trow it as if they had seen it all. Besides, when all is told, then shall we be bound together again" (201).

The argument is clear: a tale is a means of sharing experience with others, creating complementary memories of a single moment. Thereby each individual becomes part of a larger society, while retaining his or her own unique selfhood. But there is an additional attribute of the tale, which Morris has developed out of his original dialectic between direct sense-data, what we at first called "truth" but which Morris now calls "history" in its etymological sense of "information,"[10] and the data transmitted through an aesthetically crafted tale, believed in "as if [the listener] had seen it all"; this second form of belief, an act of faith, is what previously was called "LIES."

Morris is not, of course, the only artist of the nineteenth century to employ such a distinction. Even Anthony Trollope recognized "two kinds of confidence which a reader may have in his author... a confidence in facts and a confidence in vision."[12] In Trollope's vocabulary, Birdalone holds unique possession of the facts; what she engenders through her tale, however, is a vision--unverifiable, yet standing to her audience as firmly as the facts of their own memories. Viridis, the other woman, cannot tell the tale as a surrogate, because she neither participated in the action nor--the alternative which provides space for a later, reconstructive poet like Morris himself--has been initiated into the role of "a proper minstrel." Birdalone, of course, qualifies on both grounds at once.

This dilemma has also been articulated in our own time, most concisely by Philip Roth, in *The Facts: A Novelist's Autobiography*. There Roth asserts that what saved him from the effects of his disastrous marriage was "having been able to find ways of reimagining it into a fiction with a persuasive existence independent of myself."[13] But he gives the last word to Zuckerman, that very "persuasive existence" who has "counterlived" Roth's recent years, who attacks his motives: "You are not an autobiographer, you're a personificator" (162). In conclusion, Zuckerman claims, the ultimate struggle lies between fiction's "fundamentally aesthetic" motive and autobiography's "primarily ethical" one. But that, of course, is simply "truth" and "LIES" at odds yet again.

It is now that the importance of Morris's first romances becomes clear. *The House of the Wolfings*, with its wealth of details about the economy, society, and religion of the fourth century A.D., appears to be a "history"; yet it stands or falls as a work of art, a "LIE". If the tale has been well told, we will believe it "as if we had been there"; if not, we will reject the people and their world alike. Similarly, there is little room in our modern version of history for faery godmothers and magic boats; yet we listen to Birdalone's tale and, like Arthur, assent to it "as if it were written in Holy Gospel" (221). We make not an intellectual commitment but an emotional, almost a religious, one; and in the process history and lies alike become things ruled not by our logical sense but by a problematical "as-if." The tale-teller thereby assumes a power above any other worker with words, certainly more than the preacher or the propagandist.

But that power is double-edged. As Cardinal Newman noted, in his analysis of religious belief, "the images in which [belief] lives... have the power of the concrete upon the affections and passions."[13] The vision engendered by the tale-teller has the power to change the lives of those who hear the tale--even the life of the tale's creator. When Birdalone finishes her tale, it is clear that she has won Arthur's love away from its first object, Atra. The fellowship is not broken by Birdalone's encounter with the evil Red Knight, but it is shattered by the power of her narrative. Fearful of her new-found power, Birdalone flees the fellowship; but the next time she starts to recount her autobiography, she finds that it has begun to entrap her as well: "the memory of those days seemed to lead her along, as though she verily were alive in them now" (268). Once the tale achieves dramatic resolution, the teller becomes irrelevant, imprisoned within the bounds set by her past self. It is the same fate Thiodolf verged on when, donning the magic armor, he dreamed himself back into days of youth and peace: "and he felt as if he were stiffening into stone" (XIV, 150). The vision-making power threatens to advance far beyond "as-if," into "nothing-but."

Birdalone faces, in other words, the very dilemma confronted by William Morris or any artist who truly seeks to "make it new." If the tale is so well fashioned that the audience "trow it as if they had seen it all," then the teller becomes superfluous; and when that happens there is no one left to sustain the distinction between true tales and false, "histories" and "LIES." Romances assume the importance of "Holy Gospel"; every narrative becomes a tract, not for the times, but for all times. Morris had, earlier in his career, adopted a pose of detachment to downplay that danger; he called himself simply "the idle singer," thinking thereby to disclaim responsibility for his narrative. But the narrator of autobiography has no such disguise to don. Pressed to tell her story to a chance acquaintance, Birdalone late in the romance replies, "It wearies me to think thereof" (XX, 306). Each retelling ties her in a double bind: like a parent trapped by her children's repeated urgings to "tell it again," she has lost the freedom to live a further life; and like a star performer known only by her works, she has become her performance.

For Morris the entrapment of the successful tale-teller is all the more perilous because it furnishes a nightmarish paradigm for the consequences of Socialist political success. With the success of the revolution, the motivation that has impelled it will disappear; the revolution will become a completed tale, locked in the same cycle of wearisome repetition that Birdalone faces. Yet the alternative to that tale of success would be a litany of repeated failures, misprisions and distortions of the true tale that would cut the deeper for their obvious inadequacies. Birdalone must leave the fellowship, or else doom it to sterility. The pattern of self-sacrifice, so familiar to Victorian readers and writers alike, looms before her, seemingly inescapable. If she would save the fellowship, she must lose it.

What, then, can save her? The only way is for Morris to break the pattern of his own developing tale, and allow his narrative to break free of dialectical necessity. Morris's epic poem *Sigurd the Volsung*, whose narrative defined the external conditions in which it was to be read, could not do that; neither did his avowedly Socialist works, defined in their turn by the "hopes and fears" of their readership, have any means of "changing their life," as Morris described the transition from a material to a spiritual plane. Therefore Morris in his last work looks beyond these literary and political traditions, to one which he and his audience imbibed in their youth: the tradition of Nature. In the naturalists whose works Morris pored through at Marlborough, and in the Romantic writers whose spirit filled the pages of his first tales and poems, there is traceable a different, yet complementary dialectic: that between *natura naturans* and *natura naturata*, Nature as an imminent, abiding presence and Nature as a consumable yet inexhaustible product of that presence. There is even, in St. Augustine and other medieval Christian writers, a parallel to Morris's *topos* of the tale which assumes the identity of its creator: the *liber naturae* or great Book of Nature, the visible Word of its Creator.[14] In both its pagan and its Christian forms, this tradition successfully embraces product and process, Being and Becoming; the principle of life which lies behind the "book" or the "speaking face" of Nature is never threatened by the "stiffness" of its material form, as Thiodolf had been by his armor or Guest by his insistent doubts.

For the Romantic poets, engaged in unmediated intercourse with Nature, such a possibility of dual identity had been vital. It allowed them, to return to Guest's words in *News from Nowhere*, to "look upon the course of the year as a beautiful and interesting drama," but at the same time to be "a part of it all, and feel the pain as well as the pleasure in my own person" (XVI, 206-7). Woods decay, sedge withers, the thorns of life make one bleed--all the joys and sorrows of temporal life surge through the Romantic sufferer; but precisely because the poet is never drawn totally into those "fairy lands forlorn" he retains the distance necessary for aesthetic judgment. For Morris and other Victorians, however, the potentialities of immediacy had given way to the ambiguities of narrative: the poet is "an idle singer," engaged merely in filling time, not redeeming it--caught, as J. Hillis Miller puts it, "in a sterile self-enclosed circling in which the self talks to itself."[15] The convergence between Miller's image and Caudwell's image of the "walled-in peepshow" reveals the broad validity of this seemingly inevitable entrapment.

How, then, can Morris--or at least his heroine--escape this enthrallment by single vision? Precisely by doubling it. Where many Romantics were haunted by the nightmare of the Doppelganger, that image of the self which augurs one's death, Morris creates a benign second self, Birdalone's faery godmother Habundia. With the clear reference to "abundance" in her name, she is no mere faery tale sprite; she is "another form of Diana, Venus, and the German goddess Folla."[17] Habundia thus embodies *natura naturans*, the principle of natural fertility; but she is also the "image" (19) of Birdalone as she was when her tale began. Correspondingly Birdalone's tale, which embodies the principle of *natura naturata*, may be transferred to Habundia simply by being told one last time. At that moment "natural supernaturalism" will transform the autobiographical dialectic; twinned, it will achieve synthesis. Birdalone's tale will "change its life" and become Habundia's, define the godmother's life rather than/in addition to Birdalone's; from the seeming "either/or" of the finished tale will arise "both/and." Then, from the young woman's perspective, her autobiography will at last lapse back into history, and she can assume a new identity of *narrator narratans*, tale-maker.

    Birdalone's transmittal of her story to her alter ego Habundia is an act of liberation equivalent to her physical traversal of the islands in the Great Water: it removes the spell of the past. One by one, the members of the old fellowship arrive to rebuild their union; like Birdalone they have freed themselves from their pasts. Even Atra returns; though she will never marry, she can participate in this new, free fellowship not as a thrall to passion but as a partner. With the liberation of narrative, the social contract too is rendered for the first time truly free. For the rest of her life, Birdalone makes "feigned tales" (325), "LIES" that never evoke the dialectic of truth-telling; her stories are "forms of words" like other stories, but they bind no one, enthrall no one, convert no one. Birdalone's new world of playful tales therefore still belongs to her, for it lives only in words; her "game" (353) threatens neither creator nor listener; she is fertile; her world truly reaches "an era of rest."

And her readers? Do they find in her creator's "LIES" a similar paradigm of narrative openness, a fulfillment complementary to hers? We, after all, inevitably read any narrative which describes knights and their ladies seeking to form a perfect fellowship under the rule of Arthur with a certain amount of skepticism. We lie under the spell of the consummated story of that earlier Arthur no less than Birdalone lay under the spell of her own tale; we expect his bride to be unfaithful, his relatives to seek his harm, his dreams to end in horror and waste--for that primal catastrophe satisfied us so! It had been one of Morris's youthful dreams to retell the story of England's first fellowship, a dream crushed by Tennyson's achievement. Now, at the end of his career, Morris recognizes that his teenage dream had been a trap; no matter how the "tales of old time" satisfy us, we must ultimately break free of them and become the makers of our own tales. Only true "LIES" can satisfy our insatiable appetites for resolution. It is William Morris's achievement to have found the way to grant that satisfaction, yet not be swallowed up himself.

The result is not closure, but rather an eternal succession of creative tales and tellings, running parallel to that "eternal recurrence of lovely changes" which is the created world. Each item within that succession is at once a comprehensive product of the past and a visionary image of the future; and with them "we must be content." For had Roland beaten back the Moors at Roncesvalles, or Sigurd lived happily ever after with Brunhild, we might have seen their monuments, or felt the impact of their lives; but we would not have had poems. Only immersed in the unbroken yet ever-changing stream of events does the artist achieve that amphibious, dialectical "fruition... which fills a man as he receives from the minds of those who came before him to give to his fellows now living and to those that shall live."[17] There are worse fates.

Notes

1. Quoted in J. M. Mackail, *The Life of William Morris* (1899; rpt. New York, 1968), II, 147.
2. Roderick Marshall, *William Morris and his Earthly Paradises* (New York, 1981), 279.
3. Letter of 19 October 1885 to Fred Henderson, quoted in E.P. Thompson, *William Morris: Romantic to Revolutionary* (New York, 1961), 876.
4. All quotations in this essay are taken from the *Collected Works of William Morris*, ed. May Morris (24 vols. London, 1910-1915), and given as (volume, page).
5. Christopher Caudwell, *Romance and Realism: A Study in English Bourgeois Literature*, ed. Samuel Hynes (Princeton, N.J., 1970), 55-56.
6. Quoted in H. Halliday Sparling, *The Kelmscott Press and William Morris Master-Craftsman* (London, 1924), 50.
7. See the famous Fenwick note to the "Immortality Ode," in *The Prose Works of William Wordsworth*, ed. A. Grosart (London: E. Moxon, 1876) 194.
8. *William Morris Artist Writer Socialist*, ed. May Morris (London, 1924), II, 420-21.
9. For a full explication of this process, see Hartley S. Spatt, "Morrissaga: *Sigurd the Volsung*," *ELH*, 44 (1977), 355-375.
10. Letter of 29 January 1889 to May Morris, in Mackail II, 218.
11. At least according to Skeat, who was the most recent source Morris had.
12. *The Autobiography of Anthony Trollope* (1883, rpt. New York, 1905), 113.
13. *The Facts: A Novelist's Autobiography* (New York, 1988), 152.
14. *Grammar of Assent* (1870, rpt. Garden City, 1955),

86.
15. For fuller discussion of these underpinnings, see M.H. Abrams, *Natural Supernaturalism* (New York, 1971), chapter 2; and E.R. Curtius, *European LIterature and the Latin Middle Ages*.
16. See *The Linguistic Movement* (Princeton, N.J., 1985), 30.
17. Carole Silver, *The Romance of William Morris* (Athens, Ohio, 1982), 182.
18. *William Morris Artist Writer Socialist*, II, 394.

Marxism, Medievalism and Popular Culture

Chris Waters

It is not often that we are asked to forget the past. Indeed, historians often invoke Santayana's claim that those who do not learn from the past are doomed to repeat it. But Nietzsche once suggested that the ability to forget the past was sometimes more important than the lessons one might learn from it, particularly if the past inhibited action in the present: "... we need [history] for life and action," he wrote, "not as a convenient way to avoid life and action."[1] Despite his own obsession with the past, William Morris also subscribed to such beliefs, struggling to create a society in which robust living in the present would put an end to the Victorian obsession with books and the past. As Clara suggests in *News from Nowhere*, history was of little importance in utopia, and book-learning no substitute for the riches of everyday life: "As for your books, they were well enough for times when intelligent people had little else in which they could take pleasure, and when they must needs supplement the sordid miseries of their own lives with the imaginations of the lives of other people."[2]

Nineteenth-century Britain was no Morris-like utopia, peopled by individuals who enjoyed life to the fullest in the present. Instead it was a nation obsessed with the past, particularly the medieval past. From the French Revolution until the First World War, numerous writers invoked images of the Middle Ages in their critique of Victorian society. Nonetheless, the Middle Ages that existed in their minds was largely a myth, an invention of the nineteenth century. Indeed, medievalism owed more to a dislike of the urban present than to an understanding of the rural past. The present was the enemy, comprehensible only by reference to its antithesis: the Middle Ages.

Thus did medievalism emerge as a powerful discourse -- a repository of images and attitudes, beliefs and metaphors--through which Victorians could articulate their discontent with the present. Moreover, it was a discourse which incorporated the sentiments of individuals of various political persuasions. By the late nineteenth century, so many writers had contributed to medievalism, to this particular structure of perception, that it became *the* most important discourse through which individuals might organize and give expression to their understanding of the ills of the present. Thus, by 1900, the present had become a prisoner of the past, for only in the past--largely a mythical past--could a way out of the dilemmas of the present be found.[3]

Victorian medievalism was a complex phenomenon that evades simple analysis and has yet to find a historian attuned to all its varied manifestations. While other essays in this volume explore the nature of literary medievalism, this essay will focus on the relationship between medievalism and late Victorian socialism, and on the manner by which socialists invoked the medieval past in their critique of Victorian popular culture. Nietzsche's belief that people "must know the right time to forget as well as the right time to remember"[4] is of some importance for an understanding of the dynamics of socialist thought in Britain. Socialists did indeed "remember" the past, inheriting in medievalism a century-old discourse for making sense of the present. But while they borrowed selectively from it, and while they also worked to transform some of its premises, their comprehension of society was often constrained by a discourse which, for the most part, had been constructed before the advent of the socialist movement. Medievalism was a means by which socialists could invoke the past in order to attack the present. But, as we shall see, medievalism could also incapacitate socialists in their search for a more desirable future.

The Uses of the Past and the Politics of Medievalism

Victorian medievalism can be interpreted in a number of ways. First and foremost it can be seen as a functional response to the problems of a rapidly industrializing society. Just as charivari served to bind members of pre-industrial communities together by imposing on them ritualized codes of conduct, so individuals working through medievalism offered their own images of order and stability, which, they hoped, would be important in generating solutions to the problems occasioned by industrial growth. As Craig Calhoun has written in his study of early factory villages, instead of "trying to make common sense of their communal experiences, [individuals] created their own idealized version of a moral past."[5] The basis of that "moral past" was to be found in medieval England, for it was there that Victorians found--or at least pretended to find--an organically vital society that in every way appeared to be the antithesis of their own. What constituted Victorian medievalism, then, was "a set of ideas and images, constructed in the present and inscribed into the past, that redescribed it as wholesome, prosperous, sociable and active."[6]

If the medieval past seemed to offer important antidotes to the industrial present, this is not to suggest that medievalism was a coherent discourse, a series of agreed upon images and metaphors which all could share. The lasting appeal of medievalism was that it was suitably vague and malleable enough for individuals to assume various understandings of the medieval past within its frames of reference. Paul Meier, for example, in his discussion of the unfolding of William Morris's thought within the context of medievalism, has distinguished between its "negative" and "positive" manifestations. Individuals who merely found in medievalism a means of escape into an aestheticized golden age were responsible for its "negative" attributes. By contrast, "positive" medievalism characterized the work of critics who attempted to draw from the medieval past guidance for the transformation of Victorian society. Meier attributes to Ruskin the role of bridging these two strands of medievalism. And he considers Morris to be the most important of the "positive" medievalists, for it was Morris who managed to articulate a Marxist critique of Victorian social conditions within a system of representation derived largely from medievalism.[7]

Numerous individuals and events contributed to the complexity of medievalism. In the late 1830s, the infatuation with the Middle Ages displayed by aristocrats who attended the Eglinton Tournament indicated the extent to which discontent could breed escapism. While implicitly critical of the vulgarities of middle-class utilitarianism, the tournament was little more than a decorative aristocratic romp, marked by its yearning for a lost world of chivalry. William Cobbett, however, developed in medievalism an analytical metaphor and a critical weapon, invoking the past in order to argue for the positive virtues of both medieval democratic institutions and a social hierarchy in which a benevolent Church and a responsible gentry served to maintain social order. Cobbett's deployment of medievalism remained important for many decades, influencing Tory paternalists in the 1840s and later fueling socialist-inspired Merrie England myths. But while for Cobbett medievalism offered a way of talking about primitive democracy, Carlyle read into the medieval past a more narrow concern for order and leadership. Carlyle worshiped the Middle Ages because its inhabitants knew how to worship heroes. Medievalism allowed Carlyle vehemently to articulate his belief that an anarchic present was no improvement over an ordered and deferential past.

Ruskin's relationship to medievalism was more problematic. On the one hand, Ruskin, like Carlyle, desired an ordered and hierarchical society. On the other hand, Ruskin prepared the way for socialists like Morris to focus on social conditions in the Middle Ages and to criticize conditions in the nineteenth century by contrasting them with their medieval antecedents. Like several nineteenth-century historians, Ruskin began to develop an interest in everyday life in the Middle Ages-- or at least to contribute to a growing myth as to what constituted the everyday life of the past. The starting point for such investigations was always a disenchantment with day-to-day existence in the present, supporting Patrick Wright's recent claim that "the thematic repertoire of the... past comes to be defined in close relation to everyday life...."[8] Not only did such forays into the past help to facilitate the legitimation of social history as a new field of academic enquiry, but it also allowed critics, inspired by medievalism, to search for an "authentic" everyday life amidst the social conditions of the past.

Marx and Engels were also interested in social life in the Middle Ages, albeit for different reasons than Ruskin. Both writers discussed the extent to which late medieval society lacked a pronounced division of labour. They emphasized the importance of the cooperative nature of guild production, and they depicted a world in which individual producers were truly independent. Production, they claimed, was aimed at satisfying the wants of individuals, rather than the demands of capital, and personal fulfillment was never divorced from the process of work itself: "Thus there is formed with medieval craftsmen an interest in their special work and in proficiency in it, which was capable of rising to a narrow artistic sense."[9]

Although they focused on a mode of production unique to the later Middle Ages, neither Marx nor Engels romanticized this past. While guilds afforded their members many freedoms, they were doomed to extinction as soon as merchant capital established the basis of a new mode of production. Moreover, a number of landless serfs, abandoning the countryside for the town, seldom enjoyed the privileges shared by an elite stratum of craftsmen. In short, Marx and Engels were more cautious in their praise of the Middle Ages than many British critics, who often yearned for the restoration of an earlier way of life. Such individuals, according to Marx and Engels, by desiring to escape into the past, were totally incapable of comprehending "the march of modern history." Their "feudal socialism," as the *Manifesto* labelled it, was "half lamentation, half lampoon, half echo of the past, half menace of the future."[10]

In the 1880s and 1890s British socialists attempted to transcend "feudal socialism." Working within the confines of Victorian medievalism, subject to its highly charged rhetoric, they were also influenced by continental marxism. Although the writings of Marx and Engels were largely unknown in Britain until the 1880s, a few British socialists articulated Marx's analysis of economic life in the Middle Ages in terms of a native discourse. This resulted in the emergence of a "Marxist medievalism," central to British socialist thought at the end of the century. As Raphael Samuel has noted, the Middle Ages were of crucial importance for socialists because they offered both a "historical representation of class struggle" and "a benchmark by which to measure subsequent degradation and loss."[11]

One of the earliest Marxist texts to appear in Britain was Hyndman's *The Historical Basis of Socialism in England*. The first chapter, appropriately entitled "The Golden Age," suggested that the period between the end of the fourteenth century and the first quarter of the sixteenth century could be characterized by its "rough plenty" for men and women who worked with their hands. Relations between individuals were personal rather than contractual, production was carried on for use, not exchange, and individuals worked for the good of the community.[12] In the 1920s Hyndman elaborated these arguments. In *The Evolution of Revolution*, for example, he suggested that in more primitive societies, such as the Middle Ages, one could discover early forms of communism, for it was then that the "interest of each individual merged itself, unconsciously but harmoniously, in the interest of the whole gens or tribe...." Such harmony was lacking in the nineteenth century: "Ordered communism among savages; anarchical individualism among civilised people--That is the rule."[13]

Victorian social critics, in their idealization of the medieval past, often focused their attention on specific periods and places. For example, individuals who merely yearned for a more chivalrous age were usually infatuated by French court culture of the twelfth and thirteenth centuries. But because Marxists like Hyndman wished to develop in medievalism a critical weapon in their battle against nineteenth-century capitalism, they usually focused on economic conditions in Britain in the late fourteenth and fifteenth centuries. As historians now recognize, this was a period in which, due to the demographic catastrophe occasioned by the Black Death, many labourers were freed from feudal obligations and no longer competed with each other for scarce resources. Although socialists were not aware of the specific manner by which demographic change led to a wholesale restructuring of the relations of production, they were certainly aware of various manifestations of that change. Given the fact that after the Black Death conditions were often better for those who survived its ravages, it is not surprising that Hyndman believed "Merrie England" to have existed largely in the fifteenth century.

For others, the "Golden Age" existed before the Norman Conquest, rather than after the Black Death. In fact, the myth of the "Norman yoke" played an important role in the mental repertoire of British radicals, entering Victorian medievalism and complicating the equation of medievalism with any specific time period. As the myth has it, prior to 1066 Anglo-Saxons lived as free and equal citizens through their representative institutions. But then came the Norman Conquest, after which time those institutions and ways of life collapsed, only to be dreamt of and sought after by Britons ever since.[14] Members of the London Corresponding Society and various Chartists deployed this myth in their early nineteenth-century struggles, as did several socialists at the century's end. Edward Carpenter, for example, held that modern civilization had destroyed the natural bonds of community that existed prior to 1066, resulting in a chronic sense of loss, of "exile" from an earlier paradise. In "The People to Their Land," one of the songs Carpenter wrote for the socialist movement, "Norman yoke" imagery is pronounced: "A robber band has seized the land / And we are exiles here."[15] In traditional mythology the "robber band" consisted of Norman adventurers. But for Carpenter marauding Normans were interchangeable with rapacious capitalists.

By 1800 historians were questioning the validity of the "Norman yoke" argument. While many individuals continued to believe that the freedoms supposedly enjoyed by the Anglo-Saxons were lost, some historians came to view the Conquest as a watershed, essential for the creation of democratic political institutions.[16] This placed socialists in a dilemma: was the golden age to be located prior to the Conquest or much later on? As we have seen, Hyndman opted for the importance of the later Middle Ages, while Carpenter kept alive the myth of the "Norman yoke." On the whole, socialists shared Hyndman's focus, although they often described the later period in a language appropriated from "Norman yoke" mythology. Thus Morris and Hyndman wrote of the need for a "restitution" of rights and freedoms, drawing from the rhetoric of the "fall" occasioned by the Conquest.[17] Borrowing from Freeman's *History of the Norman Conquest* (1867-79), Morris also suggested that the Conquest led to the destruction of communal privileges, but that the desire to regain them lay dormant, to be rekindled by heroes like John Ball in the fourteenth century. It was Morris's self-imposed task to reawaken that desire once more in his own society.[18]

The imagery of the "Norman yoke" thus played an important role in socialists' arguments about the *later* Middle Ages. And in discussing this period they had at their disposal both an important repertoire of British medievalist sentiments--especially Ruskin's accounts of the aesthetic life of the Middle Ages--and, increasingly, continental Marxist analyses of the late medieval economy. Through Belfort Bax's familiarity with the classical texts of Marxism, British socialists were able to reinvigorate Victorian medievalism, and to work within a discourse which could now offer an analysis of everyday life in the past. The extent to which Marxism subtly transformed medievalism can be seen in *Socialism, its Growth and Outcome*, written by Morris and Bax in 1893. Although its authors argued that there was a "rough" side to the Middle Ages, that it lacked material comforts and was full of violence and superstition, they also suggested that the "whole of our unskilled labouring classes are in a far worse position as to food, housing, and clothing than any but the extreme fringe of the corresponding class in the Middle Ages." Moreover, they also argued that popular art flourished in the late Middle Ages. Medieval craftsmen, they claimed, "left behind them works to show that... happiness and cheerful intelligence were possible...."[19]

In his essays, "Feudal England" (1887) and "Art and Industry in the Fourteenth Century" (1890), Morris reiterated these beliefs. In so doing he was indebted to Marx's analysis of a pre-capitalist social formation. The late Middle Ages were for Morris a period in which the upper classes had "not got hold of those material means of production which enable them now to make needs in order to satisfy them for the sake of profit...."[20] Those needs, as we shall see, included the need for spurious gratification created by a new leisure industry. Needs in the late Middle Ages were simple, and individuals produced for personal consumption rather than for the profit of others. Moreover, work was itself enjoyable and genuine craftsmanship flourished, displaced in the nineteenth century by the advent of "shoddy" machine-made goods and exploited wage labour.

Much has been made of Morris's medievalism,[21] and here I would like merely to emphasize two of its more salient aspects. First, by adopting a Marxist critique of medieval economic conditions, Morris--along with Hyndman and Bax--infused Victorian medievalism with a series of new concerns pertaining to everyday life in the past. As a result, a transformed medievalism could itself give rise to a more potent critique of the

Victorian present. And second, because socialists were reformulating a discourse that already exerted a major influence in Victorian society, they were able to articulate their concerns in a language that was recognizable and popular.

Prior to World War I, numerous articles appeared in the socialist press which attempted to disseminate the ideas we have been concerned with. In 1908, for example, John Bruce Glasier wrote two articles for the *Labour Leader*, "Was there Once a Merry England?" and "Socialism in the Olden Time." For Glasier, the Middle Ages offered an important example of a whole way of life organized around socialist principles: "The towns, the guilds, and . . . the parish churches," he wrote, "preserved for the people an underlying structure of Socialism, stored with collective property, common obligations, traditions, and customs of song, art and play, which fortified the life of the people. . . ." This golden age, however, was not to last: "The advent of the Industrial Revolution. . . sounded the knell of this olden village and town communism. . . ." Nonetheless, because the vague memory of its achievements lingered on, socialism would eventually bring about a "new commonwealth," full of the joys of the old one.[22]

But would it? In the hands of less imaginative thinkers than Morris and Bax, such discussions tended to be devoid of analytical rigour, loaded with empty rhetoric about lost golden ages. While a few socialists in Britain attempted to attach to medieval discourse more formidable tools for a critique of industrial society, medievalism, as it existed prior to the advent of the socialist movement, had achieved such dominance as a means of shaping social criticism that attempts to transform it could be coopted or deflected. Indeed, the pull of the past could often block the emergence of a critique of the present which might actually assist in the struggle for a socialist future. For Marx and Engels there was no returning to the past. But the desire to see the past re-emerge in the present could blind Glasier and many of his radical contemporaries in Britain to their nostalgia.

The dangers of such forms of nostalgia can be understood if we turn to examine the ways in which socialists and other critics of Victorian society discussed the popular culture of their age in terms of its medieval antecedents.

Medievalism and the Critique of Popular Culture

Writing in the socialist *Glasgow Commonweal* in 1896, William Mackay claimed that in the Middle Ages May Day was a day of popular festivity and rejoicing, and that the labour movement should struggle to reinvigorate everyday life with the festive spirit that capitalism had destroyed: the "paradise that Labour has lost," he wrote, "must be regained."[23] Mackay's discussion supports Patrick Brantlinger's recent contention that the critique of popular culture often embodies nostalgia for earlier cultural forms.[24] For Mackay, as for many of his contemporaries, the Middle Ages offered a model of a more robust popular culture against which that of the nineteenth century could be judged. It was in the later medieval period, they claimed, that play was undirected and spontaneous, part of the natural rhythms of pre-industrial life: capitalism, in its demand for a disciplined workforce, had not yet severed the bonds that had presumably existed between work and leisure; nor had it created a separate sphere of leisure, cut off from work and subject to exploitation.

When critics of Victorian popular culture invoked the past in order to substantiate their beliefs about the present they often followed one of two lines of reasoning. First, they expressed nostalgia for the "genuine" pleasures of an earlier golden age, pleasures that had, they believed, been destroyed by the industrial revolution. Such beliefs surfaced in the writings of Charles Dickens--"We cling with peculiar fondness to the customs of days gone by"[25]--and they characterize George Eliot's account of "Old Leisure" in *Adam Bede*: "Leisure is gone---gone where the spinning wheels are gone--and the pack-horses, and the slow waggons, and the peddlars who brought bargains to the door on sunny afternoons."[26] This critical tradition was particularly pronounced in the early decades of the nineteenth century. It was then that radicals and rural apologists like Samuel Bamford and Pierce Egan catalogued the pastimes of pre-industrial society in order to show that industrialization had not only left a void in the recreational life of the nineteenth-century worker, but had also reoriented the temporal and spatial dimensions of everyday life in ways that were detrimental to the health of the community.

While some critics believed that industrialization had destroyed an ancient popular culture, others were aware that a new popular culture was taking its place. But they considered it to be lamentably shoddy and vulgar, and by measuring it against its more robust and vital antecedents they established in the critique of popular culture the theme of "moral decline."[27] Such individuals responded to the development of a new world of urban entertainment, characterized by singing rooms and penny gaffs in the 1850s and by music halls, spectator sports and bank holiday excursions later on. By the end of the century rising real wages, shorter working hours and a new entrepreneurial spirit in an emerging leisure industry had transformed popular culture. But for the critics the change was not particularly welcome. "True" leisure, they insisted, meant rest, renewal and genuine fulfillment, not the frivolous amusements and compulsive search for excitement that seemed to them to characterize the age: "In the 'fine old days of leisure,' which George Eliot laments," wrote one critic, "there was nothing like the same industry in pursuing recreation as there is in these days of perennial shop and unceasing work."[28]

It was assumed by these critics that in the Middle Ages people did not require artificial stimulants in order to be happy. Chartists who could recall the last vestiges of an earlier popular culture were particularly vociferous in their condemnation of the new trends. In the 1880s, for example, Thomas Cooper spoke of the pastimes of his childhood:

> Maypoles were yet in existence. But five miles from the little Lancashire town where I passed my boyhood and youth, the maypole was lowered and readorned with garlands every Mayday.... And dancing on the green, where the maypole had stood in the memories of their grandfathers and grandmothers, was still practised by the lads and lasses in hundreds of villages.[29]

Not only did Cooper lament the loss of these pleasures, but he believed that the radical culture he had once encouraged was also being displaced. Music hall, sport and dancing were all anathema to him: "The increasing passion for dancing, among you, is to me very grievous," he once told his working-class audience. "How will you fill your brains by dangling your heels?"[30]

While general pessimism with regard to Victorian popular culture was widespread, there were a number of reformers who thought they had discovered an answer to the problem in "rational recreation." Healthy and "improving" pastimes, designed to fill the void supposedly left by industrialization--or to counter the less savoury aspects of the culture it had given rise to--were encouraged by Tory aristocrats and bourgeois reformers. Rational recreation, they hoped, would remake popular culture, often by drawing upon medieval antecedents. In the 1840s, Lord John Manners, a member of the "Young England" circle, urged the revival of medieval pastimes and holidays in *A Plea for National Holydays*. And in the same decade the middle class offered workers its own version of medieval pastimes, often in mechanics' institutes. In Manchester, for example, the Free Trade Hall was once decorated as an "Old Baronial Hall of England" for a series of festivities which were to include Maid Marion and her maidens dancing around a thirty-foot maypole.[31]

Not only were such revivals symptomatic of a deep-seated disgust with Victorian popular culture, but they also represented a fear of the distance between the classes. Reformers hoped that rational recreation would encourage class reconciliation: as in the Middle Ages, individuals from all walks of life would take their pleasures together, albeit this time in somewhat artificial environments contrived by advocates of reform. But the language of "peer" and "peasant" in which the activities of rational recreation were often framed was archaic. Moreover, advocates of reform often failed to understand that a maypole was no solution to the ills of society. As Peter Bailey has suggested, "Visionary indulgence [of rational recreation] was limited to the occasional invocation of a bowdlerised Merrie England."[32] Critics of Victorian popular culture may have discovered in medievalism a powerful way of articulating their grievances. But while they were able to offer a critique of popular culture and class relations by invoking the medieval past, they were unable to suggest viable ways of transforming that culture.

Both arguments examined here--that the industrial revolution destroyed the last vestiges of a culture that grew out of the experiences of everyday life, or that it created new pleasures which, while popular, were inferior to those which had been destroyed--were articulated by socialists. Like Cooper they held capitalism responsible for the existence of cheap and ephemeral pleasures which blocked the emergence of a radical working-class culture. And like Bamford and Cobbett they suggested that the demand for a rational, disciplined workforce had destroyed the very desire for pleasure that had once been the basis of an earlier and more wholesome way of life.

In various essays, Ernest Belfort Bax offered a historical explanation for the "decline" of popular culture. According to Bax, workers had been robbed of pleasure by a bourgeoisie which insisted on the utility of its own puritanical ideology. Contrasting the Victorian Sunday--a day of "idleness and gloom"--with its medieval counterpart, Bax claimed that the Church had once guaranteed the people "as many additional holidays in the year as there were Sundays." This "Old English Sunday" was celebrated in mystery plays, fairs and morris dances, all of which flourished until the Puritans suppressed the "catholic fete days of old 'merry England'" and instilled in the general populace a belief in the "sinfulness of pleasure." Bax believed that pleasure had once flourished, a natural and spontaneous eruption of communal existence. But the industrial rationalization of everyday life had replaced "genuine" pleasure with "a mass of little wants with the means of satisfying them ready to hand for those who can purchase them...."[33]

In articulating these ideas, Bax, like Max Weber, located the roots of modern bourgeois ideology in the ascetic ideals of Calvinist theology. If George Eliot lamented the fact that few pleasures were available to the Victorian worker, this, according to Bax, was because nineteenth-century industrialists had little time for pleasure. For Bax, the bourgeoisie had brought about "the dethronement of pleasure and beauty as the end of life" in its never-ending quest for business success. Moreover, he suggested that the middle class first attacked the "luxury, ease and vice" of the feudal nobility and then demanded that workers adopt a more rational approach to life. The result was a world that had abandoned the passionate enjoyments of earlier times. As he once asked, "Is the Bourgeois world in which we are all 'puritans' despising pleasure as frivolous and [a] waste of time, all thrifty and industrious or pretending to be so... intrinsically better and happier than... the Feudal world...?"[34]

The myth of the Middle Ages as a golden age of popular pleasure was given added weight by another myth: that of the evils of puritanism. While historians suggest that Cromwellian attacks on popular culture were limited,[35] socialists attributed the decline of a robust culture of everyday life that had flourished in the Middle Ages to the growth of puritanism. By blaming religious asceticism for the impoverishment of popular culture, by relating this to the rise of capitalism, and by seeing the triumph of the ascetic ideal in nineteenth-century bourgeois ideology, socialists were able to introduce an important historical argument into their critique of popular culture. No longer was the past invoked nostalgically merely to suggest that culture had once been healthier. Rather, the historical agents of the change could now be pinpointed and attacked. This allowed socialists to dwell at length on the evils of an ideology, central to capitalism, which had brought about such a state of affairs.

Because, for socialists, the puritanical spirit of Victorian capitalism had undermined a whole way of life in which "genuine" pleasure had once flourished, it became necessary for them to develop an alternative politics of pleasure. Labour's *Daily Citizen*, for example, urged socialists to repudiate bourgeois asceticism and preach "the Play Spirit, the cult of the Right to Play."[36] Moreover, various Christian Socialists not only preached the "Play Spirit," but attempted to put it into practice as well. Conrad Noel, a member of the SDF and founder of the Christian Socialist League, recognized that not all capitalists were puritans, that some of them were beginning to market new pleasures which undermined the old ascetic ideal. Still, the pleasures they offered were, according to Noel, debased: capitalism could do little more than offer "the sugary joys of an immediate and easily gained heaven for all."[37] Noel saw it as one of his tasks--as did other Christian

Socialists like Stewart Headlam--to make working-class life more pleasurable, often by recreating the links that had once existed between the Church, the community and popular culture.

Other socialists were eager to show how capitalism had alienated individuals in specific areas of cultural production. In so doing they also focused on the extent to which people in the Middle Ages were not constrained in their creativity by a debilitating ascetic ideal. In 1910, the socialist composer and music teacher, Edgar Bainton, lectured on the subject of "Music and Socialism." In the Middle Ages, he claimed, music was an expression of the aspirations *of* the people. This lasted until wandering minstrels began to offer music *to* the people: "the rascals," he wrote, "could not turn out original productions... but used up all the music of the folk."[38] In the nineteenth century the process was complete: people no longer made their own music, but relied on commercially-produced music-hall fare. As another lecturer claimed, people in the Middle Ages produced and performed music collectively. This was exemplary because it entailed creative, communal activity. But in the nineteenth century musical life merely revolved around a division of labour between audience and performer; space was no longer available for a musical culture to grow out of the popular experience of everyday life.[39]

Edgar Bainton was content to draw attention to the discrepancy between the "popular" pleasures of the Middle Ages and the "manufactured" pleasures of his own age. But, as we have seen, other socialists--like Bax--accounted for the transformation that had taken place. And still others--like Noel--drew upon medieval antecedents in an attempt to revitalize Victorian popular culture. What united them all was the intellectual framework in which they operated: medievalism, a means of producing and organizing knowledge and of framing social criticism. Socialists who appropriated medievalism expressed their concerns about industrial society and its culture in particular ways. This appropriation also facilitated socialists' efforts to envisage a world in which "genuine" pleasure might flourish. As is well known, William Morris was interested in the connection between "art" and "work-pleasure," and he attempted to imagine an ideal society in which such pleasure would again be important. In this he was not alone. Harry Lowerison, a Fabian and a Durham miner's son, claimed that it was the degradation of work that bred the desire for "artificial" pleasures. If workers demanded "human conditions" of labour, he claimed, then more desirable forms of play would emerge. Likewise, William Diack, a member of the Aberdeen Socialist Society, wrote of the Victorian worker: "His work must grow more like his recreation, his recreation more like his work. Only artificial pleasure and degrading toil have drawn the present line of demarcation between the two."[40]

In an ideal society the work/leisure divide might thus be bridged. But what would popular culture consist of in such a society? Obviously, "work-pleasure"--pleasure at the point of production--was important in socialist thought, and it is central to Morris's *News from Nowhere*. But while Morris's novel explores pleasure *in* work, along with the pleasures of social intercourse, it is also subject to many medieval anachronisms. For example, there is a "solemn feast" to commemorate "The

Clearing of Misery" (239-40), marked by music and dancing, "merry games" and "happy feasting," and the "prettiest" girls adorned with flowers. Despite the general merriment, the whole ceremony appears flat and lifeless, a contrived account of obsolete medieval rituals. By assuming that workers were once happy in their work, Morris believed that regenerating the social bases of handicraft production would solve the problem of popular culture. Thus did his understanding of the Middle Ages shape Morris's concern with "work-pleasure." But in seeking inspiration from the medieval past, Morris could not envisage other pleasures, less centrally related to work, except in terms of medieval pageants.

At least Morris attempted to explore the nature of pleasure in work. Others merely read their own concerns for more "improving recreations" onto the society of the future. Philip Frankford, whose socialist utopia set in Croyden is the subject of "The Coming Day," believed the masses would be content if the authorities gave them an occasional Merrie England Day.[41] Frankford's festival to commemorate "The Emancipation of Humanity and the Clearing of the Slums"--rational recreation in medieval dress--borrows its central idea from Morris. But in depicting an event created largely for the people, Frankford ignores the fact that for most medievalists such festivals were only valid because they were created by the people. Critics of socialist thought pointed to this discrepancy in their own anti-socialist novels. Moreover, Edward Herbert, in *Newaera*--a novel which offers a parody of socialist festivities--attacks their medievalism in general. For

Herbert, attempting to fit the pleasures of the golden age into a utopian society was myopic and impractical.[42]

The relationship between Marxism, medievalism and popular culture is thus a complicated one. Medievalism could provide socialists with a cognitive map for life in an impersonal world. But it could also channel aspiration into a nostalgic dead end. Take socialist attitudes towards May Day, for example. Aware of the importance of May Day in the Middle Ages, socialists could attempt to harness its festivities to the struggle for socialism. But they could also, in generating a day of pleasure in the present, provide workers with a sense of well-being that would effectively block, rather than encourage, the struggle for a society in which pleasure might be enjoyed every day. Finally, May Day celebrations could merely console those who sought to escape present-day ills by entering a make-believe past.

The attempt to attach residual celebrations from the medieval past to the socialist cause is indicative of the fact that historical traditions both inspire and confer legitimacy on radical political struggles. In fact, socialists often invested traditional holidays with new meanings "as occasions for affirming the community of the movement in a pleasurable way."[43] In 1899, for example, the International Socialist Congress in Paris decreed that May Day should be a general labour holiday. William Diack praised such moves because they suggested to him that May Day might gain a new significance in the battle against the "gloom and feverish anxiety" brought about by capitalism.[44] And in West Ham, following the socialist triumphs in the municipal elections of the 1890s, May Day was proclaimed an annual holiday. As Morris once wrote, this was the most "fitting" day "for the protest of the disinherited against the system of robbery that shuts the door betwixt them and a decent life."[45]

How many workers in West Ham viewed May Day as Morris did? How many treated it as another Bank Holiday, a twenty-four hour break from work? Socialists hoped that May Day celebrations would awaken in workers a desire to struggle for a society in which pleasure would not be alienated by unceasing toil. But those hopes could be thwarted if workers merely viewed periodic festivities as a compensation for the demands of the workplace. In 1894, the Halifax branch of the ILP sponsored a "Merrie England Bazaar and Village," held on the Tudor estate of John Lister, the party treasurer. Entertainment was provided, handicrafts were displayed and several hundred pounds were raised. By all accounts it was a success: "Here in Halifax, at the ILP bazaar," wrote one observer, "we have lived and moved in 'Merrie England,' and it is well with us."[46] But it was only "well with us" for a day, and many workers may have found little fault with a world in which such pleasures existed. As Ross McKibbin has argued, it was in part the continued importance for workers of sports, hobbies and pastimes rooted in an earlier way of life that prevented in England the "catastrophic alienation" that accompanied industrialization on the continent.[47] The ILP bazaar--and various May Day celebrations--might have functioned in a similar way, blunting the demand for a total transformation of society.

Finally, many socialists paid little attention to the politics of pleasure and simply treated May Day as an occasion for displaying nostalgia for a lost way of life.

Katharine Bruce Glasier, the socialist lecturer, once wrote: "And surely there is nothing nearly so pretty and happy in our modern celebrations as the garlanding of the May-pole with real flowers, the crowning of the May Queen, and the... games and dancing on the village green."[48] Here wistful nostalgia for a lost golden age is triumphant. Somewhere politics got lost, or became subordinated to a desire for the mere revival of the pastoral. Moreover, sentiments like these were widespread and long-lasting. As late as 1934, George Lansbury claimed that he desired to see the "reclaiming" and "recreating" of rural England: "I can see the village greens with the Maypoles, and the boys and girls, young men and maidens, all joining in the mirth... of May Day."[49]

By the time Lansbury paid homage to May Day, medievalism did not occupy the strategic place in socialist thought that it once had. Marxism no longer posited an escape from the proletarian condition but a realization of workers' power; no longer did it articulate its concerns through the aesthetics of idealized medieval workers but through the strength of the "proletarian giant."[50] The ritual invocation of the medieval past gave way to an emphasis on the historical destiny of the proletariat, a destiny which did not require the prop of medievalism.

Today, morris dancers invariably make their appearance on festive occasions. But popular medievalism no longer exists--at least not as an important discourse for organizing knowledge about the present. Following World War II, affluence and relative prosperity marked Britain's entry into a different world from that which bred wholesale flight into the past a century ago. If Lansbury's attempted resurrection of the Middle Ages was already dated in the 1930s, it was positively archaic by the 1950s. Because Britons had never had it so good, there was no use pretending that the Middle Ages were a golden age. The golden age was here, now. While the "first" Elizabethan age was often invoked at the beginning of the "new" Elizabethan age in 1952, it was largely to the future--not to the past--that Britons turned. The Left pointed to the triumphs of the Welfare State; history need not extend back before 1945, let alone to the Middle Ages.

More recently, particularly since the crises of the 1970s and 1980s, nostalgia has again become important. This time, however, it is the past of Victorian values and imperial glory--not the medieval past--which attracts attention. Margaret Thatcher and her successors can invoke nostalgia to deflect criticism of everyday life in British society, although it is of no help in fighting the serious problems faced by the nation. Nor, in the nineteenth century, was a longing for the golden age much help in overcoming the social crises of industrialization. But medievalism was more than mere nostalgia. While some socialists succumbed to a simple yearning to re-invoke a lost way of life, others sought to transcend the limitations of a backward-looking medievalism. They emphasized aspects of the Middle Ages that hitherto had not been emphasized, and they drew from the past guidance in their struggle for a new society. But this particular "Marxist medievalism" was arrested in its development, swallowed up in successive waves of nostalgia for the past that was the main hallmark of Victorian medievalism. Perhaps it could not have been otherwise, given the fact that medievalism began as a rejection of the present for the more comfortable abode of an idealized, lost past.

Notes

1. Friedrich Nietzsche, *The Use and Abuse of History* (Indianapolis: Bobbs-Merrill Co., Inc., 1957), 3. On the past in Victorian England in general, see John Clive, "The Use of the Past in Victorian England," *Salmagundi* 68-69 (Fall 1985-Winter 1986), 48-65.
2. William Morris, *News from Nowhere* (London: Routledge and Kegan Paul, 1970), 129.
3. Medievalism was one of many discourses through which Victorians comprehended their world. In this analysis of nineteenth-century discourses I am indebted to Edward Said, *Orientalism* (New York: Pantheon Books, 1978).
4. Nietzsche, 8.
5. Craig J. Calhoun, *The Question of Class Struggle: Social Foundations of Popular Radicalism During the Industrial Revolution* (Chicago: University of Chicago Press, 1982), 43.
6. Joanna Banham, "'Past and Present': Images of the Middle Ages in the Early Nineteenth Century," in Joanna Banham and Jennifer Harris, eds., *William Morris and the Middle Ages* (Manchester: Manchester University Press, 1984), 24. See also Alice Chandler, *A Dream of Order: The Medieval Ideal in Nineteenth-Century English Literature* (Lincoln: University of Nebraska Press, 1970).
7. Paul Meier, *William Morris, the Marxist Dreamer* (Brighton: Harvester Press, 1978), vol. 1, 94.
8. Patrick Wright, *On Living in an Old Country: the National Past in Contemporary Britain* (London: Verso, 1985), 22.
9. Karl Marx, "The German Ideology," in Robert C. Tucker, ed. *The Marx-Engels Reader*, 2nd ed. (New York: W. W. Norton and Co., 1978), 178. See also "Socialism: Utopian and Scientific," in the same

volume, 701-706.
10. "Communist Manifesto," in Tucker, 491.
11. Raphael Samuel, "British Marxist Historians, 1880-1920: Part One," *New Left Review* 120 (March-April 1980), 21-96.
12. H. M. Hyndman, *The Historical Basis of Socialism in England* (London: Kegan, Paul, Trench and Co., 1883), 1-23.
13. H. M. Hyndman, *The Evolution of Revolution* (New York: Boni and Liveright, 1921), 22-23.
14. Christopher Hill, "The Norman Yoke," in Hill, *Puritanism and Revolution* (London: Secker and Warburg, 1958).
15. Edward Carpenter, *Chants of Labour* (London: Swan Sonnenschein, 1888). See also Carpenter's *Civilisation: its Cause and Cure, and Other Essays* (London: Swan Sonnenschein, 1889).
16. Asa Briggs, "Saxons, Normans and Victorians," in *The Collected Essays of Asa Briggs. Volume Two: Images, Problems, Standpoints, Forecasts* (Brighton: Harvester Press, 1985).
17. H. M. Hyndman and William Morris, *A Summary of the Principles of Socialism* (London: Modern Press, 1884), 60.
18. See Meier, vol. 1, 108-109; Chandler, 220-22.
19. William Morris and E. Belfort Bax, *Socialism: its Growth and Outcome* (London: Swan Sonnenschein, 1893), 79, 84.
20. William Morris, "Art and Industry in the Fourteenth Century," in May Morris, ed., *The Collected Works of William Morris* (London: Longmans, Green and Co., 1910-15), vol. 22, 380. "Feudal England" can be found in vol. 23, 39-58.
21. For more detailed discussions, see Banham and Harris; Chandler, 209-30; Margaret R. Grennan, *William Morris: Medievalist and Revolutionary* (New

York: King's Crown Press, 1945); Meier, vol. 1, 94-164; Michael Naslas, "Medievalism: a Major Part of Morris's Aesthetic Theory," *Journal of the William Morris Society* 5 (Summer 1982), 16-24; E. P. Thompson, *William Morris: Romantic to Revolutionary*, 2nd ed. (New York: Pantheon Books, 1976).
22. *Labour Leader*, 21 and 28 August 1908.
23. William Mackay, "May Day, Old and New," *Glasgow Commonweal*, May 1896, 1-2.
24. Patrick Brantlinger, *Bread and Circuses: Theories of Mass Culture as Social Decay* (Ithaca: Cornell University Press, 1983), 17.
25. Charles Dickens, *Sketches by Boz* (London: Chapman and Hall, 1867), 186, 188.
26. Quoted in Raymond Williams, *The Country and the City* (Oxford: Oxford University Press, 1973), 177. For a more detailed discussion of these points, see Chris Waters, "'All Sorts and Any Quantity of Outlandish Recreations:' History, Sociology, and the Study of Leisure in England, 1820-1870," *Historical Papers/Communications Historiques*, 1981, 8-33.
27. On this theme, see Geoffrey Pearson, "Falling Standards: A Short, Sharp History of Moral Decline," in Martin Barker, ed., *The Video Nasties: Freedom and Censorship in the Media* (London: Pluto Press, 1984), 88-103.
28. "Leisure Thoughts," *All the Year Round* 67 (September 1890), 228. For an elaboration of these themes, see Chris Waters, *British Socialists and the Politics of Popular Culture, 1884-1914* (Stanford: Stanford University Press, 1990), chapter 1.
29. Thomas Cooper, *Thoughts at Fourscore, and Earlier. A Medley* (London: Hodder and Stoughton, 1885), 8.
30. Cooper, 176.

31. Hugh Cunningham, *Leisure in the Industrial Revolution c. 1780-c. 1880* (London: Croom Helm, 1980), 101-2.
32. Peter Bailey, *Leisure and Class in Victorian England: Rational Recreation and the Contest for Control, 1830-1885* (London: Routledge and Kegan Paul, 1978), 169.
33. Ernest Belfort Bax, "Socialism and the Sunday Question," in *The Religion of Socialism; Being Essays in Modern Socialist Criticism* (London: Swan Sonnenschein, 1886), 55-57; Bax, "The Curse of Civilisation," in *The Ethics of Socialism* (London: Swan Sonnenschein, 1889), 109.
34. Ernest Belfort Bax, "Luxury, Ease and Vice," in *Outspoken Essays on Social Subjects* (London: William Reeves, 1897), 126.
35. See Percy Scholes, *The Puritans and Music* (London: Oxford University Press, 1934); Margaret Heineman, *Puritans and Drama* (Cambridge: Cambridge University Press, 1980).
36. 'JG', "Workers and Sport," *Daily Citizen*, 31 December 1912.
37. Conrad Noel, *The Day of the Sun* (London: David Nutt, 1901), 12. The links between socialism and puritanism are further explored in Waters, *British Socialists*, 148-52.
38. Edgar L. Bainton, *Music and Socialism* (Manchester: Fellowship Press, 1910), 10.
39. "How Commercialism Affects Our Music," *Justice*, 26 October 1895).
40. Harry Lowerison, "On Organised Games," *Daily Herald*, 1 June 1912; William Diack, *The Moral Effects of Socialism* (Aberdeen: Aberdeen Socialist Society, 1893), 14.
41. "The Coming Day" was serialized in the Huddersfield *Worker* between February and April 1908.

For this particular ceremony, see 18 April, 4.
42. Edward Herbert, *Newaera: A Socialist Romance* (London: P. S. King and Son, 1910), 77.
43. Eileen Yeo, "Culture and Constraint in Working-Class Movements," in E. and S. Yeo, eds., *Popular Culture and Class Conflict 1590-1914* (Hassocks: Harvester Press, 1981), 169. On May Day in particular, see Eric Hobsbawn, "Mass-Producing Traditions: Europe, 1870-1914," in Hobsbawn and Terence Ranger, eds., *The Invention of Tradition* (Cambridge University Press, 1983), 283-87.
44. William Diack, "May Day," *Justice*, 27 April 1895.
45. *Justice*, 1 May 1896; quoted in Banham and Harris, 305.
46. "Floreat Halifaxium," *Clarion*, 13 October 1894.
47. Ross McKibbin, "Why was there no Marxism in Great Britain?" *English Historical Review* 99 (April 1984), 306-307.
48. 'Iona', "Our Women's Outlook," *Labour Leader*, 4 May 1906.
49. George Lansbury, *My England* (London: Constable and Co., 1934), 93.
50. Raphael Samuel, "Enter the Proletarian Giant," *New Socialist* 29 (July/August 1985), 24-27.

Ralph Adams Cram: Last Knight of the Gothic Quest

Charlotte H. Oberg

Ralph Adams Cram (1863-1942), architect, author, art critic, social critic, political commentator, city planner, educator, and spokesman for Catholic theology, was in his time the leading figure of the Gothic Revival movement in the United States. Throughout the first four decades of the twentieth century, he and his associates made a significant mark upon ecclesiastical and collegiate architecture in this country. In designing buildings for important institutions, Cram has literally shaped significant though small portions of this nation and has undoubtedly influenced the lives of many thousands of Americans who have worshipped or been educated in Cram-designed structures. Although sometimes stigmatized by modernist critics as dated or of chiefly historical interest, Cram's buildings nonetheless continue to be widely esteemed for their informed and flexible traditionalism.[1] Likewise, although Cram's neo-medieval Christian doctrines are now largely forgotten, in his day he was also a popular public speaker and prolific author on these topics. Cram's long and successful career is in many respects a poignant American reprise of nineteenth-century British neo-medievalism.

Cram's autobiography, *My Life in Architecture*, and his many other writings on the Gothic revival and on the need for social and political reform, reveal the story of an intellectual and artistic life both complex and intense. The story begins as an impressionable and brilliant young Ralph Cram responds to the early influences of Carlyle, Ruskin, D. G. Rossetti, and Morris, and ends ironically with the elderly Cram experiencing even the disappointments and frustrations of these artist-prophets whose writings and examples had first fired his imagination and then illumined his way.

The son of a New Hampshire Unitarian minister who could not afford to send him to college, Cram was to become one of the most erudite of autodidacts. Taught Latin by his father, he began his self-education in his father's "small but singularly well chosen library," where he read voraciously: all of Ruskin and works by Carlyle, Arnold, Dickens, Scott, Browning, and Tennyson, among many others.[2] Thus was the ground prepared for his future development when Cram came to Boston in 1881 to study architecture in the offices of the Boston architects Arthur Rotch and George T. Tilden. Here he encountered a heady world of ideas, music, and art, in which "everything seemed to open out around [him] like the bursting of enormous fireworks." This was not merely the naive effusion of a boy from a country parsonage on first visiting a provincial capital; Boston in the 1880's was alive to all the intellectual currents of Europe, and Cram was reacting to the amalgamated force of all of the "great personalities of the time." In Boston, the young Cram experienced a profound moment of discovery:

> I suppose that to everyone there comes a moment when a certain definite thing, not necessarily in itself of major importance or even appositeness, acts as the precipitant on a fluid and amorphous personality, bringing some sort of order out of the chaos and dark night of immaturity, and in a way lifting self-consciousness out of the unconscious. With me, I know, it was music,--particularly that of Richard Wagner. . . . Almost simultaneously came the Pre-Raphaelites revelation, through the small showing at the old Art Museum, and the appearance of the Rossetti poems [no doubt the editions of 1881]; and these three things--music, painting, and poetry--will always remain associated in my mind as a dynamic unit of inspiration. The ground had already been measurably prepared for the pictorial seed, for by that time I had read everything that Ruskin had written (*Life* 8-9).[3]

Cram must have become a Wagner devotee in April of 1884 when there was a highly successful Wagner festival at the Mechanics Institute. The "Pre-Raphaelites revelation," which indirectly resulted in Cram's brief excursion into journalism, seems to have occurred in the following November, when the *Transcript* printed a series of five articles by Cram on Rossetti and the Pre-Raphaelites. The occasion was a showing of "twenty-two photographs from the works of the greatest master of the past four centuries," which Cram felt were not being properly appreciated by the Boston citizenry. The five articles contain a history of Pre-Raphaelitism (in which Rossetti is credited with originating the movement), a sympathetic sketch of Rossetti's tragic life, and specific discussions of most of the works represented. Not yet twenty-one, Cram shows in these essays that he already had a thorough knowledge and appreciation of his subject. Cram's favorites seem to have been "The Girlhood of Mary Virgin," "How They Met Themselves," "Dante's Dream," "Mary Magdalene," "Lady Lilith," and "Proserpina."[4] For Cram, Rossetti's greatness arose not only from his love of beauty, but from the "transcendentalism which is Rossetti," that is, his devotion to the idea or motive in art:

> Rossetti paints the intense and subtle passion of the middle ages, the transcendental dreaming and visions of a superhuman soul... [he] represents the Renaissance of the idea as the soul of art, a noble and artworthy motive, appealing to the mind through the strange, mysterious offices of color, form and light ("Dante Rossettis" II).

The transcendentalism attributed to Rossetti's painting is important in light of Cram's subsequent development; clearly, Rossetti's medieval subjects and his bent for the mystical and the supernatural held a natural appeal for Cram. At this point, Cram was still a Unitarian, but he seems nevertheless to have been attracted by the Catholic associations of Rossetti's early paintings, writing with sympathetic appreciation of Rossetti's depiction of the Virgin in "Girlhood of Mary Virgin," which he terms "a veritable transcription from the fifteenth century." Commenting on "Dante's Dream," Cram was also moved to write that the love of Dante for Beatrice was "the most perfect love that we have known; the purest, most divine, most holy love that can be"; asserting that Rossetti's translation of Dante's *La Vita Nuova* is "the truest translation of the wonderful poem," Cram must have been aware of the symbolic connections between Beatrice and the Virgin ("Dante Rossettis" IV). In the *Transcript* articles, Cram several times compares Rossetti with Wagner; so lately dead, these were the two greatest heroes of his youth.

The editor of the *Transcript* was sufficiently impressed with Cram's contributions on artistic subjects to offer him a position as art critic, which he accepted after a European trip in 1886 (financed by $500 won in an architectural competition), during which he sent back "many most highly coloured special articles to the hospitable *Transcript*" (10-12). But the great significance of Cram's brief European tour was his encounter, not only with European drama, music (including Wagner at Bayreuth), and painting (including London's Pre-Raphaelite collection), but with the great Gothic buildings of Europe; his predilection for Gothic, engendered by his reading of Ruskin's *Stones of Venice*, began to mature into his major lifelong artistic interest. (Earlier, while still in the offices of Rotch and Tilden, he had felt offended by a design for a church on which he was set to work, and was impelled to try for himself an alternative Gothic design, though at this time he had no "religious superstitions... except Oriental occultism of the Madame Blavatsky type" [46]). Like his compatriots Henry James and T. S. Eliot, he was changed forever by his exposure to the artistic heritage of Europe. Cram describes the impact of European culture upon him thus:

> At the age of twenty-three, with behind me only an America where the evidences of art and their manifestations were few, rudimentary, and, in addition, disappearing fast, such a journey was not only apprenticeship, but revelation. Never afterward was I able to isolate one art from another, or these from life. It was then, I think, that I came to believe that beauty was a definite thing, immutable and everlasting in its essence, and the best test and measure of value that man has at his disposal. I knew then, and I hold now, that the unbeautiful or the ugly thing is the thing

> of the wrong and evil shape, whether in art or religion, philosophy, government, or the social fabric (52).

Cram's career as art critic was brief; he returned to architecture after two years, giving up journalism, though not literature. Not only were the "pecuniary returns" from his art columns inadequate, but Cram "developed a certain repugnance to commenting *in extenso* on exhibits of pictures [he] considered bad, even when the proprietors of the galleries implicated were generous advertisers--an inhibition which was not sympathetically accepted by the business management" (12). Early and late, Cram would always refuse to sell out to materialistic interests.

In 1888, Cram determined finally that architecture was to be his life's work. This decision was crystallized during a second trip to Europe with T. Henry Randall, an architectural student from Baltimore and "an Episcopalian of the sound Southern sort, vitalized by Catholic tendencies." Randall rekindled Cram's enthusiasm for architecture, making him realize the inadequacy of "rationalism and physical science and liberal Unitarianism," and a visit to Venice completed finally what *The Stones of Venice* had begun as early as 1876 (57, 63).

The climax of the tour, however, was a religious conversion experienced at a Christmas Eve midnight mass in the Church of San Luigi dei Francesi in Rome. The power of the ritual induced a mystical experience:

> For the half-hour after we arrived it was quite still except for the subdued rustle of men and women on their knees and the delicate click of rosaries. Then, in their white and gold vestments, the sacred ministers came silently to the high altar, attended by crucifers, thurifers and acolytes, and stood silently waiting. Sud-

denly came the bells striking the hour of midnight, and with the last clang the great organs and the choir burst into a melodious thunder of sound; the incense rose in clouds, filling the church with a veil of pale smoke; and the Mass proceeded to its climax with the offering of the Holy Sacrifice of the Body and Blood of Christ. I did not understand all of this with my mind, but I understood (59).[5]

Cram returned to Boston, underwent religious instruction, and, in accord with his lifelong Anglophilia, was confirmed in the Anglican Communion of the Catholic Church (58-60).[6] Cram would remain passionately devoted to High Church Anglicanism all his life; not surprisingly, Newman appears frequently in Cram's approved lists of prophets and thinkers. Though Cram himself never crossed the line and joined the Church of Rome, he was to become a spokesman not only for Anglo-Catholicism, but for Roman Catholicism as well, working for the reunion of Catholics and Anglicans.[7] Cram himself referred to his religious belief as "sacramental Christianity." Sacramentalism, which Cram regarded as the governing principle of the Middle Ages, became the fundamental principle of existence for Cram and remained so throughout his life. In sacramental philosophy, Cram explained

... matter takes on a new aspect, since it is a symbol, a type and a vehicle of pure spirit, the Absolute, or, as the Christian says, God the Holy Ghost.... The aspiration and the struggle are towards the spiritual reality, but through the material agent, which thus takes on an honour and acquires a reality it otherwise would not possess.[8]

Sacramentalism would profoundly influence the direction of Cram's personal and professional lives. Not only would he later write and speak publicly on matters of Catholic doctrine, but his religious faith would henceforward motivate and govern his artistic endeavors, whether architectural or literary. Further, Cram's extensive writings on social and public issues would be motivated by his religious fervor--throughout his life his aim was literally to save humanity.

Like Carlyle, Arnold, Ruskin and Morris, Cram was always ready to address issues of public concern; his first appearance in print was a letter to the editor of the *Transcript* protesting the proposed building of a "tenement house" in front of Trinity Church.[9] As time went on, his writing would take almost exclusively the form of editorials and articles addressing public issues in the realms of architecture, religion, economics and politics. But as a young man Cram had a decided penchant for *belles-lettres*, which he indulged with some success in company with a group of like-minded friends, many of whom were to become well-known in various fields. During this "Bohemian" period, Cram belonged to several "social-controversial-inspirational groups," participated in the publication of several journals, and wrote stories, poetry, song lyrics, and verse drama, now seldom read (90, 94). England's Aesthetes and Decadents were important influences on Cram and his friends; many of the interests and activities of his circle which he recounts in his autobiography strike familiar chords, reminding us that Cram was of the same generation as W.B. Yeats. In fact, Yeats and Cram were almost exact contemporaries, and their lives followed similar patterns. Like Yeats, Cram felt the influence of Blake, D.G. Rossetti, Morris, Wilde, Madame Blavatsky (Yeats, of course, actually knew these last three); like Yeats, he was interested in the supernatural and in Japanese art[10]; like Yeats he leaned toward mysticism (especially Neo-Platonism), monarchism, elitism, and everything associated with the aristocratic traditions of the past; like Yeats, he would evolve his own theory of historical cycles and, like Yeats, having become in old age a "public man," Cram would manifest unfashionably rightist political sympathies.

Also like Yeats, as a writer Cram passed through an early Pre-Raphaelite period, characterized in his case by an attraction to medieval subjects. He planned a dramatic trilogy in blank verse based on the "Arthurian legends as the perfect embodiment of the spirit and impulse of that great Christian epoch we call Mediaevalism." He was attempting "to do for the epic of our own race, and in a form adapted to dramatic presentation, a small measure of that which Richard Wagner achieved in an allied art for the Teutonic legends."[11] Cram completed only the first part of the trilogy, *Excalibur*, which he still believed in later life had been the "best thing [he] ever wrote" (94). More indebted to Malory than to Tennyson, *Excalibur* deals only with the early career of Arthur, concentrating on the machinations of Morgan le Fay and others to prevent this rightful if somewhat doltish heir from inheriting and raising "a kingdom for the King of kings" (*Excalibur* 1). The final speech by "Angelic Voices" emphasizes the epic's Christian theme:

> The Holy Grail
> the Sword and the Table
> fix the foundation of
> God's Holy City.

The quest for the Holy Grail was clearly envisioned as the main theme of the two planned sequels:

> Go forth on the Quest for the crowning

> high symbol of God in His world. (*Excalibur* 160)

The quest theme is also emphasized in the title and artwork of the short-lived journal published in 1892-93 by Cram and his circle, the *Knight Errant*, which shows clearly its Pre-Raphaelite inspiration. The cover, designed in Kelmscott Press style by Cram's friend and future partner Bertram Grosvenor Goodhue, depicts a knight amidst the wasteland looking up at the Castle Perilous.[12] The purpose of this journal was to "war against the Paynims of realism in art, to assail the dragon of materialism, and the fierce dragon of mammonism, to ride for the succor of forlorn hopes and the restoration of forgotten ideals." The quest is admittedly hopeless:

> .. the standard has been raised in England and already many true Knights have gone into the fight, some to fall in honour, many contending still, though against heavy odds. The Knight Errant follows where they have led, asking only a good fight and an honourable death, whenever that death may come, be it soon or late.[13]

Louise Imogen Guiney's poem of salutation, "The Knight Errant," which appeared in the first issue, is quoted by Cram in his autobiography (87-88) and, in its evocation of the meaning of the quest, might well serve as a comment on Cram's life. Contributors to the first issue included Charles Eliot Norton, intimate of Ruskin and friend of Rossetti, Morris, and Burne-Jones. Cram's own contribution to the first issue of the *Knight Errant*, "On the Restoration of Idealism," is essentially a call to arms "to fight the same disease" that "Dante Rossetti fought in painting, ... that Cardinal Newman fought in religion, that Wagner fought in music, to... build on the wide ruins of a mistaken civilization a new life more in

The Knight Errant, volume one, number one (1892), title page. Fogg Art Museum, Harvard University.

harmony with law and justice."[14] Cram would return to this theme; in his 1907 introduction to *The Gothic Quest*, which includes "On the Restoration of Idealism," he likens the Gothic quest (the quest of Ruskin, Morris, Rossetti, Newman, and others, who are "the Knights of the Gothic Quest") to the quest of the Grail:

> The wild riders rode in vain in their quest of the unattainable, but they brought back a wonderful thing in its place, none other indeed than the mystical knowledge of Art, what it is, and what it does, and what it signifies. Therefore, the quest was not in vain, for Christian Art was the guerdon gained. (*GQ* 9)

Cram later characterized as "ignominious" the failure of most of the movements espoused by these earlier "knights," yet he was never daunted by the prospect of failure[15]; his quester is in fact Browning's Childe Roland, who comes all unprepared to the inevitable defeat of the Dark Tower, "the first barrier that balks all those that course on the Gothic Quest; and yet not one draws rein, nor rides aside, but with unsheathed sword rises in his stirrups and takes upon his lips the words of Childe Roland: . . . 'Childe Roland to the Dark Tower came'" (*GQ* 10-11). Thus Cram characterizes the nineteenth-century English neo-medievalists as heroic though doomed questers and enlists himself among their band.

The verse Cram wrote during this early period includes "Two Sonnets for Pictures of Our Lady," published in the second issue of the *Knight Errant* (1, 2 [July 1892], 44-45). The pictures are by actual "Pre-Raphaelites"--Botticelli and Fra Angelico; writing sonnets for pictures was, of course, a practice characteristic of Rossetti. (The Fronticepiece to this issue is a photogravure production of Walter Crane's illustration for "La Belle Dame Sans Merci," that favorite poem of the Pre-Raphaelites.) The third issue of the *Knight Errant* contained Cram's "An Ave Maria of Arcadelt" (1, 3 [October, 1892], 72). These very Catholic compositions seem to complete the pattern begun when Cram responded so fervently to Rossetti's painting, "The Girlhood of Mary Virgin Mary." Though devotion to Mary is not a conspicuous theme in Cram's mature writings, he does in one of them allude to the central place of the Virgin in sacramental Christianity when describing how, during the Middle Ages, "religion came down from heaven and became human." He writes:

> Our Lady, Queen of Heaven, was the eternal Mother of every erring child, and mercy, comprehension, intercession to forgiveness, were hers in *saecula saeculorum*. And then philosophy, elaborating and applying the original deposit of sacramental truth, gave significance and something of sacramental character to everything in nature and life, building up the tangible symbols and media of spiritual verities until men had something to take hold of at every turn, while the great art of liturgics created a series of beautiful forms, and an equally beautiful mise-en-scene for their presentation, so that it is little wonder that religion achieved a new life and smote itself into human living as never before.[16]

From this period also come the lyrics for "a sort of secular cantata" called "The Boat of Love," the music for which was composed by Cram's friend Fred Bullard. In his autobiography, Cram regretted that the piece was never produced, and toward the end of his life published his lyrics for it as a "masque for music" (94).[17] Typically for Cram, the setting is medieval and celebrates the "inscrutable Wisdom" of God, whereby two lovers in their "Boat of Love" are saved from a tempest to continue their voyage toward the "Land of

Love," an earthly paradise where they will be safe from the "hard world's hand," represented in the masque by merchants and crusaders who mock the lovers before their own destruction in the storm. The theme of regressive abandonment to human love is of course central to William Morris's *The Earthly Paradise*, although, aside from his many general references to Morris, there is no evidence that Cram was familiar with this work. Yet Cram reminds us again briefly of *The Earthly Paradise* in the opening pages of *The Decadent* (1893), which begins, like Morris's "Prologue," with a description of a hideous nineteenth-century industrial town much like the Coketown of Dickens's *Hard Times. The Decadent*, whose main character lives in a style reminiscent of that of Des Esseintes in Huysmans's *A Rebours*, is structurally a political debate in the manner of Plato's dialogues. It expresses Cram's revulsion against the horrors of the modern world, "seething with impotent tumult,--festering towns of shoe factories and cotton-mills, lying tradesmen and legalised piracy; pork-packing, stock-brokers, quarreling and snarling sectaries, and railroads; politicians, mammonism, realism, and newspapers." Aurelian Blake, "the Decadent," who has gathered together all his "treasures of art and letters" and is waiting out the "evil days" much as did the "wise monks" in the "monasteries of the sixth century," joins in the debate to denounce "Democracy, Public Opinion, Freedom of the Press,--the idolatrous tritheism of a corrupt generation."[18] At thirty years of age, Cram's opinion of the modern world was fixed forever.

    The only one of Cram's early literary works still in print is a collection of ghost stories entitled *Black*

Spirits & White (1895), for which its author claimed no particular originality.[19] The stories are well-written and agreeably horrifying; one feels that Rossetti would have approved. Their chief interest is, however, what they reveal about Cram's thinking at this time. The settings are appropriate for Gothic fiction, and the haunted buildings (including a town house, a villa, a castle, a convent, and a church) are described with some attention to architectural interest.[20] There are no rationalizations of the supernatural; the various hauntings are real impingements of the spirit world upon the ordinary daylight world of human existence. But most important, the stories reveal a concern not only with evil and retribution, but with salvation. The most interesting is "Sister Maddelena," in which a knowledge of architecture enables the narrator to discover the walled-up but unquiet tomb of a long-dead nun, put to death in all her youth and beauty by her cruel Mother Superior in punishment for meeting her lover. The climax of the story is the gaining of peace by the soul of Sister Maddelena through the rites of the church. The young architect saves the tormented soul of the beautiful murdered nun, much as the knights of the Round Table saved damsels from various perils.

Cram's literary works during his Pre-Raphaelite period reveal him as an intelligent and fluent writer who might possibly have gone on to develop a distinctive voice and become a name in American literature. But Cram's genius lay elsewhere; in light of his accomplishments, we cannot regret that he chose architecture. His early admiration for the Pre-Raphaelites, especially Rossetti, would bear fruit of a different sort from poetry or fiction.

In later life, Cram somewhat modified his youthful enthusiasm for the art of the Pre-Raphaelites. Lamenting that "the whole tradition of religious art was dead" at the end of the nineteenth century, he acknowledges that "the Pre-Raphaelites had revived it in a measure, ... but what they did was just a little artificial and made-to-order" (194). But to the end Cram continued to include Rossetti and Burne-Jones among his lists of the great.

Cram was also acutely aware of Morris's ideas and accomplishments in his youth, and indeed throughout his life. William Morris's own youthful attraction to Anglo-Catholicism and his brief architectural apprenticeship in the offices of the Gothic Revival architect G. E. Street prefigure the major directions of Cram's life. Cram, like Morris before him, was profoundly influenced in youth by Ruskin and by Rossetti. And Morris's pioneering work in what is now called historic preservation was echoed in Cram's first public utterance, the letter to the editor protesting the proposed architectural insult to Trinity Church. Cram had experience with nearly all the activities and interests which had engaged Morris, even for a time trying his hand at designing wallpaper and furniture, though not with conspicuous success (53). Inspired by the example of Morris's Kelmscott Press, he was tangentially involved with Bertram Goodhue in the revival of the art of bookmaking. Like Morris, Cram was for all his life a student of the Middle Ages; both were medievalists in every sense of the word. Cram's Gothicism was based on a wide-ranging knowledge of the history, institutions, and important people of the Middle Ages. The names of such thinkers and writers as St. Thomas Aquinas and

St. Bernard (of Clairvaux) appear frequently in his writings; Cram was among the founders of the Mediaeval Academy of America and its highly regarded journal, *Speculum* (225-26). Cram shared Morris's tastes, preferring, for example, the stained glass work of Morris's firm over that of La Farge and Tiffany (191); he shared Morris's fundamental convictions about Gothic architecture, for instance, disliking, as did Morris, slavish archaeological copies of Gothic buildings (78; *GQ* 27).[21] Following the lead of the Arts and Crafts Exhibition Society in London, which Morris had helped to found, Cram and Goodhue participated in the founding of the Boston Society of Arts and Crafts in 1897, of which Charles Eliot Norton was the first president.[22] Although Cram was in later life opposed to socialism, his monarchist leanings in early manhood did not preclude entirely the possibility of some features of the socialism advocated by Morris. He and his friends "were socialists because we were young enough to have generous impulses. We were William Morris enough to hate industrialism. . . ." (20). Like Morris, Cram deplored both the Renaissance and the rise of Protestantism.[23] Finally, Cram, like Morris, was skeptical of formal education (56, 205-08).

Cram's religion would after 1888 part him irrevocably from the philosophical viewpoints expressed by Ruskin and by Morris (the one vaguely Evangelical and the other avowedly pagan[24]), but he continued to admire both these mentors and repeatedly paid them homage in his copious writings. In his judgments of people, Cram was broadminded enough to be simultaneously aware of merits as well as demerits. Thus, Ruskin, along with Morris and Wagner, is a "prophet of the New Life," one who has "seen beyond the accidents of existing conditions; beyond the manifest reasons for these conditions, even to the root of the great decadence itself" (*GQ* 29, 26); yet Ruskin was unreliable as a guide to the truth:

> Here was a man of stupefying ability, an extraordinary species of artistic Calvinist; invincibly dogmatic, narrow as Geneva, honest, enthusiastic, inspiring, and quite the most unreliable critic and exponent of architecture that ever lived, but gifted with a facility in the use of perfectly convincing language such as is granted to few men in any given thousand years.[25]

Though Cram never forgot what he owed to Morris and Ruskin in his development as a Gothicist, after 1888 his advocacy of High Church principles would provide the direction not only for his writing, but for his architectural practice. In 1890, he formed a partnership with Charles Francis Wentworth, and their firm shortly afterwards began to specialize in Neo-Gothic designs for churches. Cram explains:

> My idea was that we should set ourselves to pick up these threads of the broken tradition and stand strongly for Gothic as a style for church building that was not dead but only moribund, and perfectly susceptible of an awakening to life again. I therefore evolved a theory that this particular style, which had been the perfect expression of Northern and Western Christianity for five centuries, and belonged to us, if we claimed it, by right of descent, had not suffered a natural death at the beginning of the sixteenth century, but had been most untimely cut off by the synchronizing of the Classical Renaissance and the Protestant Revolution. (72)

Cram's theory was, of course, not new, as he must have known--he was consciously "very High Church" in the eighties and wrote knowledgeably of the Oxford Movement (19, 97).[26] Members of England's Ecclesiological

Society, founded in the heyday of the Oxford Movement, had made much the same argument, as had Augustus Welby Pugin, whom Cram mentions many times.

The firm's first important church project came in 1891 when Cram and Wentworth won the commission for All Saints' in Ashmont, Massachusetts. The death of Burne-Jones (never more famous than at this time) frustrated Cram's plan to invite him to design the altarpiece (Muccigrosso 73-77). In the years following this notable triumph, Cram generally adhered to his architectural aims throughout his increasingly successful career in company with a succession of partners, although his firm did occasionally design in other styles, and even built a skyscraper, the Boston Federal Building. (In 1895 the firm became Cram, Wentworth & Goodhue and, upon the death of Wentworth in 1899, it became Cram, Goodhue & Ferguson. Bertram Goodhue left the firm in 1913, and it was afterward known simply as Cram & Ferguson, although it included other full members.)

Over the years, Cram's firm built many churches in the Gothic style. Their culminating achievements in the ecclesiastical line were to be the designs for St. Thomas Church in New York, completed in 1913, and for the Gothic conversion of the New York Cathedral of St. John the Divine. The plans for St. Thomas, regarded by many as the firm's masterpiece, were, according to Cram, "developed in accordance with my own theories as to design." He characterizes its stylistic qualities as "French of the latest, almost Flamboyant, type." His partner Bertram Goodhue disliked Cram's French Gothic tendencies; the friends had begun to disagree on

St. Thomas' Church, New York City. Architectural drawing by Cram and photograph.

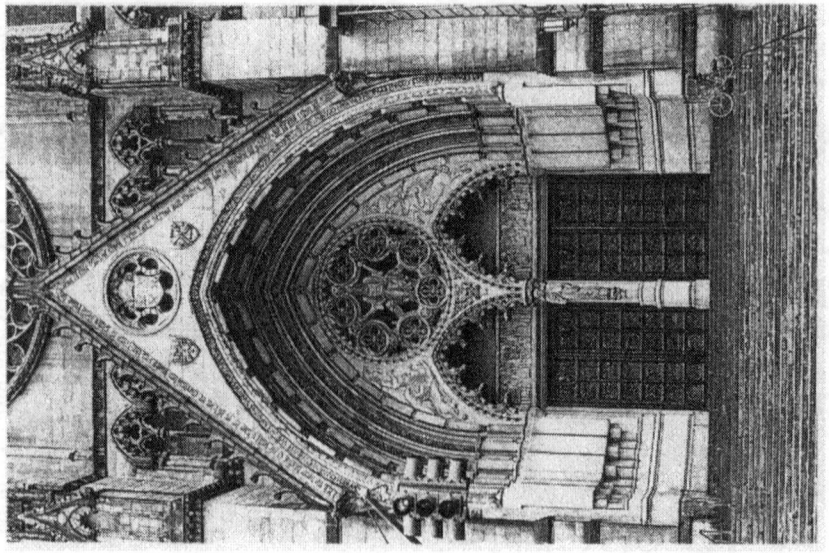

St. John the Divine, New York City, front arch, entrance, and interior, looking towards nave. Photographs by Mary Bloom.

artistic and other matters and were shortly to dissolve their partnership.[27] Goodhue alone would later design the "great reredos for the high altar together with all the other chancel furniture, fittings, and embellishments, all of it work of singular originality, richness, and charm," as Cram describes it (116-17).

The most mammoth and quite likely the most challenging commission of Cram's career was the Gothicizing of the Cathedral of St. John the Divine, the largest cathedral in the world, even now still under construction. The Romanesque design of Heins & La Farge was partially completed at the death of George Heins in 1907. Construction difficulties and design problems had brought much criticism, and the cathedral authorities took advantage of Heins' death to terminate the existing contract in order that Cram's firm might "go on in Gothic and furthermore, as far as possible, to Gothicize what already existed" (172). Cram succeeded so well with this seemingly impossible commission that some commentators regard St. John as his masterpiece (Tucci 38-39).

But the real turning point in Cram's fortunes had come earlier in 1903 when the firm won the competition for the rebuilding of the United States Military Academy at West Point. Although, because of government red tape, the firm was never paid in full for its work, this commission won national recognition for Cram and his partners and marked the beginning for them of an important series of architectural commissions in Collegiate Gothic style. The firm found the task challenging. Cram writes:

"...it was apparent from the first that the sort of thing we had been doing in church work would not apply here, except only so

> far as general principles were concerned. ... Hitherto we had dealt only with the religious aspect of the Mediaeval ethos; as a matter of fact we had built too many churches and were getting hidebound. West Point was secular and military, it was also very conspicuously of the modern age, and these qualities had to be our guide. (104-05)

Cram personally designed several of the buildings, including the Post Headquarters, now known as Taylor Hall, incidentally the tallest all stone-supported building in this country.

Though Cram disdained formal and institutionalized education, the adaptation of Neo-Gothic to educational buildings was not really a change in direction; the buildings were intended to act upon the students in much the same manner as churches. Speaking of architecture as the "handmaid of religion," Cram calls it

> a tremendous agency for expressing the loftiest emotions of humanity, for arousing the dormant souls of men, exciting their imagination to action, urging them to creative work, turning them from single devotion to materialism to spiritual activity.... [The old church builders] marshalled all the powers of art... as a great, silent, irresistible influence to work on the minds of all who should come within their sphere, lifting them out of the hard world with all its narrowing, soiling agencies, up to the splendour of the infinite God.[28]

According to Cram, the beauty created by architects is "primarily educational"; it works

> subtly through the consciousness of those who come under its influence, slowly building up a new civilization that, when it has come full tide, will burst the shell of archaeological forms and come forth in its new and significant and splendid shape.[29]

In 1909 Cram was appointed Supervising Architect to Princeton University, where a number of buildings in various styles, some Gothic, already stood.

United States Military Academy at West Point, New York, U.S. Army photograph (1951). Rice University (1990), photograph by Thomas la Vergne.

University Chapel, Princeton University, modeled after chapel of King's College, Cambridge. Graduate College and Cleveland Tower, Princeton University. Photographs by Robert P. Matthews.

That same year, Cram wrote an essay, "Princeton Architecture," in which he commends Princeton for its efforts "towards establishing a consistent style and logical plan."[30] In this same article, Cram explains his concept of a university, a concept which provided the basis for all his university designs:

> First of all, an university was conceived as a place where the community life and spirit were supreme, the rest secondary; a citadel of learning and culture and scholarship, at the same time inclusive and exclusive, containing within itself all necessary influences towards the making of character, repelling all those that work against the same; a walled city against materialism and all its works, with a 'way out' into the broadest and truest liberty; the heir of all the scholarship and culture of the past, its line of succession reaching back without a break, through Oxford and Cambridge, Padua and Paris, Bec and Rheims, Salerno and Salamanca, to the schools of Athens--and further (PA 24-25).

The Princeton campus henceforth was to be harmonized by adherence to a single style, "Collegiate Gothic," based upon English precedents:

> ... the style fixed forever by Oxford and Cambridge, Winchester and Eton; the style that education and learning had made their own and held for two centuries a bulwark against the tide of the secular Renaissance; the style hewn out and perfected by our own ancestors and become ours by uncontested inheritance (PA 23).

Cram designed the Graduate College and Cleveland Tower, as well as the Chapel. His comment on these designs is noteworthy for its statement of the firm's aims:

> The Graduate College was the most spacious opportunity the office ever has had for working out its, by then, fully established ideas and principles in the matter of 'Collegiate Gothic' adapted to contemporary conditions. The plan and general composition were my own particular preoccupation, the decorative detail,

> both exterior and interior, being largely worked out by Frank Cleveland and Harold Carswell. The Cleveland Tower I did by myself.... In point of style no particular precedent was followed; in general it is more or less English fifteenth-century of the domestic or collegiate type, though given as modern a connotation as possible, consistent with the preservation of that sense of historic and cultural continuity that I am persuaded is fundamental in all educational and ecclesiastical work (121-22).

Cram's firm would go on to design Neo-Gothic buildings for such institutions as the University of the South as well as the unique original buildings for Rice University. At Rice Cram departed radically from his previous work. The history and climate of Texas presented unusual problems; the site was level and lacked any "historical or stylistic precedent." The Gothic style deemed appropriate for West Point and Princeton would not answer, nor were the other East Coast styles right. The only solution was for Cram to invent a new style, and in doing so, he demonstrated unequivocally that his approach to architecture was much more than merely archaeological. He explains how he employed a method of extrapolation worthy of science fiction to solve the problem:

> Gothic was the result of an enthusiastic and fertile union of Northern blood and monastic fervour superimposed on the everlasting but latent tradition of Greek and Roman civilization. Now, suppose the Northern factor had been eliminated and the religious and energizing force initiated by Saint Benedict and precipitated by all the consequent religious orders, from the Cistercians to the Franciscans, had become operative on the Mediterranean races, that so had become regenerate and dynamic--what would have happened in the way of architecture to compare with what actually took place? By an act of will, I tried to put myself in the place of these supposititious races, and to invent something of the sort of thing they might have been

University of Richmond, Sarah Brunett Hall. Views of the front façade, door with arch and gargoyles placed above, and gargoyle of Ralph Adams Cram.

> supposed to engender.... [I] set myself the task of creating a measurably new style that, while built on a classical basis, should have the Gothic romanticism, pictorial quality, and structural integrity. (125-26)

Cram was satisfied with his work at Rice and wished that it were better known; he employed a similar design for the Library at the University of Southern California (127-28).

Over the years Cram's firm won many prestigious commissions to design ecclesiastical and collegiate buildings, primarily in Neo-Gothic style. While carrying out an extremely active architectural practice, he also served for seven years as head of the Architectural Department of the Massachusetts Institute of Technology (despite his qualms about formal education [212]), and, at the same period, served as chairman of the newly organized Boston City Planning Board. During his life he was singled out for many honors. His long professional career--he was nearly seventy-nine when he died--brought him both fame and material success, even while he publicly became ever more vocal in his denunciations of capitalism and materialism in general. What began as a young man's taste for the architecture of the middle ages had become an old man's crusade to recreate in some measure the fundamental ethos underlying medieval life. Unfortunately for Cram (and no doubt all of us), capitalism, materialism, industrialism and technocracy--all that constituted "modernism" for Cram--were becoming ever more powerful counterforces. Cram's buildings reflected his own severe judgment on modern society and the need for anti-democratic, conservative religious solutions to social problems. Though, unlike contemporary fascists, Cram advocated religious rather than political solutions to social unrest, he came to share some of their authoritarian assumptions about social hierarchy. (Of course, as we have seen, he had from youth been attracted to monarchism.) Like other prophets throughout human history, he was, as time went on, increasingly relegated to the wilderness-like fringes of public opinion, from whence nevertheless he continued to raise his voice in protest, much as the dauntless Childe Roland of the poem, with his predecessors ranged before him, blew his slug-horn in defiance of the looming Dark Tower.

During the 1930's, Cram's public speaking and writing largely supplanted his architectural practice, although his firm continued to flourish. Like Carlyle, Ruskin, and Morris, Cram wrote and spoke tirelessly in the interests of social reform. Like them, he advocated a return to what he defined as medieval values. But Cram's medievalism was at once more literal and more radical than anything advocated by most of his neo-medievalist predecessors; Cram was trying to revitalize the religion which was the supreme motive and impulse of the medieval consciousness of life and art. Cram's utopian work, *Walled Towns*, is a serious though sketchy proposal for effecting change by recreating, not only the social institutions and architecture of medieval life, but its religion as well. Although *Walled Towns* was written in 1919 during the chaotic political conditions following World War I, Cram would reiterate its basic arguments more than once in subsequent years. Toward the end of his life, he cited *Walled Towns* as well as the writings of Ruskin and Morris in support of the Catholic Land Movement, asserting that it was the duty of American Catholics to "begin the establishing of self-contained, self-supporting, self-sufficient Catholic communities, 'cities of refuge' so to speak, not only for the unemployed and dispossessed, but also as harbors from the coming storm...."[31]

Inevitably, Cram's utopian proposals in *Walled Towns* invite comparison with More's *Utopia*. In its aesthetics, *Walled Towns* reminds us of Morris's *News From Nowhere*; in other ways, Cram's ideas make us think of Ruskin's Guild of St. George. But Cram's vision of an ideal future is very much his own. Cram proposed a re-creation of medieval life in actual "Walled Towns," centers of "righteousness and beauty and salvation,"[32] which constitute his alternative to the various unacceptable directions he believed were open to the post-war world, including Bolshevism, state socialism, internationalism, and imperialism. (It is not accidental that Cram's definition of a university included the phrase, "walled city against materialism.") The Walled Towns, at first refuges, would eventually attract everyone into their regenerative precincts and thus serve to reorder the world. In his prologue to *Walled Towns* (part of which was reprinted from an article in *The Decadent* of 1893), Cram gives the reason why the world needs reordering, contrasting the Coketown-like description of a modern industrial city with an idyllic medieval walled city. Although Cram states that the phrase "Walled Towns" is "symbolical merely, and indicates the fact that around these communities there is drawn a definite inhibition that absolutely cuts off from the town itself and 'all they that dwell therein' those things from the assault of which refuge has been sought" (WT 46), it is characteristic that he should visualize these refuges as evocations of real medieval walled towns, a number of which are recalled in the rather detailed physical description of Cram's imaginary New England enclave, named "Beaulieu," or "beautiful place," an allusion to Beaulieu Abbey in Hampshire, England.[33] Various prominent medieval buildings are models for the buildings of Beaulieu: the Bar Gate has a "lofty tower something like that of St. John's College in Cambridge" and is "not unlike Warwick Castle" (WT 61-2). The parish church is "not unlike St. Cuthbert's, Wells" (WT 70), and the Town Hall has "painted and gilded statues like those on the Hotel de Ville of Bourges" (WT 75). As always with Cram, architecture has a vitally important role, not only in the formation of the individual character, but in the building of civilization itself. As Cram stated in 1913 when speaking at the dedication ceremonies for the new administration building (Ryland Hall) at the University of Richmond, which he envisioned as one of his firm's university cities walled against materialism in order to further "the development of high Christian character":

> ... [the architect's]... work must preach and teach and forever exert a controlling force on all those who come within its walls... through art of every kind, and especially through architecture, we may bring into play those elements of association, memory and tradition that are essential to the building of character and that make of civilization a continuous life... we ratify our faithfulness to the home, the school, and the church, one and indivisible, as the tripartite foundation of society, and we so build that... our brick and stone and timber be sacramentally transformed from inert matter into that "outward and visible sign of inward and spiritual grace" that is not only all art, but all human life as well, and that so they may exert that silent influence on all who dwell within its walls, as will make them also true to the same ideals.[34]

Thus Cram's buildings, like his writings, are intended to take on, in some measure, the sacramental offices of the church, or at least to aid in effecting the spiritual rejuvenation of human society.

In such "Walled Towns," Cram hoped that the major institutions of the Middle Ages could be revived and animate the neo-medieval buildings. Ideally, society would return to the one church, that is, to Catholicism and to sacramental religion. Cram writes: "There can be no sane and wholesome society in the future where there is not an universally accepted religion of perfectly definite form. . . ." But even he was forced to make concessions to variations in religious preference. As "the unity of religion has been shattered" (WT 38), each Walled Town would have its own religion:

> Each town as it is founded is made up only of those of the same religious convictions, and thereafter none is added who is not of the same belief. Denominationalism is inconsistent with unity of action, cooperation and true democracy. . . . (WT 73)

Further, although the family would be the basic unit upon which the society of the Walled Towns would be built, essential elements of each Walled Town would be convents and monasteries. Monasticism was a highly important concept in Cram's thinking. He evolved a complex "vibratory" theory of history, according to which all of human history occurs in deep throbs of "five-century intervals either side the birth of Christ." The two thousand years of the Christian era have thus seen four epochs, all characterized by developing types of monasticism. The era to come (beginning about A.D. 2000) will be one in which the family unit will supplement the older monastic modes within the Walled Towns (WT 32-36).[35] The real purpose of Beaulieu and the other Walled Towns would be to provide refuges in which beauty and righteousness would accomplish salvation. This point, so basic to Cram's thinking, constitutes the really major difference between Cram's and Morris's Utopian thinking. Although frequently infuriated by the stupidity and grossness of his actual fellow human beings, Morris never lost his faith in the essential goodness of humankind and looked for humanity's redemption here on earth. In *News From Nowhere*, walls are unnecessary as society has become redeemed through its own collective efforts and there is no evil from which humans need to be protected. Equally infuriated by similar human failings, Cram believed that redemption was possible only through the knowledge of God. Further, in Cram's thinking, human beings are not capable of self-government, and the cheerful anarchy of Morris's Nowhereians is not found in the Walled Towns.

In the Walled Towns, which would essentially function as religious, economic, and artistic centers in an agrarian setting,"all society is organized under the guild system, and every man must be a registered member of one guild or another." There would be guilds of farmers, metal-workers, cloth-makers, builders, artists, etc. (WT 80). The guilds would not only regulate economic matters, but would maintain and regulate religious services and educational programs. The Walled Towns would be governed by those who eventually rise through the ranks of the guilds to attain membership in one of the Academies, and beyond that, the Order of Knighthood. The Provost, the highest ranking individual of all, would be chosen from "amongst the Knights" (WT 92). In this hierarchical meritocracy, not only would there be no advertising, no usury, no "conspicuous consumption," but no twaddle about equality. "All men are equal before God and the Law but not otherwise" (WT 42).

The phrase "hierarchical meritocracy" best sums up Cram's political ideal, although to say that he opposed all manifestations of democracy would be an oversimplification. Democracy was, to Cram, "that form of social organization which endeavours to assure to man Life, Liberty and the Pursuit of Happiness."[36] He claimed simultaneously to favor monarchy and a properly conceived "High Democracy," agreeing in his autobiography with the saying that "democracy is possible only when there is a king on his throne" (20). In his last book, *The End of Democracy*, Cram argues that this "High Democracy," or "Monarchical Feudalism," which "was actually realized for a few centuries during the Middle Ages," was held in theory "by the Framers of the Constitution of the United States, though they thought of it as an Aristocratic Republic" (ED 19).

From his youth, Cram had been sympathetic to hierarchical modes of government; yet, in his view, one of the most attractive aspects of medieval civilization was the opportunity he believed it afforded for individuals of merit to rise in the feudal hierarchy. In *The Substance of Gothic* Cram wrote: "If democracy consists, as it does, in abolition of privilege, and equal opportunity for all, then the Middle Ages form the only democracy of record..." (183). Like De Tocqueville, Cram disliked what he saw as the modern American version of equality, in which individual merit was neither sufficiently recognized nor rewarded. In his writings he argued that the old, good, "High Democracy" has been supplanted by the new, bad, "Low Democracy," in which majority rule has resulted in the tyranny of society's lowest elements.

Like many others at the time, Cram also looked to a relative minority of superior leaders to give direction to society; his increasingly derogatory opinion of the masses was reinforced by the publication in 1930 of *The Revolt of the Masses* by Jose Ortega y Gasset, mentioned frequently in *The End of Democracy*. In his famous essay "Why We Do Not Behave Like Human Beings," Cram suggested that society has always based its standards for humanity upon the relatively few exceptional figures of every age and that most of the so-called "human" race are not really human, but part of a "basic raw material," a "Neolithic mass" which has not changed over the millennia. (Obviously, Cram did not believe in progress.) "They of the great list behave like our ideal of the human being; they of the ignominious sub-stratum do not--because they are not."[37]

Above all, Cram resented the claim that human beings could be judged by other than a spiritual and moral standard. In *The End of Democracy*, Cram asserted that the line between man and "sub-man" (or "mass-man" with his "tabloid, or Hearstian mind," arrested at the level of a fourteen-year-old's development) should be drawn, not on the basis of whether he walks upright, possesses a thumb and uses tools, but rather on the basis of whether he has "an immortal soul," that is, whether he has "power of reflection, conscience, the recognition and acceptance of moral sanctions, and a full and operative self-consciousness."[38] Majority rule cannot result in anything good when "tabloid man" controls all things:

> He [mass-man]... joins the ranks of specious organizations of the get-rich-quick or get-power-quick variety, from Communism to the latest of the share-the-wealth societies... he invents or follows after uncouth religions and uncouth philosophies, and he makes the newspapers and the pulp-magazines what they are--and steadily debases himself accordingly (ED 84).

Thus, near the end of his long life, Cram's denunciation of the masses makes us think once more of his early mentor Carlyle--but this time it is the elderly Carlyle of *Shooting Niagara*.

During the 1930's, Cram became intensely involved in political commentary, his arguments always tending toward neo-medieval solutions--Sacramental Christianity, monarchism, agrarianism. Unfortunately for his subsequent reputation as a social and political commentator, during this period Cram not only frequently contributed to the *American Review*, a periodical whose editor was sympathetic to fascism, but commented favorably if briefly about some of Mussolini's reforms, and, like several other intellectuals of the period, expressed some tolerance for dictatorship as an emergency measure.[39] To what extent Cram's architectural tastes have been discredited because of his politics cannot be determined. Certainly, his reputation as an architect has suffered not only from the triumph of modernism in this century, but from the increasing secularization (and perhaps the increasing religious diversity) of our society. Church architecture no longer seems as centrally important as it was to earlier generations, and thus Cram's most impressive architectural achievements have today become comparatively marginalized.

Cram began to withdraw from public life after the death, in 1938, of his wife, the former Elizabeth

Carrington Read, with whom he seems to have enjoyed an exceptionally long and happy marriage. His concern and disillusionment over Roosevelt's policies, Nazi aggression, the outbreak of war and, finally, the Japanese attack on Pearl Harbor combined to exacerbate his growing depression and failing health (Muccigrosso 262-63). Cram had enjoyed a long life of nearly eighty years filled with professional triumphs and material success, but at its end he was not to know the satisfaction of seeing his most deeply held convictions, artistic, religious, or political, vindicated by the course of events. In this he was neither the first nor the last; one of a glorious company including Carlyle, Ruskin, and Morris before him, it is enough that he made the journey and sounded the slug-horn of defiance, defending his views in the face of apparent defeat. Cram had foreseen the nature of his quest in 1907 when he wrote his introduction to *The Gothic Quest*, and, as always, his own words best express the meaning of his life:

> ... the hopeless quest brought marvellous adventure, and more, for it established forever a type of beauty, a method of creation and the mark of possible accomplishment never before achieved.... There is neither rest nor pause, neither final defeat, nor definite victory... the fight is never ending, for true beauty is too wonderful a thing to be lightly held and without challenge. (8-10)

Inspired in youth by the vision of medieval unity which he found in various forms in the works of Newman, Carlyle, Ruskin, Rossetti, Morris, Burne-Jones, and even Wagner, Ralph Adams Cram was sustained in maturity by his constant if idiosyncratic evocation of their views and examples. He was for all his life faithful to the cause, the Gothic quest, in which he had enlisted.

Though the prestige of overt neo-Gothicism may have lost ground in our own century, at the least Ralph Cram succeeded in creating a visible and coherent legacy of nineteenth-century medievalism for twentieth-century America (and perhaps beyond). His neo-Gothic university cities preserve an Arnoldian sense of the university as a haven of peace and order, an ideal which has influenced several generations of Americans. No mere antiquarian, Cram creatively reshaped for a new environment the traditional features of Gothic and gave to it a new impetus for his own day. In their historical evocations of earlier forms of European university and church edifices, his buildings, through their "silent influence," teach us that the past has part in us and that we can benefit from and rejoice in the cultural continuum which they represent.

Notes

1. For a thorough discussion of the decline in Cram's reputation, as well as a convincing defense of Cram, see Douglass Shand Tucci, *Ralph Adams Cram: American Medievalist* (Boston: Boston Public Library, 1975).
2. Ralph Adams Cram, *My Life in Architecture* (Boston: Little, Brown & Co., 1936); "Fulfillment" (first published in *The American Review* IV (March, 1935) 513-28), in *Convictions and Controversies* (1935; rpt. Freeport, New York: Books for Libraries Press, 1970) 101, 108.
3. Hereafter all references to *Life* will be indicated solely by page number.
4. C.A. Ralph, "The Dante Rossettis at the Art Museum, I, Pre-Raphaelitism," *Boston Evening Transcript* (5 November, 1884) 6, col. 2; "The Dante Rossettis at the Art Museum, II, Pre-Raphaelitism," *Boston Evening Transcript* (6 November, 1884) 4, cols. 5-6; "The Dante Rossettis at the Art Museum, III, The Painter," *Boston Evening Transcript* (7 November, 1884) 6, cols. 1-3; "The Dante Rossettis at the Art Museum, IV, The Pictures," *Boston Evening Transcript* (10 November, 1884) 6, cols. 1-3; and "The Dante Rossettis at the Art Museum, V, The Pictures, The Painter," *Boston Evening Transcript* (12 November, 1884) 6, cols. 1-3. Cram's autobiography seems to suggest that he wrote only one letter to the editor on this subject; it also makes no mention of the use of a *nom-de-plume*. Cram had used the same pseudonym earlier (see note 8 below), however, and their content indicates that these articles were almost certainly written by Cram. The autobiography makes reference to the "first Pre-Raphaelite water colours and photographs

show at the old Art Museum in Copley Square" (*Life* 7); the watercolors he remembers could have been those shown a year later in October and November of 1885, when the Art Museum had a well-publicized exhibit of over 450 watercolors and black-and-whites by living English artists, including Burne-Jones and Ford Madox Brown.

5. Two years earlier, Cram had felt, for the first time in his life, an "unaccountable impulse" to pray before the tomb of St. Francis of Assisi. Since his father was a "mystical philosopher" and his mother possessed "keen rationalistic convictions," Cram had not in his youth experienced "anything approaching formal religious action" (*Life*) 58. Cram's conversion was not his only mystical experience; he wrote to Louise Imogen Guiney of a religious vision which occurred during a trip to Europe in 1910. See Robert Muccigrosso, *American Gothic: The Mind and Art of Ralph Adams Cram* (Washington, D.C.: University Press of America, 1979) 222, n. 73.4.

6. According to the *Dictionary of American Biography*, Supplement Three (New York: Charles Scribner's Sons, 1973), 195, because of Cram's hatred of the Renaissance, he was repelled by "much of post-Tridentine Roman Catholicism"; T.J. Jackson Lears suggests that he simply did not wish to join the church of immigrants. See *No Place of Grace: Antimodernism and the Transformation of American Culture, 1880-1920* (New York: Pantheon Books, 1981), 204.

7. See "Christian Unity" (1934) in *Convictions and Controversies*. Cram was a founder of *The Commonweal*, the well-known Catholic periodical. For a full discussion of these points, see Muccigrosso, 209-15.

8. *The Sins of the Fathers* (Boston: Marshall Jones Co.,

1919), 88.
9. Cram's recollections of these events, which were recorded over fifty years afterwards, differ (not surprisingly) in some relatively unimportant particulars from what appears in the files of the *Transcript*. In his autobiography, he recounts that his first appearance in print was a letter to the editor protesting the proposed building of an apartment house in front of Trinity Church; Cram recalled that the letter was captioned "Have We a Ruskin Among Us?" There were actually two letters, both signed "C. A. Ralph," and the caption "Have We a Ruskin Among Us?" does not appear. See "The Danger That Threatens Copley Square," *Boston Evening Transcript* 3 October 1884: 6, cols. 2-4; and "The Copley Square Disgrace," *Boston Evening Transcript* 9 October 1884: 6, col. 1.
10. Cram travelled to Japan in 1898 in pursuance of an abortive proposal to rebuild the Japanese houses of parliament. The only fruit of his trip was to be his book, *Impressions of Japanese Architecture*. See *Life*, 98-100.
11. Advertisement to *Excalibur, An Arthurian Drama* (Boston: Richard G. Badger, The Gorham Press, 1909).
12. Like Cram, Goodhue was a devotee of Pre-Raphaelitism and especially admired Burne-Jones (Muccigrosso 77). Morris's Kelmscott Press was the major inspiraton for his rather extensive work in book design; in addition to preparing the *Knight Errant* graphics, Goodhue designed for all the presses involved in Boston's revival of printing (Elizabeth Cumming and Wendy Kaplan, *The Arts and Crafts Movement* [London: Thames and Hudson Ltd., 1991], 111). The second issue of the *Knight Errant* (1, 2[July 1891], 53-63) featured an

article by Francis Watts Lee called "Some Thoughts Upon Beauty in Typography Suggested by the Work of Mr. William Morris at the Kelmscott Press."
13. "The Quest: Being an Apology for the Existence of the Review Called the Knight Errant," *The Knight Errant, Being a Magazine of Appreciation*, 1, 1 (April 1892), 1-2.
14. "On the Restoration of Idealism," reprinted in *The Gothic Quest* (New York: The Baker and Taylor Company, 1907), 25, 30.
15. "The Test of Beauty," *The Harvard Graduates' Magazine*, 30, 117(September, 1921), 16.
16. "What Was Mediaeval Civilization?," *The Substance of Gothic*, 2nd ed. (Boston: Marshall Jones Company, 1925), 211-21 (first published in *The Forum*, 73, 3(March, 1925), 350-58.
17. "The Boat of Love (A Masque for Music)," *Poet Lore*, 46, 2(Summer, 1940), 165-77.
18. *The Decadent: Being the Gospel of Inaction: Wherein Are Set Forth in Romance Form Certain Reflections Touching the Curious Characteristics of These Ultimate Years, and the Divers Causes Thereof.* (Boston: Copeland and Day, 1893), 37-41.
19. See Postscript to *Black Spirits & White* (1895; rpt. Freeport, N. Y.: Books for Libraries Press, 1971).
20. The setting for the last story in the collection, "The Dead Valley," is haunted by a "great dead tree," surrounded by the bones of its victims. This motif would later be used by William Morris in *The Well at the World's End* (1896).
21. See William Morris, "The Gothic Revival II," in *The Unpublished Lectures of William Morris*, ed. Eugene D. LeMire (Detroit: Wayne State University Press, 1969).
22. Cumming and Kaplan 109; Lears 66. In after years, Cram was contemptuous of the "Mission" style asso-

ciated with the Arts and Crafts Movement in America (see *Life* 124-25) and considered that the Arts and Crafts Movement as a whole ("a revived guild system") had failed (see "Test of Beauty" 16). He speaks of the "deplorable results" of the Arts and Crafts Movement on the Continent in *Impressions of Japanese Architecture*, 2nd ed. rev. (1930; rpt. New York: Dover Publications, Inc., 1966), 166-67.
23. Cram's writings are full of denunciations of both; Morris frequently railed against the effects of the Renaissance and, in "The Revival of Church Architecture," specifically condemns the "stupid isolation of Protestantism." *The Collected Works*, ed. May Morris (New York: Russell & Russell, 1966), 22, 319.
24. William Morris, *Works*, 22, xxxii.
25. "The Development of Ecclesiastical Architecture in America" (first published as "Ecclesiastical Architecture, Paper V, The United States," in *The Brickbuilder*, 14[1905]), 134-39), *The Gothic Quest*, 149.
26. See *Life*, 97 and "The Oxford Movement and Public Worship" (1934) in *Convictions and Controversies*.
27. In his autobiography, Cram is both reticent and gracious about his professional relationship with Bertram Goodhue. For more details, see Tucci, 27-39, and Muccigrosso, 85-86.
28. "On the Building of Churches" (lecture first delivered in 1900), *The Gothic Quest*, 197-200.
29. *The Ministry of Art* (Boston: Houghton Mifflin Company, 1914), 210.
30. "Princeton Architecture," *The American Architect*, 96, 1752 (July 21, 1909), 21.
31. "Cities of Refuge," *The Commonweal*, 22(August 16, 1935), 380. See also "Recovery or Regeneration,"

Part I, *The Commonweal*, 21(November 2, 1934), 7-10; and "Recovery or Regeneration," Part II, *The Commonweal*, 21(November 9, 1934), 56-58. These two articles were reprinted as "Recovery or Regeneration?" in *Convictions and Controversies*. In this essay, Cram quotes from a 1921 lecture. See also "The Change Beyond," *The Commonweal*, 31(November 3, 1939, 33-35.
32. *Walled Towns* (Boston: Marshall Jones Company, 1919), 104.
33. I am indebted to Stuart L. Wheeler for pointing this out; I am also indebted to him for allowing me to read the manuscript of his history of the architecture of the University of Richmond, which first alerted me to the full significance of Cram's work. See his "Building for the Centuries: The New Jerusalem," in *University of Richmond Magazine*. 52, 2 (Winter, 1990), 2-6.
34. "Laying of the Cornerstone at Westhampton," *Religious Herald*, 86, 25(June 19, 1913), 6.
35. Cram's theory of history as presented in *Walled Towns* varies somewhat from explanations in other writings. See also *The Great Thousand Years* and *Ten Years After* (Boston: Marshall Jones Company, 1919). Cram claimed that his theory of history harked "back even to Egypt and Babylonia" (*Life* 22). According to his autobiography, Cram was familiar with occult lore, in which cyclical theories of history abound; he had in his youth flirted with the Theosophical teachings of Madame Blavatsky and had joined a group of "Visionists" who indulged in a version of the worship of Isis (*Life* 46, 91-93). The importance accorded to monasticism in Cram's scheme inevitably reminds us of the theories of Joachim de Flora who, although never to my knowledge mentioned by Cram, could not have been

unknown to such an ardent student of the Middle Ages.
36. *The End of Democracy* (Boston: Marshall Jones Company, 1937), 28.
37. "Why We Do Not Behave Like Human Beings" (first published in *The American Mercury*, 27[September 1932]), *Convictions and Controversies*, 150-51.
38. *The End of Democracy*, 64, 79, 84, 93.
39. Cram advocated the "functional representation" then being tried in Italy; he was in favor of abolishing not only the party system, but all politicians. See *The End of Democracy*, Chapters 6, 7, and 9. These chapters were previously published as follows: "The Forgotten Class, Part I," *The American Review*, 7(April, 1936), 32-46, "The Forgotten Class, Part II," *The American Review*, 7(May, 1936), 179-91; and "The Nemesis of Democracy," *The American Review*, 8(December, 1936), 129-41. See also "Post Caesarem Quid," in *Convictions and Controversies*, previously published in *The General Magazine and Historical Quarterly*, 37, 1(October, 1934), 1-14. For a fuller discussion of Cram's ideas, see Muccigrosso, 233-34, 241-42. John R. Harrison's *The Reactionaries: A Study of the Anti-Democratic Intelligentsia* (New York: Schocken Books, 1967) discusses the phenomenon of the fascist sympathies expressed by Yeats, Lewis, Pound, Eliot, and Lawrence.

Mark Girouard, An Enthusiast for Chivalry: *The Return to Camelot: Chivalry and the English Gentleman.* New Haven: Yale University Press, 1981.

Debra Mancoff

During the last decades of the eighteenth century and the whole of the nineteenth century, the code of chivalry underwent a transformation. The first edition of the *Encyclopedia Britannica*, published in 1771, defined chivalry as a hierarchy of obligation: "A tenure of service, whereby the tenant is bound to perform some noble or military office to his lord."[1] Five decades later, the protagonist of Sir Walter Scott's novel *Ivanhoe* (1819) could speak of chivalry in terms of an ideal:

> Chivalry! . . . she is the nurse of pure and high affection, the stay of the oppressed, the redresser of grievances, the curb of the power of the tyrant. Nobility were but an empty name without her.[2]

This definition, although voiced by a hero of fiction, had gained acceptance, supplanting the dry *Encyclopedia* definition. Scott, in fact, was the author of the new, lengthy essay on chivalry for the fifth edition of the *Encyclopedia Britannica* of 1814, and *Ivanhoe* exemplified in literature what Scott defined in scholarly discourse.

As the century progressed, enthusiasm for chivalry escalated, touching most aspects of British culture, from the visual arts to the concept of manhood. By the end of the century, the chivalric knight was the symbol for the nation. Frescoes of medieval champions graced the walls at the new Palace of Westminster, the late Prince Consort was commemorated as an ideal knight, and the Poet Laureate Tennyson had produced an Arthurian epic as his life's work.

To the nineteenth-century gentleman, the chivalric revival was more than a nostalgic glorification of his ancestors. Although sparked by the new regard for romance literature that arose during the Gothic Revival, interest in matters of chivalry became a manifest reality. Young men of Britain were urged to emulate their ancestors, and the knight became the paradigm for the gentleman. By the end of the century, a new form of chivalry had run full course, created for and rooted in contemporary idealism. This metamorphosis of an arcane code of behavior into an integral part of modern society is the subject of Mark Girouard's recent book *The Return to Camelot: Chivalry and the English Gentleman* (New Haven: Yale University Press, 1981).

Mark Girouard has made an estimable contribution to the literature of architectural history in Britain. His writings address diverse topics, including a monograph on the Elizabethan master Robert Smythson, an analysis of Queen Anne eclecticism, and a picture book of Victorian pubs. Girouard's major contribution has been in his observation of the symbiotic relationship of the English country house and the society that produced it. *The Victorian Country House* (1971; revised and enlarged, 1979) and *Life in the English*

Country House (1978) are without parallel on the subject.

In his writings on country house life, Girouard betrays a persistent attraction to the monuments of chivalry. His fascination for castles, medieval and modern, has been constant. Readers of *The Victorian Country House* will also recall the ironic delight implicit in his description of the gentleman at mid-century:

> The early Victorian knight galloped into the field, his bible *The Broadstone of Honor,* his political expression the Young England party, his escapade the Eglinton tournament. He was faithful to God, reverent to women, courteous in language, modest in demeanour, lacking in arrogance to his inferiors, and a shield and support to his tenantry.... He endeavoured to combine the most credible aspects of the Arthurian knight and the feudal baron.[3]

It is with sympathetic enthusiasm that Girouard regards this gentleman in *The Return to Camelot*. His position as an enthusiast is both the strength and the weakness of the book. Girouard assembled a wealth of evidence in his argument for nineteenth-century chivalry, and that wealth is astonishing in variety. The observation he makes in his preface, however, that "Once one starts looking for the influence of chivalry in this period, one finds it in almost embarrassingly large quantities," is equally true for his book. Girouard groups everyone, from Scott to Henry Newbolt, and everything, from the Empire to the Boy Scouts, under his chivalric umbrella. He has done a fine job uncovering the trappings of the new chivalry; a lucid documentary history of this movement will have to await the attentions of a scholar with a little more objectivity.

In the nineteenth century, the development of the new chivalry travelled a meandering course, shifting from sober scholarly interest to the arena of popular culture. The latter half of the eighteenth century saw increased attention to the material trappings of the medieval era, as well as attempts to recover the "lost" literature of the Middle Ages. Differentiation between the history of chivalry and its counterpart in literature was rarely made.[4] Increased familiarity with the medieval world led to the success of Scott's novels. His readers felt a real sympathy for his very human characters, and, as a consequence, they imagined that the world of chivalry was not an alien one.

In the 1820s and the 1830s, chivalry was transformed from a romantic into a practical concept. Kenelm Digby, in *The Broad Stone of Honour* (1822-23), challenged modern man to accept his position as heir to a chivalric heritage. It was a phase of mock heroics and pretense, culminating with the ill-fated Eglinton Tournament (1839), in which modern champions were prepared for fierce, armed adversaries, but not a Highland downpour.

In the 1840s, mock heroism was reformed into moralism, as evidenced in the politics of Young England and the novels of Benjamin Disraeli. The revival began to have an effect on the monarchy, and Victoria's German husband, Prince Albert, was presented to the xenophobic British populace as an ideal knight of the nation. He, in turn, directed the grandest program of government-sponsored history painting in the new palace of Westminster, and a new chivalric iconography was born. By the end of the 1850s, the new Poet Laureate, Alfred Tennyson, published the first segment of his Arthurian epic *The Idylls of the King*.

The widespread popularity of chivalry led, by mid-century, to novels and paintings featuring virtuous knights, both in medieval and modern dress. During the 1870s, the new aesthetic poets and painters chipped away at the moral pedestal built for the modern knight. At the end of the century, the new chivalry was a popular vernacular, with an audience that included aesthetes who read the Arthurian poetry of Algernon Swinburne, to the public school boys who thrilled to *The Boy's King Arthur*.

Girouard's account, which he cautions is neither an art historical nor a literary study, occurs within this time period and is restricted to Great Britain. These are plausible limitations, but there is an air of contrivance to his study. The chivalric revival is presented by Girouard as a lengthy prologue to the Great War.

Girouard has organized his material to substantiate his thesis that the ultimate challenge to the nineteenth-century knight was World War I. His first chapter "1912," contrasts a play, *Where the Rainbow Ends* (Girouard informs us that this tale of little Rosamund and Crispian Carey's adventures at the side of St. George was as popular as Peter Pan), the South Pole expedition of Captain Robert Falcon Scott, and the sinking of the Titanic, complete with stories illustrative of the motto Women and Children First! The discourse that follows explains why each member of this anomalous group was, in its way, an example of chivalry, and how the chivalrous gentleman came into being.

In turning to the sources of chivalry, Girouard declines to provide a firm definition for the concept itself, referring the reader to Richard Barber's *The Knight and Chivalry*.[5] Discussion of the literature of the

Gothic Revival is thorough, but flawed in organization. By sorting his sources into two categories, literary and historical, he has rent the seamless unity that existed at mid-eighteenth century. He presents, for example, the contribution of Thomas Percy's *Reliques of Ancient English Poetry* (1765), before his discussion of Richard Hurd's *Essay on Chivalry* (1762). Percy acknowledged his debt to Hurd in his own text. Subsequent chapters focus upon the popularizers of chivalry, including Sir Walter Scott and Kenelm Digby, and trace the material results of that popularity, including armor collecting and castle building.

To give order to the years of full-scale revival (1830-1880), Girouard divides the anachronistic trends of chivalry into small, seemingly manageable topics. As a consequence, the story becomes more complex than it need be. The reader must travel over the same decades repeatedly, chasing every form of chivalry imaginable. In addition to mock tournaments and monarchical interpretation, there is the political "Radical Chivalry" and the cult of manhood in "Muscular Chivalry." Acquisitive imperialists are dubbed "Knights of the Empire," and, in the chapter "Chivalry for the People," Christian Socialists, the Jewish Lads' Brigade and the Boy Scouts are all shown to be chivalric in intent. The nineteenth century looms as one great paean to chivalry, a dazzling display of idealism, heroism and pretense that crashed to earth with the horrifying reality of the Great War. The spirit of chivalry was indeed pervasive, but Girouard suggests that it was universal.

Among Girouard's eighteen chapters on the new chivalry, several are outstanding. The excellent chapter devoted to Sir Walter Scott defines his essential role in the revival. A strong image of Scott the popularizer is painted. Through Girouard's descriptions, it is easy to grasp the appeal of Scott's protagonists, all dashing and brave, proud of their heritage and loyal to their monarchs. What gentleman would not like to see himself cast in that mold?

Girouard gives equal attention to Kenelm Digby, the author of *The Broad Stone of Honour*, an odd, sermon-like treatise on the adaptation of chivalry to modern life. Digby's elaborate ramble is ignored today, but in the nineteenth century, it attracted a vast audience.[6] Called by Lord John Manners "the breviary of Young England," this is the book of which Julius Hare stated that if he had a son, he would place it in his hands with the admonition to "love it next to the Bible." As late as the 1880s, Sir Edward Burne-Jones kept an edition on his night table for ready inspiration.[7] Girouard is captivated with this character, whom he describes as "chivalry-mad." Digby's role as an apostle for chivalry is presented in full, and Girouard credits Digby with an enormous hand in the creation of modern chivalry; he even suggests he was the first to promote cold baths to cleanse the character and harden the body. Girouard also weaves a thrilling tale of this obscure eccentric crossing the continent and spreading his cause, a tale the reader discovers with dismay is pure fabrication. Digby's philosophy and its ramifications were colorful enough. Girouard need not have resorted to invention.

The reader may be surprised to learn that Queen Victoria and Prince Albert were advocates of the new chivalry. This neglected phase is well illustrated. Girouard even uncovers an iconographical identity developed for the prince, in painting during his lifetime and in memorials after his death. The role of Albert, however, is summarily treated, due in part to Girouard's declared geographical limitations. Albert's German background informed his own understanding of chivalry, but Girouard does not address this issue of foreign influence. The prince also played a crucial role in reintroducing the Arthurian legend into the visual arts but, as the legend is not discussed until a later chapter, this major contribution is minimized. Even the analysis of the death iconography is flawed. The reader can only surmise the importance of Tennyson dedicating his *Idylls of the King* to the Prince Consort, for a discussion of Tennyson's chivalric ideals, which closely paralleled those of Albert, awaits the reader in "The Return of Arthur," four chapters later.

Girouard's discussion of the Arthurian legend is similarly weakened by his desire to simplify and categorize. To facilitate his analysis of the visual arts, Girouard employs a fallacious formula: the moralists turned to Tennyson for inspiration and the romantics chose Malory. The first Pre-Raphaelite Arthurian pictures, however, were drawn from Tennyson, and William Dyce created his moral allegory in the new Palace of Westminster from what he read in Malory. The heroic figure style, created for Arthurian imagery, is likewise passed over in Girouard's hurry to tell spicy anecdotes about the Pre-Raphaelite painters.

Anecdotes do abound in Girouard's text. He must have done a tremendous amount of digging into contemporary memoirs and memorials. A whole chapter, "Modern Courtly Love," is devoted to lively gossip, although the saga of Wilfred Scawen Blunt, purported lover of "Doll" Fraser, Georgiana Sumner, Minny Pollen and Jane Morris, is more a portrait of a philanderer than of a chivalric lover.

There are too many chapters on sports as an adjunct to the new chivalry. The connection of physical training with knightly discipline is apt. The very concept of an ideal knight implies great physical prowess. A case can be made for calling the proponents of Muscular Christianity, Charles Kingsley and Thomas Hughes, chivalric, but subsequent chapters, "The Public Schools" and "Playing the Game," wear out the analogy, applying it to cold dips, football jerseys, and the history of cricket. To underscore the seriousness of this connection, Girouard employs a quotation from Thomas Carlyle's *Past and Present*, the call for "Sheer obstinate toughness of muscle; but much more, what we call toughness of heart,"[8] but he uses it no less than three times and understands it to be a sort of athlete's creed.

It is not until Girouard's penultimate chapter, "The Chivalrous Gentleman," that the reader encounters the synthetic results of these forms of chivalry. In a reflective, and somewhat repetitive discourse, Girouard observes that "By the end of the nineteenth century a gentleman had to be chivalrous, or at least if he were not he was not fully a gentleman." Girouard has failed, however, to sort the real from the ideal. He notes that, in the end, the English gentleman thought himself to be brave, straightforward and honorable. He was loyal to his monarch and his lady, he was fearless and the natural leader of men, and he was ready to redress any wrong he confronted. He was also ready to fight and die for his nation, and did in great numbers in the Great War. The unanswered question remains as to whether the characteristics of a true gentleman had indeed changed, or were now justified and enhanced through allusions to chivalry.

If in the end Girouard appears to be, like Kenelm Digby, a bit "chivalry-mad," the reader should be reminded that *The Return to Camelot* does not pretend to be a scholarly investigation.[9] Girouard's conversational prose, coupled with a wealth of handsome illustrations, is aimed at a popular audience. He has done well in describing the material trappings of chivalry; the castles, the armor collections and the noble monuments are all captured in vivid detail. Girouard, however, goes no further. Chivalric idealism, as an essential form of nineteenth-century medievalism, merits more extensive study. But Girouard has shed a warm light on this development, and if his enthusiasm is the salient feature of his study, it is worthwhile to observe that in this he recreates the spirit which brought the chivalric revival into being.

Notes

1. *Encyclopedia Britannica* (Edinburgh, 1771), vol. 2, 193.
2. Sir Walter Scott, *Ivanhoe*, vol. 17 of *Waverly Novels* (Edinburgh: 1829-33), 109.
3. Mark Girouard, *The Victorian Country House* (Oxford: 1971), 8-9.
4. In his *Essay on Chivalry*, Scott spoke of fictional knights and historical heroes as equal examples. He justified this practice as follows:
    > We may observe, once and for all, that we have no hesitation in quoting the romances of Chivalry as good evidence of the laws and customs of knighthood. The authors, like the painters of the period, invented nothing, but copying the manners of the age in which they lived, transferred them, without doubt or scruple, to the period and the personages of whom they treated. *Miscellaneous Prose Works of Sir Walter Scott* (Edinburgh: 1827), vol. 6, 9n.
5. Richard Barber, *The Knight and Chivalry* (London: 1970), is a non-analytical study of medieval chivalry. Girouard's choice further suggests his popular emphasis.
6. James Merriman, in *The Flower of Kings* (Wichita: 1973), 124-25, has caught the curious attraction of Digby's book.
    > An extraordinary fusion or confusion of Scottian medievalism, romantic Catholicism, English and German Gothicism and enthusiasm for chivalric romance.... Yet for all its hortatory rhetoric, its slightly crack-brained pietism, its vulgarly argued noblesse oblige, and its grossly sentimentalized version of medieval life, it is not difficult to understand the book's appeal to two generations of young men.
7. Charles Wibley, *Lord John Manners and his Friends* (Edinburgh: 1925), vol. I, 133; Julius Hare, *Guesses*

at Truth (London: 1827), vol. I, 152; and Georgiana Burne-Jones, *Memorials of Sir Edward Burne-Jones* (London: 1906), vol. I, 56.
8. Thomas Carlyle, *Past and Present* (London: 1912), Book III, chapter V, 154.
9. For a serious analysis of Scott, Carlyle and Ruskin, with reference to their own interpretation of chivalry, the reader is referred to Alice Chandler, *A Dream of Order* (University of Nebraska: 1970). See also Debra N. Mancoff, *The Arthurian Revival in Victorian Art* (New York: Garland Publishing, 1990) for a similar analysis of chivalry in Victorian painting.

Kevin L. Morris. *The Image of the Middle Ages in Romantic and Victorian Literature*. London: Croom Helm, 1984.

Carolyn Collette

Morris has all the right scholarly instincts about medievalism; he sets out to identify, define, and analyze the role of "religious medievalism" within the larger phenomenon of the nineteenth-century medieval revival. In doing so, he brings to our attention the fact that religion, in the Middle Ages as well as in the nineteenth-century, was a real issue in the revival. What's more, Morris has done what no one else has done so far--he has looked beyond the first rank of often-cited thinkers, beyond Carlyle, Pugin, Scott, and Ruskin to the second rank, as it were, to men like Neale, Paley, R.H. Froude, Manners, and Digby, who were in their time influential writers. For its attention to Kenelm Digby alone the book is a worthwhile addition to the body of literature attempting to analyze the phenomenon of nineteenth-century English medievalism. But Morris goes even further; in the pages of this slim volume one finds a rich compendium of continental and British sources. Morris includes virtually every significant figure who wrote about the Middle Ages in England during the nineteenth century, with the exception of William Morris. (This omission is in one sense self-explanatory because of Kevin Morris's thesis-- that at its center medievalism guarded a deep well of spirituality, decidedly Catholic in form and dogma. While William Morris may have on some occasions appropriated the signs and symbols of medieval spirituality for his own vision of a new society, his interest never led him to Catholicism). For a neophyte in the study of medievalism the book is a valuable guide to primary sources and seminal thinkers.

In addition, this book has substance beyond its usefulness as a reference tool or vade mecum through the world of nineteenth-century English medievalism. Over the course of its two hundred pages the book is full of insight into its subject: Morris repeatedly links the religious dimension of medievalism to a desire for social reconciliation and national unity. Writing of Coleridge, for instance, he refers to the "metaphysico-political concept of unity" in medievalism, saying that it is "...an expression of the theme of reconciliation, and connected with the perceived need of a revival of an ancient spiritual outlook." (48) In her *A Dream of Order: the Medieval Ideal in Nineteenth-Century English Literature* (Nebraska, 1971), Alice Chandler explored medievalism as a desire for social order; in his work Morris expands our understanding of social order to include a desire for universal harmony encompassing the earthly and the spiritual. Morris is similarly shrewd about how English Protestants appropriated the Catholic Middle Ages to their nineteenth-century use. They turned medieval Catholicism into a trope of symbols and signs serving the idea of medieval England. He rightly connects the leitmotif of interest in monasticism throughout the first half of the century to an interest in reviving not the form but the spirit of the past in order to restore social unity to a country that had become more an aggregation than a nation. In sentences like the following he moves to the center of the phenomenon he studies, approaching its social dimension and its reliance on language and verbal communication: "Visions of ritual were often depicted in the monastic context, and quintessentially depicted the need for a new language within a new society." (227) Under the influence of a well-established rhetoric idealizing life within its walls, the monastic system became a widely comprehended symbol, a microcosmic type of a wished-for communal society. In all these ways Morris has indicated that the idea of the medieval Church was a central, rich, complex, driving force within nineteenth-century English medievalism.

Unfortunately the wealth of material he incorporates into his book obliges him to move quickly from one figure to another. As a result he rarely analyzes the material he presents. The reader is always conscious of the work's uneasy blend of scholarly strength and analytical weakness. The book's real problem lies in its language. In the first place, the title of the book is absolutely misleading. A phrase like "Romantic and Victorian literature" conveys a specific and well-defined meaning: the reader trained in literature understands it to refer to a specific canon of texts, very few of which appear in this work. Moreover, a phrase like "the image of the Middle Ages" is virtually meaningless in its breadth. The obliquity of language represented in the title persists throughout the book. Morris repeatedly attempts to define, explain and re-define the term

"Catholicism" and then spends most of the volume attempting adequately to define both terms in respect to the sources he uses. The book also suffers from substantial stylistic faults. Not the least of these is the distressing number of typographical errors in spelling and syllabification. More important, Morris's style labors under the weight and complexity of his subject. He, like Chandler before him, has recourse to a style full of oppositions, contradictions, qualifications. A subject so full of inner complexities requires a writer's patient, painstaking exposition and a reader's patient interpretation. A book claiming to "offer a range of answers in areas fraught with imponderables," in effect to map a labyrinth fashioned out of an idea of an idea, needs as much precision and lucidity as language can provide. But Morris's analysis fails because his language fails him. He cannot master the qualifications, the oppositions he creates; as a result, he never quite directly faces his subject in all its complexity. Sentences like these are too typical of the book's style: "His (Kenelm Digby's) work was a bridge between eighteenth and early nineteenth-century romantic religious medievalism and the truer 'religious medievalism' of Victorian Catholicism, and between Continental religious medievalism and English medievalism" (103), and similarly, "The revival of interest in medieval religious art and architecture was a mental chameleon, expressing both vague romantic and precise partisan religious aspirations, a subject which focuses the general response to the Middle Ages, illustrating its depth and range, and depicting the process whereby it became more profound" (168).

Imprecision and turgidity are not merely stylistic problems. The problem of clarity, of where and how to draw the line, of how to define, to limit the investigation of frustratingly slippery phenomena (on page 178 he says of medievalism " ...the Middle Ages were really whatever individuals wanted them to be...") leads him to cast his net wider than is either useful or necessary. The section on continental sources, for instance, is fascinating but not particularly germane to late eighteenth- and early nineteenth-century English medievalism which, even in its religious aspect, was closely tied to indigenous social problems and to a long cultural history of lamenting the passing of the monasteries. (On this neglected dimension of English interest in medieval Catholicism see Margaret Ashton, "English Ruins and English History: The Dissolution and the Sense of the Past," *Journal of the Warburg and Courtauld Institutes*, xxxvi (1973), 231-55, reprinted as Chapter 10 in Ashton, *Lollards and Reformers: Images and Literacy in Late Medieval Religion* (London: Hambledown Press, 1984). At the very end of the book (221) Morris briefly acknowledges the social problems which fed comparisons of past and present. One could make a stronger case than he does for the synchronous growth of religious medievalism and social distress in England during the first half of the nineteenth century. The frustrating aspect of any scholarly approach to religious medievalism is that one can look at the subject from so many perspectives, see it as behind or beneath or part of so many other phenomena, that virtually no one book can cover all the material. Nevertheless, the reader has a right to ask Morris at least to establish the obvious connections. No treatment of English medievalism during the first half of the nineteenth century can afford to ignore the social distress of the period.

Possessed of a compelling thesis, Morris has tried to tie all medievalism together. As a result, he presents us with a host of writers, and their work, and asks us to be satisfied with generalizations and abstractions where we want analysis and interpretation. But at the least in his book Morris has opened a way, charted a broad course for those who can follow him. The next generation of works on nineteenth-century English medievalism must come to terms with the phenomena of language, rhetoric, and meaning Morris has discovered as central to religious medievalism but has not really explored.

Bibliography

Bibliography

I. Selected Biblography of Victorian Historicism and Medievalist Writings

1. Addison, Agnes Eleanor. *Romanticism and the Gothic Revival*. Philadelphia: Richard R. Smith, 1938.

2. Anderson, Olive. "The Political Uses of History in Mid-Nineteenth Century England." *Past and Present* 36 (1967): 87-105.

3. B., E.I. "On the Ethical Value of the Gothic Revival." *Architectural Review: For the Artist and the Craftsman* 5 (1898-99): 272.

4. Baillie-Cochran, Alexander. "In the Days of the Dandies, III: The Young England Party." *Blackwood's Edinburgh Magazine* 146 (March 1890): 313-330.

5. Banham, Joanna, and Jennifer Harris, eds. *William Morris and the Middle Ages: A Collection of Essays*. Manchester: Manchester University Press, 1984.

6. Bann, Stephen. *The Clothing of Clio: A Study of the Representation of History in Nineteenth Century Britain and France*. Cambridge University Press, 1984.

7. Barnes, Harry E. *A History of Historical Writing*. Norman: University of Oklahoma Press, 1937.

8. Baswell, Christopher, and William Sharpe, eds. *The Passing of Arthur: New Essays in Arthurian Tradition*. New York: Garland Publishing, Inc., 1988.

9. Bøe, Alf. *From Gothic Revival to Functional Form: A Study in Victorian Theories of Design*. Oslo Studies in English 6. Oslo: Oslo University Press, 1957.

10. Bowler, Peter. *The Invention of Progress: The Victorians and the Past.* Oxford: Blackwell, 1989.

11. Bratchel, M. E. *E. A. Freeman and the Victorian Interpretation of the Norman Conquest*. Ilfracombe: Arthur Stockwell, 1969.

12. Bradbury, Ronald. *The Romantic Theories of Architecture of the Nineteenth Century, in Germany, England, and France (Together with a Brief Survey of the Vitruvian School)*. New York: Dorothy Press, 1934.

13. Bright, Michael. *Cities Built to Music: Aesthetic Theories of the Victorian Gothic Revival*. Columbus: Ohio State University Press, 1984.

14. Brooks, Richard A. E. "The Development of the Historical Mind." *The Reinterpretation of Victorian Literature*. Ed. Joseph E. Baker. Princeton: Princeton University Press, 1950.

15. Brown, David. *Walter Scott and the Historical Imagination*. London: Routledge and Kegan Paul, 1979.

16. Buckley, Jerome Hamilton. *The Triumph of Time: A Study of the Victorian Concepts of Time, History, Progress, and Decadence*. Cambridge: Belknap Press, 1966.

17. Burrow, John W. *A Liberal Descent: Victorian Historians and the English Past*. Cambridge University Press, 1981.

18. --------. "'The Village Community' and the Uses of History in Late Nineteenth Century England." *Historical Perspectives: Studies in English Thought and Society in Honour of J. H. Plumb*. Ed. Neil McKendrick. London: Europa Publications, 1975. 255-84.

19. Butterfield, Herbert. *Man on His Past: The Study of the History of Historical Scholarship*. Cambridge University Press, 1969.

20. Chadwick, Owen, ed. *The Mind of the Oxford Movement*. Stanford: Stanford University Press, 1960.

21. Chandler, Alice. *A Dream of Order: The Medieval Ideal in Nineteenth-Century English Literature*. London: Routlege and Kegan Paul, 1970.

22. Chapman, Raymond. *The Sense of the Past in Victorian Literature*. London: Croom Helm, 1986.

    Some discussion of Victorian historical fiction.

23. Clark, Basil F.L. *Church Builders of the Nineteenth Century: A Study of the Gothic Revival in England*. London: Society for Promoting Christian Knowledge, 1939.

24. Clark, Sir Kenneth. *The Gothic Revival, An Essay in the History of Taste*. New York: Charles Scribner's Sons, 1929.

25. Clark, G. Kitson. "A Hundred Years of the Teaching of History at Cambridge: 1873-1973." *Historical Journal* 16 (1973): 535-553.

26. Clive, John. *Thomas Babington Macaulay: The Shaping of a Historian*. London: Secher and Warburg, 1973.

27. --------. "The Use of the Past in Victorian England." *Salmagundi* 5 (Fall-Winter 1985-86): 48-65.

    Political uses of history.

28. Cochran, Rebecca Ann. "The Neomedieval Works of Victorian Poets: Tennyson, Arnold, Swinburne, Rossetti, and Morris." *DAI* 46 (1985): 1632A. University of Iowa.

29. Cole, David. *The Work of Sir Gilbert Scott*. London: Architectural Press, 1980.

30. Cooksey, Thomas Lynch. "Dante's Victorians: The Use of Dante by Carlyle, Tennyson and Rossetti." *DAI* 43 (1983): 3918A.

31. Crook, J. Mordaunt. *William Burges and the High Victorian Dream*. Chicago: University of Chicago Press, 1981.

32. Crosby, Christina. *The Ends of History: Victorians and "The Woman Question."* London: Routledge and Kegan Paul, 1991.

33. Culler, A. D. *The Victorian Mirror of History*. Yale University Press, 1985.

34. Curtis, L. P., Jr. *Anglo-Saxons and Celts: A Study of Anti-Irish Prejudice in Victorian England*. Bridgewater, Conn.: Conference on British Studies, 1968.

35. Dale, Peter Ann. *The Victorian Critic and the Idea of History: Carlyle, Arnold, Pater*. Cambridge: Harvard University Press, 1977.

36. Davis, Terence. *The Gothic Taste*. Rutherford, N.J.: Fairleigh Dickinson University Press, 1975.

37. Dawson, Christopher. *The Spirit of the Oxford Movement*. New York: Sheed and Ward, 1933.

38. Day, Mildred, and Valerie Lagorio. *King Arthur Through the Ages*. Vol. 2. New York: Garland Publishing, Inc., 1990.

39. De Caro, Francis A. "G. L. Gomme: The Victorian Folklorist as Ethnohistorian." *Journal of Folklore Institute* 19.2-3 (1982): 107-117.

40. Dellamora, Richard. "An Essay in Sexual Liberation, Victorian Style: Walter Pater's 'Two Early French Stories.'" *Literary Visions of Homosexuality*. New York: Hawthorn, 1983.

41. Dellheim, Charles. *The Face of the Past: the Preservation of the Medieval Inheritance in Victorian England*. New York: Cambridge University Press, 1982.

42. Dilthey, Wilhelm. "Poetry and Experience." *Selected Works*. Vol. 5. Ed. by Rudolf Makkreel and Frithjof Rodi. Princeton: Princeton University Press, 1985.

43. Eastlake, Sir Charles. *A History of the Gothic Revival*. London: Longmans Green, 1872.

44. Feldman, Durton, and Robert Richardson. *The Rise of Modern Mythology: 1680-1860*. Bloomington: Indiana University Press, 1972.

45. Fisher, H. A. L. "Modern Historians and Their Methods." *Fortnightly Review*, o.s. 62 (1894): 805.

46. Fitzsimons, M. A. *The Past Recaptured: Great Historians and the History of History*. Notre Dame: University of Notre Dame Press, 1983.

47. Forbes, Duncan. *The Liberal-Anglican Idea of History*. Cambridge: Cambridge University Press, 1952.

48. Friederich, Werner P. *Dante's Fame Abroad: 1350-1850*. Chapel Hill: University of North Carolina Press, 1950.

49. Fry, Ruth Eckmann. "The Victorian Image of the German Revolution, 1806-1871, As Reflected in the Writings of Carlyle, Matthew Arnold and George Eliot." *DAI* 44 (1983): 1464A.

50. Fuwa, Yuri. "The Globe Edition of Malory as a Bowdlerized Text in the Victorian Age." *Studies in English Literature*. (1984): 3-17.

51. Gardiner, Patrick, ed. *Theories of History*. New York: The Free Press, 1959.

52. Gent, Margaret. "'To Flinch From Modern Varnish': The Appeal of the Past to the Victorian Imagination." *Victorian Poetry*. Eds. Malcolm Bradbury and David Palmer. Stratford-Upon-Avon Studies 15. London: Edward Arnold, 1972. 11-35.

53. Germann, Georg. *The Gothic Revival in Europe and Britain: Sources, Influences and Ideas*. Trans.

Gerald Ohn. London: Lund Humphries with the Architectural Association, 1972.

54. Girouard, Mark. *The Return to Camelot: Chivalry and the English Gentleman*. New Haven: Yale University Press, 1981.

55. Goldstein, Doris. "The Organizational Development of the British Historical Profession." *Bulletin of the Institute of Historical Research* 55 (1982): 180-93.

56. Gooch, George P. *History and Historians in the Nineteenth Century*. London: Longmans, 1913.

Discusses Hallam and Macaulay; Thirlwall, Grote and Arnold; Carlyle and Froude; the Oxford School; Gardiner, Lecky, Seeley and Creighton; and Acton and Maitland. Also contains specialized studies, such as "The Jews and the Christian Church," and "Catholic Historiography."

57. Grennan, Margaret. *William Morris: Medievalist and Revolutionary*. New York: King's Crown Press, 1945.

58. Gwynn, Denis. *Lord Shrewsbury, Pugin, and the Catholic Revival*. London: Hollis & Carter, 1946.

59. Hale, John R. *England and the Italian Renaissance: The Growth of Interest in Its History and Art*. London: Faber and Faber, 1954.

60. -------. *The Evolution of British Historiography*. London: Macmillan, 1967.

61. Hall, Sir James. *Essay on the Origin, History, and Principles of Gothic Architecture*. London: John Murray, 1813.

62. Harding, Jane D. *The Arthurian Legend: A Checklist of Books in the Newberry Library*. Chicago: Newberry Library, 1933; supplement 1938.

63. Harrison, Antony H. *Swinburne's Medieval German and Other Poetry*. Cambridge: Cambridge University Press, 1980.

64. Harte, N. B. *One Hundred and Fifty Years of History Teaching at University College, London*. London: University College, London, 1982.

65. Haskell, Francis, "The Manufacture of the Past in 19th Century Painting," *Past and Present* 55 (May 1972): 109-120.

66. Hersey, George L. *High Victorian Gothic: A Study in Associationism*. Baltimore: Johns Hopkins University Press, 1972.

67. Hill, Christopher. "The Norman Yoke," *Puritanism and Revolution*. London: Secker & Warburg, 1958. 50-122.

68. Hough, Graham. *The Last Romantics*. London: Duckworth, 1949. Pugin, Ruskin, Morris, Yeats.

69. Jackson, Thomas Graham. *Modern Gothic Architecture*. London: Henry S. King & Co., 1873.

70. Jagger, Alison M. *Feminist Politics and Human Nature*. Totowa, N. J.: Rowman and Littlefield, 1988.

Contains an account of nineteenth-century socialist views of human nature.

71. Jann, Rosemary. *The Art and Science of Victorian History*. Columbus: Ohio State University Press, 1985.

Discusses Arnold, Carlyle, Macaulay, and Froude.

72. Jann, Rosemary. "Changing Styles in Victorian Military History." *Clio: A Journal of Literature, History, and the Philosophy of History* 11 (Winter 1982): 157-64.

Discusses Carlyle, Thomas Arnold, Thomas Gardiner, and Samuel Rawson.

73. Jann, Rosemary. "From Amateur to Professional: The Case of the Oxbridge Historians." *British Studies* 22 (1983): 122-147.

74. Johnson, Edwin. "Gothic and Saracen Architecture." *Westminster Review* 136 (1891): 643-49.

75. Jones, Owen. *The Grammar of Ornament*. London: 1856.

76. Jordan, R. Furneaux. *The Medieval Vision of William Morris*. London: William Morris Society, 1960.

77. Kegel, Charles Herbert. "Medieval-Modern Contrasts Used for a Social Purpose in the Work of William Cobbett, Robet Southey, A. Welby Pugin, Thomas Carlyle, John Ruskin, and William Morris." Diss. University of Michigan, 1955.

78. Kenyon, John. *The History Men: The Historical Profession in England Since the Renaissance*. London: Weidenfeld and Nicolson; Pittsburgh: University of Pittsburgh, 1983.

79. Kinnell, Susan K., ed. *Historiography: An Annotated Bibliography of Journal Articles, Books, and Dissertations*. Santa Barbara, Calif.: ABC-Clio, 1987.

80. Lacy, Norris J. and Geoffrey Ashe. *The Arthurian Handbook*. New York: Garland Publishing, Inc., 1988.

81. Lang, S. "The Principles of the Gothic Revival in England." *Journal of the R.I.B.A.* 7 (1900): 241-48.

82. Lowenthal, David. *The Past is a Foreign Country*. Cambridge University Press, 1985.

An overview — includes sections on the Renaissance, Victorian Britain, memory, relics, creative anachronism, etc.

83. Macaulay, James. *The Gothic Revival, 1745-1845.* Glasgow: Blackie & Son, 1975.

84. Macleod, Robert. *Style and Society: Architecture Ideology in Britain, 1835-1914.* London: RIBA Publications, 1971.

85. Mancoff, Debra N. *The Arthurian Revival in Victorian Art.* New York: Garland Publishing Inc., 1990.

Contains an extensive bibliography, with sections on "Archival Sources and Unpublished Manuscripts"; "The Arthurian Tradition and the Victorian Era"; "Victorian Art"; and "Individual Artists."

86. -------. "'An ancient idea of chivalric greatness': The Arthurian Revival and Victorian History Painting." *The Arthurian Tradition: Essays in Convergence.* Tuscaloosa: University of Alabama Press, 1988. 127-142.

87. McDougall, Hugh. *Racial Myth in English History: Trojans, Teutons, and Anglo-Saxons.* Hanover, New Hampshire: University Press of New England, 1982.

88. McGann, Jerome, ed. *Historical Studies and Literary Criticism.* Madison: University of Wisconsin Press, 1985.

89. McLachlan, Jean. "The Origin and Development of the Cambridge Historical Tripos." *Cambridge Historical Journal* 9 (1947-49): 78-105.

90. McMaster, Graham. *Scott and Society*. Cambridge University Press, 1981.

91. Meinecke, Friedrich. *Historicism: The Rise of a New Historical Outlook*. Trans. J. E. Anderson. London: Routledge and Kegan Paul, 1972.

92. Mitchell, Jerome. *Scott, Chaucer, and Medieval Romance: A Study in Sir Walter Scott's Indebtedness to the Literature of the Middle Ages*. Lexington: University Press of Kentucky, 1987.

Very thorough. Scott's neo-medievalism influenced a whole generation of Victorian writers.

93. Morris, Kevin L. *The Image of the Middle Ages in Romantic and Victorian Literature*. London: Croom Helm, 1984.

Religious medievalism; anti-medievalism; Kenelm Digby; Catholics and anti-Catholics; medieval eccelstiastical architecture; Ruskin and medieval art.

94. Morton, Patricia M. "Life After Butterfield? John Burrow's *A Liberal Descent* and the Recent Historiography of Victorian Historians." *Historical Reflections* 10 (1983): 229-44.

95. Neff, Emery. *The Poetry of History*. New York: Columbia University Press, 1947.

96. Ollard, Sidney Leslie. *A Short History of the Oxford Movement*. London: A. R. Mowbray, 1915.

97. Pevsner, Nikolaus. *High Victorian Design: A Study of the Exhibits of 1851*. London: Architectural Press, 1951.

98. Roberts, Helene E. "Victorian Medievalism: Revival or Masquerade?" *Browning Institute Studies* 8 (1980): 11-44.

99. St. Louis, Ralph F. "The Middle Ages as a Political and Social Ideal in the Writings of Edmund Burke, Samuel Taylor Coleridge, Thomas Carlyle, and John Ruskin." *DAI* 1973: 3600A-3601A.

100. Saintsbury, George. "The Young England Movement." *Miscellaneous Essays*. London: Percival & Co., 1892.

101. Schenker, Mark. "Historical Transcendentalism in the Works of Carlyle, Newman, and Browning." *DAI* 49 (April 1989): 3036A.

102. Scott, Sir George Gilbert. *Personal and Professional Recollections*. Ed. G. Gilbert Scott. London: Sampson Low, Marston, Searle & Rivington, 1879.

103. Semmel, Bernard. "T. B. Macaulay: The Active and Contemplative Lives." *The Victorian Experience: The Prose Writers*. Ed. Richard A. Levine. Athens: Ohio University Press, 1982. 22-46.

104. Shaw, Christopher, and Malcolm Chase, eds. *The Imagined Past: History and Nostalgia*. Manchester University Press, 1989.

Considers the nineteenth and twentieth centuries.

105. Smith, Paul. "The Young England Movement." Diss. Columbia University, 1951.

106. Smith, R. J. *The Gothic Bequest: Medieval Institutions in British Thought, 1688-1864*. Cambridge University Press, 1987.

107. Stanton, Phoebe B. "Architecture, History, and the Spirit of the Age." *The Mind and Art of Victorian England*. Ed. by Josef L. Altholz. Minneapolis: University of Minnesota Press 1976. 146-58.

108. Strong, Roy. *And When Did You Last See Your Father? The Victorian Painter and British History*. London: Thames and Hudson, 1978.

109. Trevelyan, George Macaulay. *British History in the Nineteenth Century*. London: Longmans, Green and Co., 1922.

110. ———. *Clio, A Muse and Other Essays*. London: Longmans & Co., 1913.

111. Tuman, Myron Chester. "*Frederick the Great, Romola, The Ring and The Book* and the Mid-Victorian Crisis in Historicism." *DAI* 34 (1974): 7251A.

112. Watkin, David. *Morality and Architecture: The Development of a Theme in Architectural History and Theory from the Gothic Revival to the Modern Movement*. Oxford: Clarendon Press, 1977.

113. Whibley, Charles. *Lord John Manners and His Friends*. 2 vols. Edinburgh: William Blackwood and Sons, 1925.

114. White, Hayden. *Metahistory: The Historical Imagination in Nineteenth-Century Europe*. Baltimore: Johns Hopkins University Press, 1973.

115. White, James F. *The Cambridge Movement: The Ecclesiologists and the Gothic Revival*. Cambridge University Press, 1962.

116. Zweig, Robert M. "The Victorian Dante: Dante and Victorian Literary Criticism." *DAI* 45 (1983): 2538A.

II. Late Eighteenth Century and Nineteenth-Century Works on Historiography and on Medieval and Early Renaissance History

117. Acton, J. E. *History of Freedom in Antiquity*. Bridgeworth: C. Edkins, 1877. *The History of Freedom in Christianity*. Bridgeworth: C. Edkins, 1877. *Lecture on the Study of History*. London: Macmillan & Co., 1895.

Historian of Catholicism, who believed English political institutions had preserved much of the spirit of essential Catholicism.

118. Arnold, Thomas. *Introductory Lectures on Modern History*. Oxford: J. H. Parker, 1842.

119. Bagehot, Walter. *The English Constitution*. London: Chapman & Hall, 1867.

120. Bateson, Mary. *Records of the Borough of Leicester*. London, Cambridge, 1899.

Also published other works of medieval borough history, 1901-1904.

121. Bloxam, Matthew Holbeche. *The Principles of Gothic Ecclesiastical Architecture*. 5th edition. London: Tilt & Bogue, 1843.

122. Bowles, William Lisle. *Annals and Antiquities of Lacock Abbey in the County of Wilts.* London, 1835.

123. Buckle, Henry Thomas. *History of Civilization in England.* 2 vols. London: J.W. Parker & Son, 1857.

124. Creighton, Mandell. *History of the Papacy.* 5 vols. London: Longmans, Green and Co., 1882-94.

His accounts of the early Renaissance popes are not as unsympathetic as earlier Protestant histories had been.

125. Dickens, Charles. *A Child's History of England.* New York: G. W. Carleton & Co., 1875.

126. Dixon, R. W. *History of the Church of England.* 1878-1902. London: Beal & Co., 1886.

Anglican viewpoint.

127. Freeman, Edward Augustus. *The Chief Periods of European History: Six Lectures Read in the University of Oxford in Trinity Term, 1885.* London: Macmillan, 1896.

Freeman (1823-92) was one of the "Oxford School" and a radical historian of classical Greece. His histories place great emphasis on political events, and in contrast to Carlyle and Froude, he especially detested autocratic cruelty. Other works included: *Growth of the English Constitution*, London: n.p., 1872; *William the*

Conquerer, London: Macmillan, 1888; *Old English History for Children*, London, n.p., 1869; *Sketches of Travel in Normandy and Main*, London: Macmillan, 1897; "On the Study of History," *Fortnightly Review* 35 (1881): 330; and "The Use of Historical Documents," *Fortnightly Review* 16 (1871): 335. See also M.E. Bratchel, section 1.

128. --------. *The History of the Norman Conquest of England: Its Causes and Its Results*. 5 vols. Oxford: Clarendon Press, 1870-76.

This contains an opening description of Anglo-Saxon England, the settlement of the Norsemen in France, and a study of the Danish kings. According to Gooch, "Worshipping political liberty, [Freeman] believed that he found it among the Teutonic nations and above all in his own country."

129. Froude, J. A. *The Divorce of Catherine of Aragon*. London: Longmans & Co., 1891.

130. --------. *History of England from the Fall of Wolsey to the Death of Elizabeth*. 12 vols. London: John Parker; Longman, Green, and Co., 1856-70.

A defense of the English Reformation. Froude admired Henry VIII and disliked Elizabeth I.

131. --------. *The Life and Letters of Erasmus*. London: Longmans, 1894.

132. Gibbon, Edward. *The Decline and Fall of the Roman Empire*. 6 vols. London, 1776-88.

133. Green, J. R. *The Conquest of England*. London: Macmillan, 1883.

134. --------. *The Making of England*. London: Macmillan, 1881.

135. --------. *A Short History of the English People*. London: n.p., 1874.

    Green was a militant radical and pioneer of a populist approach to history. The hero of his history is the British people, and his account includes criticism of English treatment of Ireland, Scotland, India, America, and France. According to Gooch: "His work possesses the living interest of a biography and the dramatic unity of an epic." Green died at age 46.

136. Hallam, Henry. *View of the State of Europe during the Middle Ages*. London: J. Murray, 1818.

    Emphasis on government and law. Relatively more ample treatment of France, Italy, and Spain, more meagre treatment of Germany and Eastern Europe.

137. Hallam, Henry. *Constitutional History from the Accession of Henry VII to the Death of George II*. New York: Sheldon, 1862.

    One of first works on modern England, from a right-wing Whig view; he believed in the existence of an English "constitution" (that is, the right of Parliament to limit the Crown), but remained distrustful of public opinion.

138. Harrison, Frederic. *The Meaning of History*. London: n.p., 1894.

139. Hume, David. *The History of England from the Invasion of Julius Caesar to the Revolution of 1688*. New edn. 12 vols. J. J. Tourneson, 1789.

140. Hurd, Richard. *Hurd's Letters on Chivalry and Romance*, ed. Edith J. Morley. London: Henry Frowde, 1911.

141. James, G. P. R. *The History of Chivalry*. New York: Harper and Brothers, 1839.

142. Jameson, Anna. *Sacred and Legendary Art*. 2 vols. London: n.p., 1848.

143. Kemble, John Mitchell. *The Saxons in England*. 2 vols. London: n.p., 1849.

One of first British "Germanists," who believed that "The Englishman has inherited the noblest portion of his being from the Anglo-Saxons. In spite of every influence, we bear a marvellous resemblance to our forefathers." He collected Anglo-Saxon documents, and dominated English historical scholarship for a generation.

144. Kingsley, Charles. *The Roman and the Teuton: A Series of Lectures Delivered before the University of Cambridge*. London: Cambridge (printed), 1864.

145. Lecky, W. E. H. *History of the Rise and Influence of the Spirit of Rationalism in Europe.* 2 vols. London: Longman, Green, and Co., 1865.

   Reviewed critically by George Eliot.

146. Lingard, John. *The History of England.* 3rd edition. 14 vols. London: J. Mawman, 1825-1831.

147. Macaulay, Thomas B. *Critical and Historical Essays.* London: Longman & Co., 1843-56.

   Famous Whig polemicist; as a historian, according to C. P. Gooch, he is best on English history of the seventeenth and eighteenth centuries. He attacked Hallam's near-Tory views, and eulogized the character and policy of Cromwell in a way which prepared for Carlyle.

148. Maitland, F. W. *History of English Law before the Time of Edward I.* 2 vols. London: Cambridge University Press, 1895.

   Analyzes assumptions and mental processes behind laws.

149. Markham, Elizabeth. *A History of England.* London: n.p., 1853.

150. Mill, James. *History of British India.* London: J. Madden, 1858.

151. Mills, Charles. *The History of Chivalry, or Knighthood and Its Times.* 2 vols. London: Longman, Rees, Orme, Brown, and Green, 1826.

152. Milman, Henry Hart. *History of Latin Christianity.* London: J. Murray, 1854-55.

Indifferent to doctrinal controversy, Milman presented a detached view of Catholicism.

153. Neale, John. *The History of the Eastern Church.* London: C. F. Hodgson, 1854.

154. Newman, John H. *The Arians of the Fourth Century. The Development of Christian Doctrine. Historical Sketches.* London: J. G. & F. Rivington, 1833.

155. O'Grady, Standish. *The History of Ireland: The Heroic Period.* Vol. 1. London: Sampson Low, Searle, Marston, and Rivington, 1878.

156. Palgrave, F. T. *History of Normandy and England.* London: 1851.

Gives a "Romanist" view of British law and history.

157. Palmer, J. Foster. "The Saxon Invasion and its Influence on our Character as a Race." *Transactions of the Royal Historical Society,* 2nd ser. 2 (1885): 173-96.

158. Prescott, William Hickling. *The Conquest of Mexico.* London: R. Bentley, 1843.

159. -------. *The Conquest of Peru*. London: R. Bentley, 1847.

160. Robertson, J. R. *The Cryptic Rite*. Toronto: Hunter & Rose, 1888.

   Also wrote other histories of Freemasonry.

161. Round, John Horace. *Feudal England*. London: Swan Sonnenschein, 1895.

162. Seeley, John Robert. *The Expansion of England*. Boston: Roberts, 1883.

   Source of arguments for proponents of British imperial power; though ambivalent about the value of expansion. "Bigness is not necessarily greatness. If by remaining in the second rank of magnitude we can hold the first rank morally and intellectually, let us sacrifice mere material magnitude" (16).

163. Shaw, Henry. *Dresses and Decorations of the Middle Ages*. 2 vols. London: Henry Bohn, 1858.

164. Strickland, Agnes and Elizabeth. *Lives of the Queens of England*. 12 vols. London: Henry Colburn, 1840-48. Vol. 1: Matilda of Flanders, Matilda of Scotland, Matilda of Boulogne Adelicia of Louvaine, Eleanora of Aquitaine. Vol. 2: Eleanor of Provence, Isabella of France, Berengaria of Navarre, Isabella of Angouleme, Eleanora of Castile, Marguerite of France,

Philippa of Hanault, Anne of Bohemia. Vol. 3: Joanna of Navarre, Margaret of Anjou, Isabella of Valois, Elizabeth Woodville, Anne of Warwick. Vol. 4: Anne Boleyn, Anne of Cleves, Katherine Howard, Elizabeth of York, Katherine of Aragon, Jane Seymour. Vol. 5: Katherine Parr, Mary Tudor. Vol. 6,7: Queen Elizabeth, Anne of Denmark. Vol. 8: Catherine of Braganza, Henrietta Maria. Vol. 9, 10: Mary Beatrice of Modena, Mary II. Vol. 11, 12: Anne.

165. Stubbs, William. *Constitutional History of England in Its Origins and Development.* Clarendon Press Series, 1866.

Conservative medieval historian of the "Oxford School."

166. -------. *Seventeen Lectures on the Study of Medieval and Modern History.* 3rd ed. Oxford: Clarendon Press, 1886.

167. Turner, Sharon. *History of the Anglo-Saxons; Comprising the History of England from the Earliest Period to the Norman Conquest.* 3 vols. London: Longman, Hunt, Rees, Orme, and Browne, 1820.

168. Wood, Mary Everett, ed. *Letters of Royal and Illustrious Ladies of Great Britain from the Commencement of the Twelfth Century to the Close of the Reign of Queen Mary.* 3 vols. London: Henry Colburn, 1846.

III. A Few Works the Victorians Would Have Read to Understand the Medieval and Early Renaissance Legendary and Literary Past

169. Baring-Gould, Sabine. *Curious Myths of the Middle Ages.* 2nd ed. London: Rivingtons, 1868.

170. Boccaccio, Giovanni. *The Decameron.* London: Chatto & Windus, 1874.

171. Burckhardt, Jacob. *Die Kultur der Renaissance in Italien. Ein Versuch.* Basel, 1860.

172. --------. *The Civilisation of the Period of the Renaissance in Italy...* Trans. by S.G.C. Middlemore. 2 vols. London: Kegan Paul & Co., 1878.

173. Chaucer, Geoffrey. *Canterbury Tales, a new text, with illustrative notes.* Ed. by Thos. Wright. 3 vols. London: Percy Society, Early English Poetry, 1847.

174. --------. *Legend of Good Women.* Oxford: Clarendon Press, 1889.

175. --------. *Troilus and Criseyde.* Chaucer Society 1: 44, 65. London: Chaucer Society, 1873.

176. Child, Francis James. *English and Scottish Popular Ballads.* Boston: Houghton Mifflin, 1904.

177. Condorcet, M. J. A. N. *Sketch for a Historical Picture of the Progress of the Human Mind.* Baltimore: J. Frank, 1802.

178. Dante Alighieri. *The Divine Comedy.* Trans. H. F. Cary. London: J. Barfield, 1814.

179. -------. *Vita Nuovo.* Trans. H. F. Cary. London: J. Barfield, 1814.

180. Dasent, George Webbe. *Popular Tales from the Norse.* Edinburgh: Edmonston and Douglass, 1854.

   Translations from the *Norske Folkeventyr* collected by Peter Asbjørnsen and Jørgen Moe.

181. Digby, Kenelm. *The Broad Stone of Honor, or, Rules for the Gentlemen of England.* London: C. and J. Rivington, 1823.

182. Donald, A.K., ed. *Melusine.* Comp. (1382-1394) Jean d'Arras. London: Early English Text Society, 1895.

183. Durandus, William. *The Symbolism of Churches and Church Ornaments: A Translation of the First Book of Rationale Divinorum Officiorum.* [Introduced by John Mason Neale and Benjamin Webb.] London: Gibbings & Co., 1893.

184. Elmes, James. *Lectures on Architecture, Comprising the History of the Art from the Earliest Times to the Present Day.* London: n.p., 1821

185. Ellis, George. *Specemins of Early English Metrical Romances*. 3 vols. London: Longman, Hunt, Rees, Orme, and Brown, 1805.

186. Fitzgerald, Edward, adapt. *The Rubáiyát*. London: B. Quaritch, 1859.

187. Frazer, James, *The Golden Bough*. London: Macmillan & Co., 1890 ff.

188. Froissart, Sir John. *Chronicles of England, France, Spain and the adjoining Countries. . . .* Trans. Thomas Johnes. 2 vols. London: William Smith, 1848.

189. Furnivall, F.J., ed. *The History of the Holy Grail.* From the French prose of Sires R. de Borron. London: Early English Text Society, 1874-78.

190. Garbett, Edward Lacy. *Rudimentary Treatise on the Principles of Design in Architecture as Deducible from Nature and Exemplified in the Works of the Greek and Gothic Architects*. London: John Weale, 1850.

191. Grimm, Jacob and Wilhelm Grimm. *German Popular Stories.* Trans. Edgar Taylor from Kinder und Haus Märchen, collected by M. G. from the oral tradition. 2 vols. London: C. Baldwin, 1823.

192. Guest, Lady Charlotte, ed. *The Mabinogion: from the Llyfr Coch o Hergest, and other Ancient Welsh*

Manuscripts. 3 vols. London: Longman, Orme, Brown, Green, and Longmans, 1838-1842.

193. Hall, S. C. *The Book of British Ballads*. 2 vols. London: J. How, 1842.

194. Herrtage, S.J., ed. *The English Charlemagne Romances*. London: Early English Text Society, 1879.

195. Hyde, Douglas (An Chraoibhin Aoibhinn). *Love Songs of Connacht, being the Fourth Chapter of The Songs of Connacht*. London and Dublin: T. Fisher Unwin, 1893.

196. Keightley, Thomas. *The Fairy Mythology, Illustrative of the Romance and Superstition of Various Countries*. Bohn's Antiquarian Library 13. London: Bohn, 1850.

197. Lumby, J.R., ed. *King Horn, with fragments of Floriz and Blauncheflur and of the Assumption of Our Lady*. London: Early English Text Society, 1866.

198. Mallet, P.H. *Northern Antiquities: or a description of the manners, customs, religions and laws of the ancient Danes and other Northern Nations. . . .* Trans. from new ed. revised by J. A. Blackwell. London: Bohn, 1847.

199. Mandeville, John. *The Voiage and Travaile of Sir John Maundevile*. Ed. J. O. Halliwell. London: E. Lumley, 1839.

200. Matthew, F.D., ed. *The English Works of Wyclif hitherto unprinted*. London: Early English Text Society, 1880.

201. Morgan, Lewis Henry. *Ancient Society*. New York: Henry Holt, 1878.

202. Morris, R. *Sir Gawayne and the Green Knight*. London: Early English Text Society, 1864.

203. O'Grady, Standish James. *History of Ireland*. 2 vols. London, 1878-80.

204. Percy, Bishop. *Reliques of Ancient English Poetry*. 3 vols. London: J. Dodsley, 1765.

205. Scott, Walter. *Essays on Chivalry and Romance*. London: Chandos Classics, 1888.

206. Skeat, W.W., ed. *The Bruce; or, the Book of the most excellent and noble prince, Robert de Broyss, King of Scots*. London: Early English Text Society, 1870.

207. Skeat, W.W., ed. *Joseph of Arimathie: otherwise called the Romance of the Seint Graal, or Holy Grail*. London: Early English Text Society, 1871.

208. --------. *Lancelot of the Laik*. London: Early English Text Society, 1865.

209. --------. *The Lay of Havelok the Dane*. London: Early English Text Society, 1868.

210. --------. *Pierce the Ploughman Crede*. London: Early English Text Society, 1867.

211. --------. *The Romans of Partenay, or of Lusignan, otherwise known as the tale of Melusine*. London: Early English Text Society, 1866.

212. --------. *The Vision of William concerning Piers Plowman, together with Vita de Dowel, Dobet, et Dobest, secundum wit et resoun*. London: Early English Text Society, 1885.

213. Sturluson, Snorre. *Heimskringla. The Olaf Sagas*. Trans. Samuel Laing. 3 vols. London: Longmans, 1844.

214. Thorpe, Benjamin. *Northern Mythology*. 3 vols. London: Edward Lumley, 1851.

215. --------. *Yule-Tide Stories. A Collection of Scandinavian and North German Popular Tales and Traditions* London: n. p., 1888.

216. Tylor, Edward. *Researches into the Early History of Mankind and the Development of Civilization*. London: John Murray, 1865.

217. de Varagine, Jacobus. *The Golden Legend or Lives of the Saints, as Englished by William Caxton*.

Intro. F. S. Ellis. 7 vols. London: J. M. Dent, 1900.

218. Wackerbarth, A. Dietrich. *Beowulf*. London: William Pickering, 1849.

219. William of Malmesbury. *Chronicle of the Kings of England*. Ed. J. A. Giles. London: Bohn, 1847.

220. Worsaae, J. J. A. *The Primeval Antiquities*. Trans. W. J. Thomas. London: J. H. Parker, 1849.

221. -------. *The Pre-History of the North based on Contemporary Memorials*. Trans. H. F. Marland Simpson. London: Trubner, 1896.

222. Zupitza, J., ed. *The Romance of Guy of Warwick*. London: Early English Text Society, 1883.

IV. Victorian Prose Historicists

223. Arnold, Matthew. *On the Study of Celtic Literature*. London: Smith, Elder & Co., 1867.

224. -------. *Culture and Anarchy*. London: Smith, Elder & Co., 1869.

225. Blatchford, Robert. *Merrie England*. London: Walter Scott, 1894.

226. Carlyle, Thomas. *Early Kings of Norway: Also an Essay on Portraits of John Knox*. London: Chapman & Hall, 1875.

227. -------. *On Heroes and Hero-Worship*. London: James Fraser, 1841.

228. -------. *Past and Present*. London: Chapman & Hall, 1843.

229. Engels, Friedrich. *Der Ursprung der Familie des Privateigenthumus und des Staats*. Zürich: Hottingen, 1884.

230. -------. *The Origin of the Family, Private Property, and the State*. English translation. Chicago: C. H. Kerr, 1902.

231. Lee, Vernon. *Euphorion*. 2 vols. London: T. Fisher Unwin, 1884. A study of Renaissance art.

232. ———. *Renaissance Fancies and Studies*. London: Smith, Elder & Co., 1895.

233. Morris, William, and Eirikr Magnússon. *Grettis Saga*. London: F.S. Ellis, 1869.

234. ———. *The Saga Library*. London: Bernard Quaritch, 1891-95.

Also, several essays on medieval art and labor, such as "Art and Labour," "The Literature of the North," "Early England," in *Hopes and Fears for Art*, London, 1882, and *Signs of Change*, London, 1888.

235. Morris, William and E. Belfort Bax. *Socialism: Its Growth and Outcome*. London: Swan Sonnenschein, 1893.

Contains chapters on European economic development from a Marxist perspective.

236. ———. *Völsunga Saga*. London: F.S. Ellis, 1870.

237. Pater, Walter. *Studies in the History of the Renaissance*. London: n.p., 1873.

Pater's Renaissance includes twelfth century French romances.

238. Pugin, Augustus N.W. *An Apology for the Revival of Christian Architecture in England*. London: n.p., 1843.

239. --------. *Contrasts: or, A Parallel between the Noble Edifices of the Middle Ages and Corresponding Buildings of the Present Day; Shewing the Present Decay of Taste. Accompanied by Appropriate Text.* London: n.p., 1836.

240. --------. *The Present State of Ecclesiastical Architecture in England.* London: n.p., 1843.

241. --------. *A Reply to Observations Which Appeared in "Fraser's Magazine," for March 1837, on a Work Entitled "Contrasts."* London: James Moyes, 1837.

242. --------. *Some Remarks on the Articles Which Have Recently Appeared in the "Rambler," Relative to Ecclesiastical Architecture and Decoration.* London: Charles Dolman, 1850.

243. --------. *The True Principles of Pointed or Christian Architecture.* London: John Weale, 1841.

244. Rosenberg, John D. *Carlyle and the Burden of History.* Oxford: Clarendon Press, 1985.

245. Ruskin, John. *The Seven Lamps of Architecture.* London: Smith Elder & Co., 1849.

246. --------. *The Stones of Venice.* London: Orpington, 1879-81.

Includes "The Nature of Gothic," set-piece of Victorian medievalism. Also, portions of *Modern*

Painters, London: Smith Elder & Co., 1843, are historical criticism.

247. Sidgwick, Henry. "The Historical Method." *Mind* 11 (1886): 203.

248. Symonds, John A. *The Renaissance. An Essay.* Oxford: H. Hammans, 1863.

249. --------. *The Renaissance in Italy.* 7 vols. London: Smith, Elder & Co., 1875-86.

250. --------. *The Renaissance of Modern Europe.* London: T. Scott, 1872.

251. Yonge, Charlotte. *Unknown to History. A Story of the Captivity of Mary of Scotland.* 2. vols. London: Macmillan & Co., 1882.

V. Some Examples of Nineteenth-Century Historical Fiction Set in the Middle Ages and Early Renaissance

252. Ainsworth, W. Harrison. *Cardinal Pole; or, the Days of Philip and Mary.* 3. vols. London: Chapman & Hall, 1863.

Mary Tudor's marriage.

253. --------. *The Constable of the Tower: An Historical Perspective.* London: Chapman & Hall, 1861.

The fall of Edward Seymore, first Duke of Somerset (The Protector), 1506-1552.

254. --------. *Guy Fawkes.* London: Richard Bentley, 1841.

Causes of and reaction to the Gunpowder Plot, circa 1605.

255. --------. *The Lancashire Witches.* London: Henry Calburn, 1849.

Deals with the witchcraft trials in Lancaster in 1612.

256. --------. *The Tower of London.* London: Richard Bentley, 1840.

The story of Lady Jane Grey's reign and execution, 1537-1554.

257. --------. *Windsor Castle.* London: Henry Colburn, 1843.

Romance involving the stories of Henry VIII, Anne Boleyn, Jane Seymour, Cardinal Wolsey, the Earl of Surrey and others.

258. Baker, James. *The Cardinal's Page*. London: Chapman & Hall, 1898.

Henry Beufort and the Hussites in Bohemia.

259. --------. *The Gleaming Dawn: A Romance of the Middle Ages*. London: Chapman 7 Hall, 1896.

Presents the Wycliffe Movement in England and the Hussite Wars in Bohemia.

260. Baring-Gould, S. *Domitia*. London: Methuen & Co., 1898.

Rome at the time of Domitian and Nero, circa A.D. 67-96.

261. Baring-Gould, S. *Guavas, the Tinner*. London: Methuen, 1897.

Life revolving around a tin mine in Dartmoor, circa 1572.

262. --------. *Noémi: A Story of Rock-Dwellers*. London: Methuen & Co., 1895.

Domestic conditions and the struggle between England and France during the reign of Charles VII, circa 1450.

263. -------. *Pabo, the Priest*. London: Methuen & Co., 1899.

Henry I's attempt to subjugate the Welsh, circa 1100-1135.

264. Barr, Robert. *Tekla: A Romance of Love and War*. London: Methuen & Co., 1898.

A romance of adventure set in the Rhine area of Germany, circa 1275, wherein, with many perils along the way, a countess is wooed and won by an emperor in disguise.

265. Bray, Anna Eliza. *The White Hoods*. London: n.p., 1828.

The struggles of the citizens of Bruges, Ghent, and Antwerp, led by Philip von Antevelde, against Louis III, Count of Flanders, circa 1381-81.

266. Bunbury, Selina. *Coombe Abbey*. Dublin: W. Curry Junr & Co., 1843.

An historical tale of the reign of James I.

267. Butcher, C.H. *Armenosa of Egypt*. Edinburgh: Blackwood, 1897.

A tale about the Arab conquest of Egypt in the seventh century.

268. Coleridge, Christabel Rose. *Minstrel Dick. A Tale of the XIVth Century.* London: Gardner, Darton & Co., 1896.

269. Crockett, Samuel R. *Joan of the Sword-hand.* London: Lock & Co., 1900.

　　The warlike adventures and amours of an Amazonian princess in north Germany in the time of Pope Sixtus IV, circa 1470-80.

270. Davidson, Mary M. *Edward the Exile.* London: Hodder & Stoughton, 1901.

　　The life of Edward the Atheling (1017-57).

271. Davies, Naughton. *The King's Guide.* London: Simpkin Marshall & Co., 1901.

　　Thirteenth-century Welsh fight for independence.

272. deMinto, Walter. *The Meditation of Ralph Hardelot,* London, 1888.

　　Peasant's Revolt of 1381.

273. Dole, Nathan Haskell. *Omar the Tentmaker.* London: Duckworth & Co., 1898.

　　Romance of Omar Khayyám, circa 1050.

274. Doyle, Sir Arthur Conan. *The White Company.* 3 vols. London: Smith Elder & Co., 1891.

A company of English bowmen in France and Castile, under John of Gaunt, Duke of Lancaster, circa 1366-67.

275. Eliot, George. *Romola*. London: Smith Elder & Co., 1866.

Tells of a saintly life in the time of Savonarola, fifteenth century Italy.

276. James, G. P. R. *Atilla: A Romance*. 3 vols. London: Routledge, 1837.

The experiences of a young Roman exile in the camp of Atilla the Hun (ruler of the Huns 434-453).

277. Kingsley, Charles. *Hereward the Wake, "Last of the English"*. Cambridge: n.p., 1866.

An account of Hereward's 1070-71 resistance to the Norman invasion of England.

278. -------. *Hypatia*. 2. vols. London: n.p., 1853.

Clash between Christianity and paganism in fifth century Egypt.

279. Lawless, Emily. *Maelcho. A Sixteenth-Century Narrative*. 2 vols. London: Smith Elder & Co., 1894.

An account of the hard conditions of the Irish under English oppression, circa 1577-82.

280. -------. *With Essex in Ireland*. London: Smith Elder & Co., 1890.

Tale of British invasion in 1599.

281. Lytton, Edward Bulwer. *The Caxtons*. 3 vols. Edinburgh and London: W. Blackwood & Sons, 1849.

282. -------. *Harold*. London: n.p., 1848.

The Norman invasion, the Battle of Hastings, and the fall of the last Saxon king.

283. -------. *The Last of the Barons*, 3 vols. n.p., 1843.

Edward IV (1442-1483) and Warwick the King Maker (Richard Neville) are central characters.

284. Manning, Anne. *The Household of Sir Thomas More*. London: n.p., 1851.

Written as the diary of More's daughter Margaret, this pictures the saint as a family man.

285. Manning, Anne. *The Maiden and Married Life of Mary Powell, Afterwards Mistress Milton*. N.p., 1855.

286. Meinhold, Wilhelm. *Sidonia the Sorceress*. Trans. Lady Wilde. London: Parlour Library, 1847.

Vivid account of the woman who supposedly destroyed the reigning ducal house of Pomerania [Poland] by black magic. No precise date is given, but these events would have to have occurred between the twelfth and sixteenth centuries, after which the ducal political structure changed in Poland.

287. Morris, William. *A Dream of John Ball*. London: Reeves and Turner, 1888.

    Peasants' Revolt of 1381.

288. -------. *The House of the Wolfings*. London: Reeves and Turner, 1889.

    Set in third-century Germany.

289. -------. *Roots of the Mountains*. London: Reeves and Turner, 1890.

    Set in fourth-century Germany.

290. Newman, John Henry. *Callista: A Tale of the Third Century*. N.p., 1856.

    The savage persecution of Christians by the Emperor Decius (201-251).

291. O'Byrne, M. L. *Art M'Morrough O'Cavanagh, Prince of Leinster*. Dublin: M.H. Gill & Son, 1885.

    Romance set in late fourteenth-century Ireland, with bitter portrayal of the English laws which suppressed Irish culture and proscribed intermarriage between the Irish and English.

292. -------. *The Court of Rath Croghan, Or, Dead But Not Forgotten*. Dublin: M. H. Gill and Son, 1887.

Set in twelfth-century Ireland.

293. --------. *The Pale and the Septs: An Irish Romance of the Sixteenth Century*. Dublin: M. H. Gill and Son, 1885.

A story of rebellious Ireland under English domination in mid-century.

294. Palgrave. Francis. *Truths and Fictions of the Middle Ages: The Merchant and the Friar*. London: n.p., 1837.

The reign of Edward I (1272-1307).

295. Reade, Charles. *The Cloister and the Hearth*. 4. vols. London: Trübner & Co., 1861.

A travelogue of Western Europe in the fifteenth century, with the father of Erasmus as hero.

296. Robinson, Emma. *Whitefriars: or, The Days of Charles the Second: An Historical Romance.* 2 vols. London: Routledge, 1844.

297. Scott, Walter. *Anne of Geierstein: Or, The Maiden of the Mist*. 3 vols. Edinburgh: Cadell & Co., 1824.

298. --------. *The Antiquary*. 3 vols. Edinburgh: Archibald Constable & Co., 1816.

299. -------. *The Bridal of Triermain, or The Vale of St. John.* Edinburgh: John Ballantyne and Company, 1813.

300. -------. *The Heart of Midlothian.* Edinburgh: A. Constable & Co., 1818.

301. -------. *History of Scotland.* London: The Cabinet Cyclopaedia, 1830.

302. -------. *Ivanhoe.* 3 vols. Edinburgh: A. Constable and Co., 1820.

303. -------. *Redgauntlet.* 3 vols. Edinburgh: Archibald Constable & Co., 1824.

304. -------. *Tales of the Crusaders.* 4 vols. London: Hurst, Robinson & Co., 1825.

Contains *The Betrothed*, which chronicles a border war in the time of Henry II, and *The Talisman*, a vigorous romance of the Third Crusade (1189-1192), set in Palestine.

305. Shorthouse, Joseph Henry. *Sir Percival: A Story of the Past and of the Present.* London: Macmillan, 1886.

306. Yonge, Charlotte, *The Lances of Lynwood.* London: Macmillan, 1855.

An adventure tale set in mid-fourteenth-century Spain: the Black Prince of Spain allies himself with

Pedro the Cruel, King of Castile, to defeat Pedro's brother Enrique at the Battle of Navarrete.

VI. Criticism

307. Boos, Florence S. "Morris's German Romances as Socialist History." *Victorian Studies* 27 (1984): 321-42.

308. Fleishman, Avrom. *The English Historical Novel: Walter Scott to Virginia Woolf.* Baltimore: Johns Hopkins Press, 1971.

309. Lukacs, Georg. *The Historical Novel.* Trans. Hannah Mitchell and Stanley Mitchell. Boston: Beacon Press, 1963.

310. Sanders, Andrew. *The Victorian Historical Novel, 1840-1880.* London: Macmillan, 1978.

VII. Victorian Historicist Poetry and Drama

311. Arnold, Matthew. *The Poems of Matthew Arnold*. Ed. Miriam Allott. New York: Longman, 1979.

"The Church of Brou" (1853) celebrates the tomb of Philibert II of Savoy, (d. 1504), and his wife Marguerite d'Autriche (1480-1530). In "Stanzas From the Grande Chartreuse" (1855), the poet visits the Grande Chartreuse, a monastery founded by St. Bruno in 1084, where he debates the nature of right action and the role of faith in the world. "Tristan and Iseult" (1852), Arnold's most famous medieval poem, is a set-piece on the destructive effects of passion. In "Saint Brandon" (1860), while on a seven year voyage to "the land of the saints," Brandon (circa 484-578, the Benedictine Abbott of Clonfert, Galway) experiences a vision of Christ's betrayer, Judas, with whom he converses regarding God's mercy and the possibility of redemption for all.

312. Aytoun, W. E. *Lay of the Scottish Cavaliers*. Edinburgh and London: W. Blackwood & Sons, 1849.

313. Blind, Mathilde. *The Prophecy of Saint Oran and Other Poems*. London: Newman and Co., 1881.

In the title poem, Saint Columba orders the death of the monk Oran in punishment for his liaison with Mona, daughter of a converted Pictish chieftain. Before burial St. Oran rises from his grave to deny the existence of an afterlife and affirm the value of earthly love.

314. Borrow, George. *The Death of Balder. A Tragedy in Three Acts and in Verse*. Translated from the Danish of Ewald. London: Jarrold & Sons, 1889.

315. Bowles, William Lisle. *Poetical Works*, ed. George Gilfillan. 2 vols. Edinburgh: James Nichol, 1855.

316. Browning, Elizabeth Barrett. "Lady Geraldine's Courtship." *Poems*. London: Edward Moxon, 1844.

317. Browning, Robert. *Dramatis Personae*. London: Chapman & Hall, 1864.

318. -------. *Men and Women*. London: Chapman & Hall, 1855.

319. -------. *Poems*. 2 vols. London: Chapman & Hall, 1849. Later published as *Dramatic Romances and Lyrics*. London: Walter Scott, 1897.

Browning's monologues are often set in fifteenth and sixteenth-century Italy.

320. -------. *The Ring and the Book*. 4 vols., London: Smith, Elder & Co., 1868.

321. Buchanan, Robert. *Idyls and Legends of Inverburn*. London: Alexander Strahan, 1865.

322. Bulwer-Lytton, Edward George. *"Eva, A True Story," and Other Tales & Poems*. London: Saunders and Othey, 1842.

In "The Last Crusade," a departing soldier looks on the Holy Land, and implores God to assure him that the Crusades have not been fought in vain. "The Lay of the Minstrel's Heart" is a lyric on lost love set in a medieval context.

323. -------. *The Poetical and Dramatic Works*. 3 vols. London: Chapman & Hall, 1853.

The ending of the epic poem "King Arthur" explains how Arthur's line, despite no known male heir, has influenced the destiny of modern England. According to Bulwer-Lytton, this poem came from the "best powers of my maturer years [and is] the worthiest contribution that my abilities enable me to offer the literature of my country."

324. Carr, J. W. Comyns. *King Arthur: A Drama in a Prologue and Five Acts*. London: Macmillan and Company, 1895.

325. Coleridge, Mary E. *Poems*. London: Elkin Matthews, 1908.

"The Merciful Knight," with epigraph: "For a Picture by Burne-Jones," expresses the sentiments of a knight who kneels before the cross to seek forgiveness for his own transgressions and those of his foe.

326. Cook, Eliza. *"Melaia," and Other Poems*. London: Charles Tilt, 1840.

"The King's Old Hall" comments on the transient nature of life and kingly magnificence.

327. Davidson, John. *The Poems of John Davidson*. Ed. Andrew Turnbull. 2 vols. Totowa, New Jersey: Rowman and Littlefield, 1973.

"The Ordeal" (circa 1893) portrays the tragic results of a false charge of adultery in a medieval setting. "Serenade (1250 A.D.)" (1895) is a love lyric with medieval touches, and "A Ballad of Tannhäuser" (1896) a love ballad. "A Ballad of Lancelot" (1898) presents Lancelot's interior struggle between good and evil.

328. Dawson, C. Amy. *Idylls of Womanhood*. London: William Heinemann, 1892.

"Woman's Wit," set in 1138, recounts the legend of the Duchess of Wittenberg's rescue of her condemned husband. "A Woman's Faith," set during the Crusades, tells how the daughter of Baldwin IV of Jerusalem rejects the proferred throne in order to remain faithful to her husband.

329. Dixon, R. W. *Historical Odes*. London: n.p., 1864.

330. -------. *Mano*. London: Routledge, 1883.

Epic in four books set in the tenth century. The narrator Fergant recounts the struggles of his friend Mano, a chivalric Norman knight who struggled to gain Norman support for an Italian campaign waged by his liege. With its complicated plot, sudden reversals, and moments of horror and pathos, *Mano* won G. M. Hopkins's commendation as one of the best poems of the century.

331. Dobell, Sydney. *Balder*. London: Smith, Elder & Co., 1854.

332. Eliot, George. *Poems of George Eliot*. New York: White, Stokes, and Allen, 1886.

"How Lisa Loved the King" is a chivalrous romance which recounts a woman's obedience to her benefactor.

333. Ferguson, Samuel. *Congal: A Poem, in Five Books*. Dublin: Edward Ponsonby, 1872. *Lays of the Western Gael*. London: Bell and Daldy, 1865.

334. Hardy, Thomas. *Collected Poems of Thomas Hardy*. New York: Macmillan, 1925.

In "The Lost Pyx: A Mediaeval Legend," at the behest of a mysterious voice, a priest carries the Pyx (sacrament) in a storm to shrive a dying man near a medieval stone pillar called Cross-and-Hand. Although he loses the Pyx, he regains it through a miracle.

335. Hopkins, Gerard Manley. *The Poems of Gerard Manley Hopkins*. Oxford University Press, 1967.

"Duns Scotus' Oxford" expresses Hopkins' kinship with the eleventh century philosopher.

336. Hopper, Nora. *Songs of the Morning*. London: Grant Richards, 1900.

Contains "Robin Hood's Goodnight," a short love poem; "The Rowing Song of King Atli," love ballad of the Norse hero; and "The Last Viking," a sea-faring song of exploration and destiny.

337. Ingelow, Jean. *19th Century British Minor Poets*. Ed. W. H. Auden. New York: Delacorte, 1966.

"The High Tide on the Coast of Lincolnshire, 1571" is a ballad which recounts the loss of a loved one in an unexpected flood-tide.

338. Jones, Henry. *The Crusaders*. London: Macmillan & Co., 1893. A play.

339. Kipling, Rudyard. *A Choice of Kipling's Verse*, ed. T.S. Eliot. London: Faber & Faber, 1941.

In "Sir Richard's Song (A.D. 1066)," a Norman invader celebrates his new land after the Battle of Hastings. "A Tree Song" (A.D. 1200) praises the rustic, natural charms of Britain. "The Roman Centurion's Song (A.D. 300)" is a dramatic monologue in which a soldier who has served all his life in Britain, and whose family is buried there, regrets that he has been ordered back to Rome. "Dane-Geld (A.D. 980-1016)" contains an exhortation to courage and heroism. "Norman and Saxon (A.D. 1100)" celebrates the resilience and moral uprightness of the Saxon.

340. Lucas, Mrs. Henry. *Songs of Zion by Hebrew Singers of Mediaeval Times*. Trans. Mrs. Henry Lucas. London: J.M. Dent & Co., 1894.

341. Meredith, George. *The Poems of George Meredith*. Ed. Phyllis B. Bartlett. 2 vols. New Haven and London: Yale University Press, 1978.

Medieval poems include "Song of Theolinda," "King Harald's Trance," "The Nuptials of Atilla," "Aneurin's Harp," "The Glastonbury Thorn," "The Story of Sir Arnulph," "St. Therèse," and "Richard Lionheart."

342. Meredith, Owen. *Clytemnestra, The Earl's Return, The Artist, and Other Poems*. London: n.p., 1855.

343. Meynell, Alice. *"A Father of Women" and other Poems*. London: Burns and Oates, Ltd., 1917.

"To Tintoretto In Venice" celebrates the courage of Tintoretto's powerful use of light and shade.

344. Morris, William. *The Defence of Guenevere*. London: Bell & Daldy, 1858.

345. ---------. *The Earthly Paradise*. London: F.S. Ellis, 1868-70.

346. ---------. *The Life and Death of Jason*. London: Bell & Daldy, 1867.

347. ---------. *Love Is Enough*. London: Ellis & White, 1873.

348. ---------. *Sigurd the Volsung*. London: Ellis & White, 1877.

349. Noyes, Alfred. *Collected Poems*. New York: Stokes Co., 1913.

"A Song of Sherwood" retells the Robin Hood story. Told in a series of chronological leaps, "The Progress of Love" narrates love between Etain and Anwyl, with reference to Arthur, Guenevere, Lancelot.

350. Proctor, Adelaide. *The Poems of Adelaide Proctor*. Boston: James Osgood and Co., 1873.

In "A Knight-Errant," a knight defends his "mistress" Truth against Ignorance, Prejudice, Custom, and Opinion.

351. Rossetti, Christina. *Goblin Market and Other Poems*. Cambridge: London (printed), 1862.

352. --------. *The Prince's Progress and Other Poems*. London: n.p., 1866.

353. --------. *A Pageant, and Other Poems*. London: Macmillan, 1881.

Especially note "Monna Innominata," a response to the Petrarchan tradition.

354. Rossetti, Dante G. *Dante and His Circle*. London: Ellis & White, 1874.

355. Rossetti, Dante G. *Poems*. London: F. S. Ellis, 1870

Includes "The Blessed Damozel," "Sister Helen," "Dante at Verona," "The Staff and the Scrip," "The King's Tragedy," "The White Ship," "Rose Mary," and several sonnets on pictures.

356. ———. *The Lady of the Lake*. Edinburgh: John Ballantyne and Co., 1810.

357. ———. *Marmion, A Tale of Flodden Field*. Edinburgh: Constable and Company, 1808.

358. Scott, William Bell. *A Poet's Harvest Home: Being 100 Short Poems*. London, 1893.

In "Oisin" the speaker mourns the death of the third century Gaelic warrior-bard Ossian. "Dante in Exile" reflects on the injustices and bitternesses of the past.

359. Smith, Alexander. *Edwin of Deira*. London: n.p., 1861.

360. Stevenson, Robert Louis. *The Poems and Ballads of Robert Louis Stevenson*. New York: Scribner's, 1913.

"Heather Ale, A Galloway Legend" narrates Pict resistance to invasion.

361. Swinburne, Algernon. *Bothwell*. London: Chatto & Windus, 1874.

362. ———. *Poems and Ballads*. London: E. Moxon & Co., 1866.

Includes "The Hill of Venus."

363. ———. *Rosamund, Queen of the Lombards*. London: Chatto & Windus, 1899.

364. -------. *Tale of Balen*. London: Chatto & Windus, 1896.

365. -------. *Tristram of Lyonesse*. London: Chatto & Windus, 1882.

366. Symonds, Arthur. *Wine, Women, and Song*, 1884.

   Translation of medieval Latin students' songs.

367. Tennyson, Alfred. *Becket*. London: Macmillan, 1884.

368. -------. *Harold*. London: H.S. King, 1877.

369. -------. *The Idylls of the King*. London: E. Moxon, 1856-69.

370. -------. *Poems*. London: E. Moxon, 1832.

   Includes "Lancelot and Guenevere."

371. -------. *Poems*. 2 vols. London: E. Moxon, 1842.

   Includes "Lady Clare."

372. -------. *The Princess*. London: E. Moxon, 1847.

373. Thompson, Francis. *Poems and Essays*. Westminster, Maryland: Newman Bookshop, 1947.

   In "Orison-Tryst," the lover celebrates his lady according to courtly tradition.

374. Tynan, Katherine. *New Poems*. London: Sidgwick & Jackson, Ltd., 1911.

In "The Little Brethren," after praying on the Eve of St. John, Saint Brendan falls asleep in the woods. The Queen of the Faery Kingdom appears to him and pleads for access to Life Everlasting. After questioning her, Brendan concludes that fairies do not possess souls, and cannot be saved. The poem ends with the sound of the weeping Faery Kingdom.

375. Webster, Augusta. *Dramatic Studies*. London: n.p., 1866.

376. -------. *Portraits*. London: n.p., 1870.

Portraits include one of "Joan of Arc."

377. Yeats, William B. *Cathleen Ni Houlihan* (a play). London: Cara doc Press, 1902.

378. -------. *The Celtic Twilight. Men and Women, Dhouls and Faeries*. London: Lawrence & Bullen, 1893.

379. -------. *The Collected Poems of William Butler Yeats*. London: Macmillan, 1933.

Includes "The Wandering of Oisin" (1889), "Cuchulain's Fight by the Sea," and other Irish Renaissance lyrics based on Gaelic folklore. According to Yeats, these combine "much that is medieval with much that is ancient."

For Product Safety Concerns and Information please contact our EU representative GPSR@taylorandfrancis.com
Taylor & Francis Verlag GmbH, Kaufingerstraße 24, 80331 München, Germany

www.ingramcontent.com/pod-product-compliance
Lightning Source LLC
Chambersburg PA
CBHW050838230426
43667CB00012B/2050